SOLO

Vicki McAuley

SOLO

MACMILLAN
Pan Macmillan Australia

First published 2010 in Macmillan by Pan Macmillan Australia Pty Limited
1 Market Street, Sydney

Copyright © Vicki McAuley 2010

The moral right of the author has been asserted.

All rights reserved. No part of this book may be reproduced or transmitted by any person or entity (including Google, Amazon or similar organisations), in any form or by any means, electronic or mechanical, including photocopying, recording, scanning or by any information storage and retrieval system, without prior permission in writing from the publisher.

National Library of Australia
Cataloguing-in-Publication data:

McAuley, Vicki.

Solo: a man, a kayak, an ocean / Vicki McAuley.

ISBN: 9781405040136 (pbk.)

McAuley, Andrew.
Sea kayakers – Australia – Biography.
Adventure and adventurers – Australia – Biography.

797.224092

Typeset in 12/16 pt Fairfield LH Light by Midland Typesetters, Australia
Printed in Australia by McPherson's Printing Group
Cartographic art by Laurie Whiddon, Map Illustrations

Papers used by Pan Macmillan Australia Pty Ltd are natural, recyclable products made from wood grown in sustainable forests. The manufacturing processes conform to the environmental regulations of the country of origin.

For my two angels, Ant and Finlay

Andrew's Route

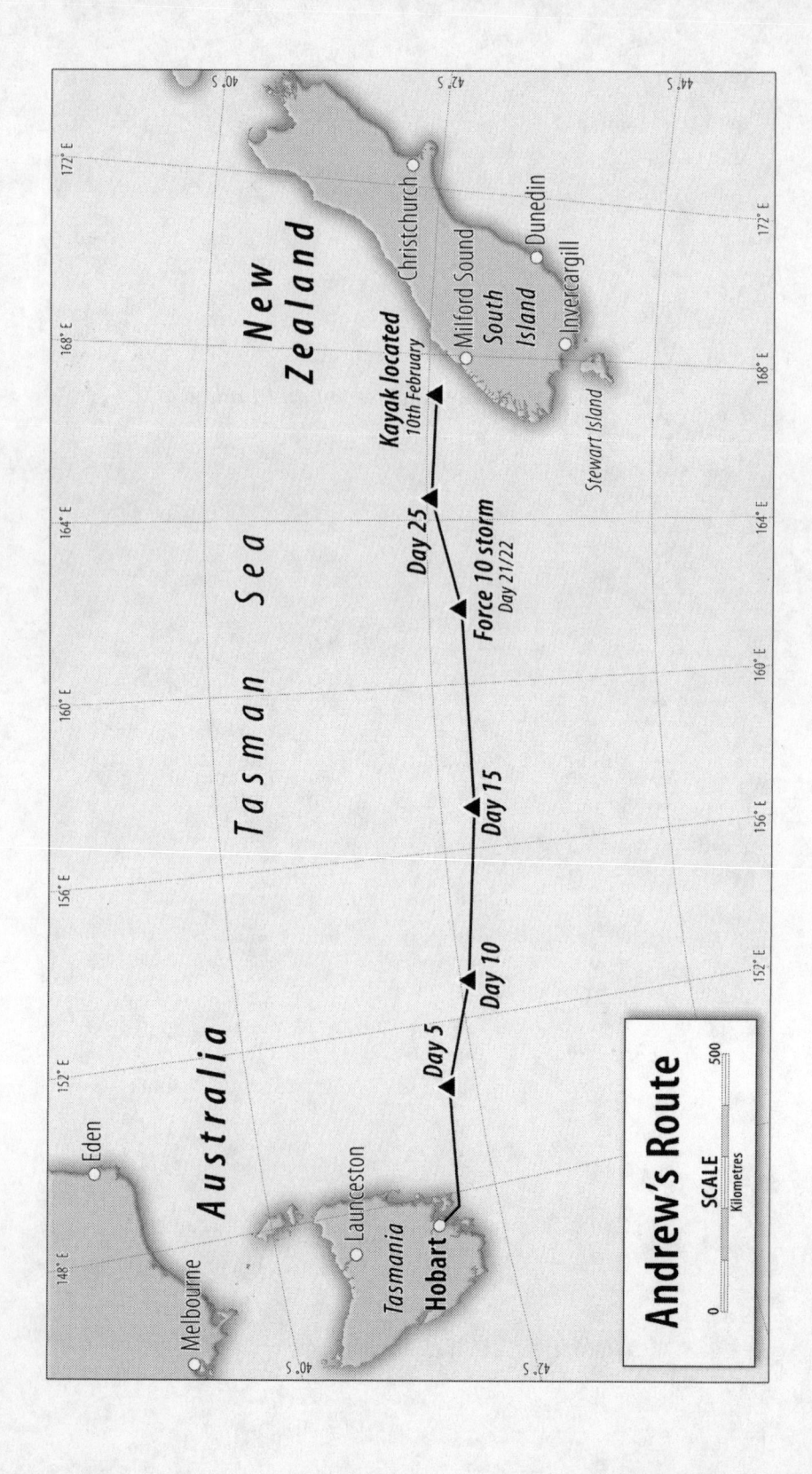

SCALE
0 — 500
Kilometres

Australia
Eden
Melbourne
Tasmania
Launceston
Hobart

Tasman Sea

Day 5
Day 10
Day 15
Force 10 storm
Day 21/22
Day 25
Kayak located
10th February

New Zealand
Christchurch
Milford Sound
South Island
Dunedin
Invercargill
Stewart Island

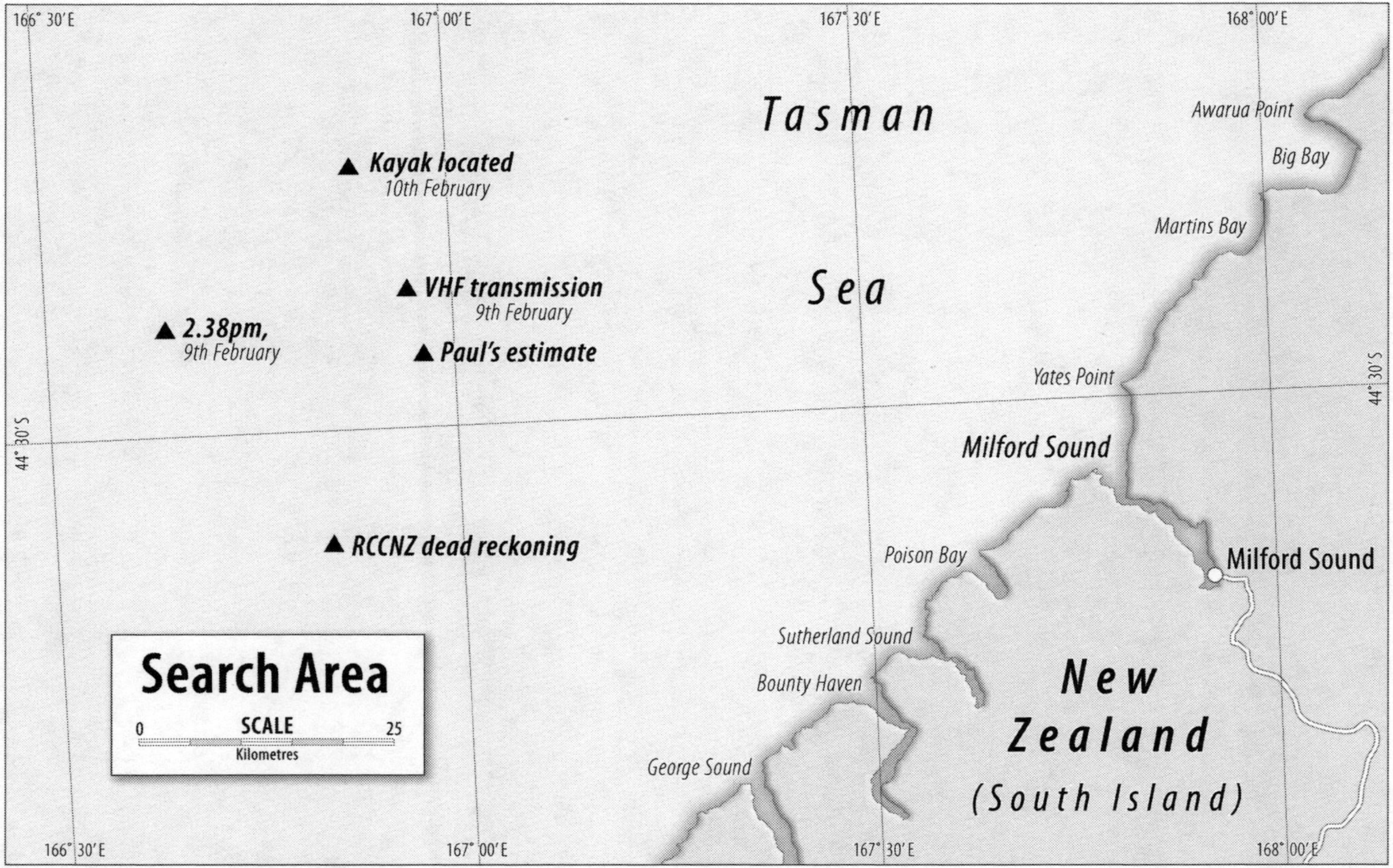

Search Area
SCALE
0
25
Kilometres
Tasman
Sea
Kayak located
10th February
VHF transmission
9th February
2.38pm,
9th February
Paul's estimate
RCCNZ dead reckoning
Awarua Point
Big Bay
Martins Bay
Yates Point
Milford Sound
Milford Sound
Poison Bay
Sutherland Sound
Bounty Haven
George Sound
New
Zealand
(South Island)
166° 30′E
167° 00′E
167° 30′E
168° 00′E
44° 30′S

PREFACE

Andrew McAuley had many dreams. One was to cross the Tasman Sea in a kayak. Another was to write a book about it. He crossed the Tasman, but to my utmost devastation he was unable to write the book.

On 26 February 2007 a crowd exceeding five hundred gathered in the shadow of Australia's oldest lighthouse, Macquarie Lighthouse overlooking the Tasman Sea. I made a promise to him then to write his book.

On that windswept February afternoon I asked him to watch over me and help me find the words, and when I eventually summoned the courage to tackle this overwhelming project, I discovered that he'd already written quite a few of them for me. He had told me he'd been writing, but he refused to show me, claiming it would be better for me to read it after he succeeded in his challenge. Thus, upon my return from New Zealand, I found files of his writings, and film footage that has haunted me from the day I unearthed them.

So, at last, my Ant, here 'tis. Your story, my catharsis.

PART ONE

CHAPTER 1

Fortescue Bay, Tasmania 2 December 2006 2.45 pm

'See you in New Zealand.'

'See you in New Zeelum,' the small child echoes.

A light westerly blows. A sliver of sunlight filters through the clouds. History is unfolding before us. One man is about to depart from Tasmania, bound for Milford Sound, New Zealand.

The distance, some 1600 kilometres, his vessel a kayak.

A lifetime of adventure has led to this, the ultimate challenge for the 39-year-old. Two video cameras in waterproof casings are mounted on the deck to capture the journey for posterity.

He adjusts the camera casing on the front deck and tucks the small waterproof satchel containing the camera remote controls under his life vest. He presses play, takes a deep breath, swallows hard, turns and waves. 'See you, gorgeous.' His voice betrays his emotions as he casts one final, longing glance at his wife and young son who sit huddled together on the shore, calling out to him. He pushes off from the boat ramp and his eyes well up with tears. He digs his paddle in for a sweep stroke to bring the bow around, manoeuvring his heavily laden craft with difficulty, and paddles off to a chorus of cheers from the small crowd. With each stroke of the blade, tears flow.

Some years ago, Andrew McAuley had a dream. That dream involved a sea kayak, and an open ocean. And some tough questions. What distance of open ocean can be safely crossed in a kayak? How much can a man endure, physically, emotionally, psychologically?

And now, the time for answers.

Overwhelmed by raw emotion, the floodgates open. He sobs uncontrollably. Water flicks off the paddle blade with each laboured stroke, splashing up into his face to mingle with the tears. A river runs down his cheeks. He stops, turns, waves back at the shore and sobs louder with the sounds of 'See you daddy, love you' fading away in the distance.

He sniffs, wipes his nose with the back of his hand and spits overboard. The hypnotic sound of each stroke is inconsistent with his short, shallow breaths, which verge on hyperventilation. A wave of desperate sobbing ensues. *Oh God.* Minutes pass, but not the tears, nor the agony of leaving his wife and child.

Oh God. Please let me finish in one piece. Please let me finish in one piece.

He turns back to wave again. *I love you, gorgeous.* He rests the paddle over the cockpit and slumps, head in hands. *I love you, beautiful.* Weeping without restraint, he picks up the paddle again.

Oh gorgeous, I love you. I love you, Finlay. His face distorts with the intensity of emotions. *Finlay and Vic – I love you more than anything.* His voice wavers. He sobs, stops, reaches forward, and adjusts something on the deck. This simple physical act seems to stimulate a mental response because his voice becomes suddenly strong and forceful.

I must make it. I must make it . . . I will. I will. I must make it . . . I will make it! The mantra continues, although the resolve weakens and his voice trembles again. *I love you, Finlay and Vic. I must make it. I must make it. My beautiful wife, I'll never put you through this again.* More tears flow. *I love you too much. I love you, gorgeous. I'll never put you through this again.* He stops to adjust the paddle leash.

Cliffs rise to his starboard as he progresses further out of the bay and clouds wisp overhead, exposing larger patches of blue sky.

I love you. I love you. I just want to get there in one piece. I really do . . .

Tears cascade down his face, threatening to wash the thick layer of sunscreen away. *Oh beautiful, what am I doing? I love you.* A raw, rasping animal noise escapes his throat.

He splashes water onto the camera lens to rinse it clear, another subconscious cleansing act. He paddles again, stronger now, more composed, more confident.

He lets out a heavy sigh. *Well, I've just left Fortescue Bay. I'm still in the bay . . . and we had a small crowd at the boat ramp there. It was 'Take two' actually, because I left early this morning but I had a problem with the camera. So I turned around. Well, I pretended to leave and all the media left – left us in peace, which was nice because I found them a bit intrusive for a very difficult moment, and I waited a few hours and the weather has settled down a little bit.*

It's now quite favourable, actually. It's a nice westerly . . . and now I can paddle in conditions that are a lot easier than they were going to be when I left. And so I can be a little bit more relaxed about the conditions that I'll find out here. They'll still be hard today. The whole trip is going to be very hard.

Another deluge of tears overwhelms him. His voice becomes very weak, almost frightened. *I'm really worried I'm not going to see my wife again, and my little boy. And I'm very scared . . . I'm very scared. I've got a boy who needs a father . . . and a wife who needs a husband, and I'm wondering what I'm doing here. I'm wondering why I'm doing this, I really am. And I don't have an answer.*

He scans the shoreline on his starboard side.

People ask me why, and I love adventure. There's no doubt about that. I love adventure. But . . . it's not worth it if you die . . . And this is a big dangerous ocean . . . and all I want right now . . . is to come back in one piece . . . 'cause I . . . want to see my little boy again . . . I want to see my beautiful wife again.

But, if there's one thing that gives me strength, it's the knowledge that I have to hold it together, if I'm gonna get there in one piece . . . I have to, and so I will. I must do it . . . I know I can do it, so I will.

And then after this, I'll put my feet up, and I don't think I'll ever do anything as dangerous as this trip ever again. And I hope to God that I live through it, because I know I might not . . . The big problem with this trip is that it involves the weather, and the weather is a random variable, over which we have no control. And the ocean is a big, scary place. And I'll just have to be very, very, very careful . . . that I don't take any unnecessary risks and that I make it to New Zealand in one piece.

You know, it's 2006 now, and it's about 20 years ago that someone else paddled out of this very bay, and attempted the Tasman in a sea kayak. And he turned around and he came back and he was only an hour off shore. Well, some people have said that it wasn't a fair dinkum effort, but I tell you what, right now, I totally understand anyone who wants to turn around and go back to shore. It was a very sensible decision.

His voice breaks with emotion. *I think he was a very smart man... I'm wondering if I shouldn't do that very same thing, right now. Turn around, and go back to shore. I wonder... Might be a smart thing to do.*

Guess I'm not always known for doing the smart thing. So, instead of turning round, I'm gonna keep going, keep paddling east, until I hit New Zealand. I'll tell you what, I can't wait to get there. I just hope I do.

I must. He digs the paddle in with more determination. *I must. I must. I must.* He throws another glance back over his shoulder. *I must. I know I can. I just need a little bit of luck with the weather. A little bit of luck.* He inhales deeply. *But I reckon I can. I just need to relax. I'm sure I can do it. I'm sure I can.*

He stops paddling, adjusts his legionnaire's hat, with the square of foam sewn into the back of the flap so it will float if it goes overboard. Turning fully at the waist, he allows a lingering gaze back to the safety of land, the shoreline now steep with cliffs rising high out of the water. *I'm sure I can. I love you, beautiful. I love you.*

Overwhelmed again by sobbing, he picks up the paddle and continues his seemingly impossible easterly course. *I love you, gorgeous. I love you. I love you, Finlay, I really do.* More tears flow and the paddling is laboured under the weight of his heavy burden. And at this pivotal moment the burden is far more psychological than physical.

He stops again, reaches forward to retrieve his drink bottle from the deck netting, takes a long swig, has a look around to his port side, another big gulp, scratches his nose, adjusts the peak of his hat, and replaces the bottle in its designated place. A place for everything, and everything must remain in its place for 30 gruelling days at sea. Give or take.

He sneaks one more quick glance towards the shore. He stops paddling again, and gives a frustrated sigh. He pulls off his spray skirt at the front, just enough to reach his hand underneath, and fiddles around with whatever it is that is sticking into his leg. The cockpit is ridiculously tight. Every available space is filled with essentials to sustain life at sea in this tiny vessel for a month.

I might see you again, beautiful. And if I do, I'm not going to do any of this shit again. I'm not. His voice breaks. *This is too crazy.*

Water splashes rhythmically off the paddle blades, the light chop sloshes against the hull.

Funny thing is, a lot of people seem to be genuinely inspired by what I'm doing. Which is nice. It's encouraging. Let's hope I don't die doing it. That's my main concern. They did seem to be genuinely inspired. It's not why you do it, but if they are inspired, that's nice.

Deep breath. *Well trust me, I don't normally get this emotional.*

I'm coming to think of the camera as my friend, already. Someone to talk to, share my thoughts with . . . but I can't leave it on all the time.

All I want to do is live. All I want to do is live, man.

To what extent does one go to live, to truly live, to seek out and find the truth in life, the essence of life? And who dares, really? It takes a rare individual to delve so deeply into themselves and their environment in search of answers. Perhaps, to find the answers, one must go to the very edge of living, to the very edge of life.

Part of me says that fear is a bit illogical, because it's only water, you know. The ocean's only water. The kayak's not gonna sink. I know I can do it. I know I can do it. But then the reality hits.

The ocean really is a big and scary place. And it can get very, very angry. And it's going to get very angry . . . The ocean is the boss. There's no doubt about it. I've got a lot of respect for it.

He turns around to check how far he's come. The headland recedes behind him. Ominous grey clouds blanket the sky again.

Only 1600 kilometres to go.

CHAPTER 2

What do you do when you love someone more than your own life? And when that someone tells you they have an uncontrollable urge to attempt some improbable feat, inherently fraught with danger, what do you do? When you've nursed that someone back to health after falling from a cliff; when you've watched, horrified, through binoculars from a distant ridge, that someone disappearing from view as the side of a mountain was swept by an avalanche; what do you do?

When that someone is your heart, your soul, your life, and the father of your child, what do you do? *I chose to believe.*

I came to believe in a lot of things back in the spring of 1995. Well, I'm not sure if I ever really believed in love at first sight, but *something* happened one warm September evening, something that changed my life forever, something that was to develop into a bond stronger than I would ever have imagined possible.

I grew up in the country town of Bathurst and worked at the local fitness club, Cityfit, as a gym instructor, although my work involved more than just teaching aerobics. I did the accounts, I designed advertising campaigns for press, radio and television, I wrote a fortnightly health and fitness article for the local Bathurst newspaper, led a bushwalking club, organised ski trips and golf days. It was a good job. In fact, it was so good that when I asked for a pay rise one day, my boss responded, 'Quality of life, Vic. Quality of life,' by which he meant that I lived ten minutes walk from work, stayed fit on the job, and my work was varied enough to keep me interested for almost nine years. What more could I want? I couldn't dispute his logic, although I'm sure the boss was more concerned with the quality of *his* life than mine. But then, I did meet some very interesting people on the job.

It was 7 pm. I stood at Cityfit's reception, warmly greeting the crowd rushing in for their evening aerobics class. I saw, out of the corner of my eye, two men coming down the stairs from the weights gym. One was shortish, with cropped dark hair, a goatee, John Lennon glasses, and huge calf muscles – Arthur Henry. The other, tall – about six-two, very lean, with beautifully high, chiselled cheekbones and effervescent eyes – was that man I'd done a fitness assessment on last year. He'd been training for a mountaineering trip to the Nepalese Himalayas at the time. Fascinating. Andrew McAuley. Big M, little c, big A. U. L. E. Y.

Our eyes met. Oh! My heart skipped a beat and I clutched at my chest. Tears glistened. A thrill of electricity ran through my entire body as we maintained our gaze. That was the moment I started to believe in life, in love, in everything.

Our first date, of sorts, was rock climbing. Arthur chaperoned. Our destination, the Wolgan valley in the south-western corner of the Wollemi National Park, west of Sydney. As the road wound its way through the valley floor, I stared in wonder at the majestic beauty of the rugged sandstone cliffs towering above us and wondered why, given its close proximity to Bathurst, I'd never been here before. It was simply stunning country.

Back in the early 1900s, Newnes was a thriving township in the heart of the Wolgan, supported by an oil-shale industrial development. The 1930s saw the closure of the industry, resulting in the death of the settlement. Extensive ruins can still be found throughout the area, although I felt quietly comforted to witness the triumph of the natural environment as it suffocates the evidence of mankind. We walked past the remains of some fascinating brick structures that reminded me of the beehive catacombs of ancient Mesopotamia. Andrew informed me that they were once coke ovens, giving name to the climbing crag we were heading for.

We harnessed up after reaching the base of the cliff and Andy tossed me a pair of his smelly old climbing shoes, assuring me that the rubber soles would stick to the rock like glue. This was my first foray into climbing, so I was bit apprehensive. The boys chose a two-pitch bolted route for my introductory climb. Arthur led the first pitch. Andy tied me into the rope in preparation and then followed Arthur up to the belay about 30 metres overhead. Too soon, he yelled that it was my turn to climb. I was feeling more than a little uneasy by now, and slightly numb.

'OK. What do I do?' I yelled up at him, trying not to let my voice betray my anxiety.

'Just climb!' was his helpful reply.

Alright, so I *just* climbed. And he was right. The boots did stick to the rock! In a few exhilarating minutes, I'd reached him at the belay. Arthur had already headed up the second pitch, leaving Mr McAuley to tie me into a very flimsy little sapling that was growing, miraculously, out of the rock on a narrow ledge.

He cleared his throat and said, rather shyly, 'Excuse me while I put my arms around you to tie you into the belay.'

'Mmm' was all I could manage as he squeezed around the sapling and squashed his body against mine while locking my harness into the carabiners on the belay. Since there was nowhere to move, all I could do was blush furiously, breathe deeply and enjoy the spectacular scenery.

Life, from that day onwards, became an adventure. Not that life before that was in any way boring. It was just, well, a normal, routine, country town sort of life. Predictable. Satisfactory. Unfulfilled.

Sweat poured from my body as I sprinted laps of the aerobics room floor, yelling at Arthur beside me to run faster, faster. Billy Idol screamed out for more, more, more, then the buzzer sounded, and I shouted, 'OK. Everyone on the floor! Pushups!' I positioned myself next to Andy and commenced the countdown, reminding the class to keep bodies straight, and touch noses to the floor.

'Since when have you been doing circuit classes?' I whispered. Then, 'Eight to go!' I shouted to the class.

'Uh, just thought I'd . . .' groan 'try something different.'

'Six and a half!' Pushup. Then, 'So, did you enjoy it?' I whispered again.

'Uh . . .' pushup.

'Seven and three-quarters', pushup, 'seven and seven-eighths.' They hated it when I did that.

'Enjoy isn't the word that springs to mind!' he gasped.

The music blasted its final chord, and bodies collapsed en masse to the floor for the cool-down.

The class exited amidst comments ranging from 'Great class, as always' to 'Man, I'm never doing one of her classes again!'

Andrew loitered until the last of the participants had departed, and then asked if I'd like to go caving this Saturday. The only problem was that I'd have to meet him in Oberon, a small town 45 kilometres south-east of Bathurst, and I didn't have a car. I thought him exceedingly generous when he offered to drop his car off at my place on Friday afternoon, so I could drive out in the morning to meet him in the main street at 7 am.

I walked home from work in the dark, and noticed a vehicle in my driveway. Red. Excellent. Must be a good car.

Appearances can be deceiving when seen only from the dim lighting of the street lamp. When I rushed out the front door and into the driveway early the next morning, I realised that my previous night's assessment of the car wasn't entirely accurate. The rusty old Mazda 323 with balding tyres would have been more at home in a wrecking yard. I pulled the door handle. It wouldn't budge. I yanked harder and the entire door nearly came off in my hands. Very gingerly, I climbed in and turned the key in the ignition.

Nothing.

Again.

Nothing.

On the third attempt, the engine sputtered to life, and I pulled out of the drive, wondering if I'd actually make it to Oberon.

There he was, that unmistakable lanky frame, leaning against the shopfront of the local bakery.

A party of eight cavers was waiting at Matthew McMahon's house. I recognised Arthur, of course, and a couple sitting with him on the lounge looked familiar. They were in my Thursday night circuit class. Although I couldn't have known it at the time, Mark and Teena Windsor were to become two of my closest friends and pillars of support when my world was later to fall apart.

The Tuglow caving system, in the Kanangra–Boyd Wilderness area south-west of Sydney, is known by speleologists to be one of the best wild caves in New South Wales. Three species of kangaroo, white cockatoos, rosellas and lyrebirds are endemic to the region, and the scenery both outside and in the caves is spectacular.

We abseiled down through a tiny hole in the ground, that opened, 60-odd metres below, into a large cavern.

After several hours beneath the earth, exploring the natural beauty of the rock formations and underground river, Arthur recommended a visit to the Crystal Pools. This was, by all accounts, a stunning formation that simply should not be missed. Since the rest of the party had allegedly visited this amazing spectacle on a previous visit, only Arthur, Andy and I made the side trip.

'So, where is this wonder?' I asked eagerly.

'Through there,' Arthur claimed, pointing at what appeared to be merely a crack in the rock at floor level.

We slithered on our bellies through the narrow squeeze. We pushed on for what seemed an eternity beneath an ever lower roof of solid rock. Before long, it became necessary to remove our headlights – they wouldn't fit through the confined space, so we pushed them along ahead of us. The space between roof and cave floor diminished even further. We had to stop, expel all the air from our lungs, wiggle forward a few centimetres, stop, inhale, exhale and repeat this painstaking procedure for several metres until finally the floor sloped down, creating a space of about half a metre between floor and roof. A small puddle of muddy water lay at the very back of this 'chamber' (for want of a better word). Behold – the Crystal Pools!

I made no attempt to avoid kicking the boys as we rolled our bodies into the foetal position, twisted and then, with great effort in the extremely confined space, performed a 180 degree about-face.

Now, Matthew McMahon is not a small man, and I can't fathom how it would be physically possible for him to have ever fitted through there, unless he did it when he was ten years old. He guffawed so loudly when our mud- and sweat-drenched faces reappeared through the slot that I thought the noise might bring the roof down.

The early days of romance – you never know where it might lead, do you? You just want to love and appreciate every moment you have together. Make the most of it while it lasts. I guess I thought it was all too good to be true. But it just kept getting better. Didn't want to think about commitment or anything. But thinking, hoping there might be something more. Yes indeed. There was a *lot* more.

My next bushwalk club weekend was coming up, and I thought the Pipeline Track in the Wolgan would be a good objective. I ran the idea by that handsome, unique young man I was now spending most of my spare time with. He suggested a reconnaissance walk, maybe camping the night, with some climbing the next day.

From the campground, we followed the path north along the river, past evidence of the old settlement, until the trail headed up and traversed around the hill, the river now far below. The track eventually came to a steep gully, scant evidence remaining of the pipes that 100 years earlier fed the shale oil from the Newnes settlement over to Glen Davis.

At the top of the gully the trail flattens and continues north for another few kilometres and eventually winds its way down into the tiny settlement of Glen Davis. Before we continued along the track, we detoured east to the clifftops, where we were rewarded with superb views along the valley. Andy draped his arm around my shoulders as we sat dangling our legs over the edge, looking 200 metres or so down into the valley floor. From our clifftop vantage point we could just make out the coke oven cliffs on the other side of the river. I felt an extraordinary sense of oneness in this place with this man. 'When I die,' he told me then, 'I'd like my ashes spread from up here.'

The afternoon was hot as we descended the gully and by the time we reached the river, we were in need of a dip. Andy stripped off his shirt and tossed it onto a rock. I stifled a scream as it landed on a brown snake. The snake hissed, then slithered off the rock, over a sandbank and away into the bush on the far side of the river. We watched it go, then jumped in, hoping it wouldn't decide to come back.

The last of the sun's rays had long disappeared before we made our way back to the campground. He held my hand tight. We'd only gone a few hundred metres from the river when we came upon a magnificent sight. Fireflies. These amazing little light bulbs guided us back along the track. I was mesmerised.

We climbed on 'Old Baldy' the next day – the huge buttress of rock that we had skirted on the previous day's walk. Andy dragged me up several challenging climbs. I think he had forgotten that I was only a novice. I swore under my breath often as I fought my way up that sheer cliff face. I'm sure he was quietly cursing at my incompetence, but he shared a great pearl of wisdom that day – 'Whether you think you can, or you think you can't, you're right.' A mantra that has served me well these past years.

About a month later we went back to 'Old Baldy' with Arthur and a few other friends, only to find that the exact rock face we were climbing just weeks before was rubble on the forest floor, leaving a trail of destruction. Seems we thought too hard that day.

It's a peculiar Australianism that we tend to enjoy reducing people to a single syllable. During our first date, Andrew became Andy. By the end our weekend of camping with the fireflies he was Ant.

CHAPTER 3

Andrew Peter McAuley. Born on the seventh day of August 1967 – the firstborn child of Peter and Jill McAuley of Goulburn, New South Wales. A beautiful baby he was, or so his mother said. But then, if you'd ask my dad, no newborn baby is beautiful. They are crumpled up, wrinkly little pink things, with scrunched up little eyes, and ear-piercing wails.

Beauty is in the eye of the beholder, and I know that when our son Finlay was born, he was the most beautiful, perfect little thing I had ever laid eyes on. And he is the image of his father.

Siblings soon followed for young Andrew. Michael was born 18 months later, just after the family moved from their 200-acre property to Sydney. Peter had taken a position with Stockland Trust. Then, two years after that, the boys' baby sister Juliet was born. As they progressed from toddlerdom to childhood, the threesome did what most kids did back in the early seventies – explored the great outdoors from dawn till dusk. No Playstations, Wiis or X-Boxes. Just active, healthy fun, running, riding, wrestling, climbing, playing, until they were called in for dinner. They shared germs with the neighbourhood kids as they all drank from the same drink bottle, shared blood from each other's cuts and grazes. Didn't eat Big Macs or KFC because there was no such thing. Ah, the good ol' days. It's a wonder anyone survived. Their father built them an amazing treehouse, and it was always Andrew who climbed right to the very top of that big old tree while the other kids settled safely somewhere in the middle.

When Andrew was nine, Stockland transferred the McAuley family to Brisbane. With new territory to explore, Andrew and Mike, the dynamic duo, would sometimes ride from their Pullenvale home right out to Lake Manchester near the back of Ipswich to jump off huge 60-foot [18-metre] cliffs into a deep waterhole, then ride all the way home again, stealing pineapples as they went.

'In those days,' the grown-up Mike once told me, 'we'd be gone pretty much all day. No contact with the folks or anything, but they never worried too much. I don't think so anyway. We would compete and push each other as brothers do – who could jump from a higher spot, who could catch the biggest wave, get the first barrel, ride the fastest, without using brakes, down the gnarliest hill.'

His adventurous spirit was spawned from the many family camping trips of his youth. Of particular note was the night on the banks of the Norman River at Karumba. The barramundi were biting and so, unbeknown to the McAuley family, were the crocs. The womenfolk slept on the roof of the campervan while the boys roughed it in the sand. And as the two youngsters sprang to life at dawn, they were delighted to find their patch of sand littered with croc tracks. The delight was confined to the two boys; the grown-ups and Juliet were simply relieved that all limbs were accounted for. It was not the sort of adventure they had planned.

I remember, on one of our many drives home from visiting my sister Robyn in Coffs Harbour, we camped the night at South West Rocks. Ant wanted to show me the sight of his most memorable childhood adventures. We drove to the old house, now somewhat run-down, but still standing, where his family would holiday each year. We peeked through a smeared window so he could point out the room he and Mike slept in, and that same window they would sneak out of during the night.

We walked up to the old sandstone gaol on the hill where, one year, he and Mike deliberately allowed themselves to be locked in, to see if they could escape. It proved harder than they thought. The sheer 10-feet-high walls were built to stop grown convicts from climbing over. The two young boys somehow managed to shimmy up and along the wall until they found an overhanging tree that they hauled themselves up into, climbed, and then jumped to freedom.

Ant drove me down a seriously rutted four-wheel-drive track in our Mazda 626 to show me the beautiful secluded beach where the brothers would dare one another to climb the most radical cliff face and then jump off into the sea and swim back to shore.

Then, of course, Andrew travelled to the place we've all been, that dreaded state of teenageism. That search for independence, maybe rebellion, when it's not cool to hang out with your parents. Andrew's father, Peter, recalls a time when he decided to call in on the young Andrew, who was deejaying for his University of Queensland station. The radio station was just across the road from the tennis courts. Andrew, with his unruly long hair and skin-tight black jeans, was mortified to see his conservative father in pristine tennis whites walk into the totally hip, cool graffiti-covered studio. So embarrassed was he that he failed to press the mute button as 'Dad! What are *you* doing here?' was broadcast over the airwaves.

In retrospect Andrew's folks can laugh at the time when he brought a girl home to dinner for the first time. His parents had other guests that night too. The four adults waited in eager anticipation for the teens to arrive. Peter paints quite a description of the young lass. 'She had a skirt that came up to not far beneath her navel and a plunging neckline that went down to her navel.' Peter didn't tell me this bit, but from Ant's account, his father dragged him into the study and told him, 'Whatever you do, boy, just don't get that girl pregnant!'

As a parent now, I dread that time. Can't we skip the teens? Jump straight to the twenties?

Most kids grow out of the need to seek daredevil adventures. Adulthood tends to stifle our imaginations, and perhaps our dreams. But one little prison escapee continued throughout his life to seek that esoteric freedom. The adventure in this one McAuley child never died with his youth. Or perhaps, the child never died in the adventurer.

Maria Coffey boldly states, in the opening pages of her book *Where the Mountain Casts its Shadow*, 'The world needs risk-takers. They inspire, challenge and encourage. They set off sparks, ignite fires that burn long after their passing. They dare the impossible. But not without cost.'

Indeed, not without cost.

CHAPTER 4

Summer 1995/96

Ant made the first Australian ascent of Torre Centrale in the Torres del Paine National Park, Patagonia. He spent six weeks in Chile, climbing with his German friend Carsten von Berkhan. I spent the six weeks climbing with Arthur and friends – the weekends at least – in the Blue Mountains. When Ant returned, jobless, he took Arthur and me to New Zealand to teach us the rudiments of mountaineering in the Mount Cook region. He threw us down mountains to teach us self-arrest skills; he dropped us into crevasses and made us prusik out.

And it was there in New Zealand, as we were hut-bound on the Murchison Glacier due to a white-out, that I truly came to unearth the phenomenon of Andrew McAuley. 'There's more to life than climbing,' I said to him. He stared as if I'd blasphemed. And in utmost sincerity asked, 'What?'

1996

And then winter was upon us. I loved the bitter Bathurst winters, especially that year when I'd walk Noushka up to Ant and Arthur's place on Suttor Street. I never thought of Noushka as a dog. She was my beautiful girl, my little angel, not that you could ever call a 45 kilogram Alaskan Malamute little. She'd lie outside in the frost while Ant stunned me with his culinary expertise. Rumour has it that he once served a girl a bowl of raw cauliflower in an attempt to get rid of her. Arthur would serenade us with his guitar. Then we'd take Noushka for long walks in the cold, dark night. Arthur was dumbfounded. Wondered what we were doing, when all we were doing was what we *said* we were doing – walking the dog. Why would anyone walk a dog at midnight in the fog and frost and minus 8 degrees? Because precious moments like that you treasure forever. And because it was a time for us to talk, to dream, to turn those dreams into something tangible. Andrew taught me that dreams are nothing if you can't make them something more.

His dreams involved conquering mountains. Mine were less esoteric – a change in life's direction, a university degree. I was never encouraged down that path when I left school. I always thought I was just smart enough to know that I wasn't smart enough, which is never a good thing. But Andrew had a profound influence on me. He made me believe in myself. So I took a leap of faith. I applied for and was accepted into the Bachelor of Design – Visual Communication at the University of Technology, Sydney. At twice the age of some of my fellow students, I left the security of my job and my home town and boldly, for me at least, stepped into the unknown.

CHAPTER 5

1997

Sea kayaks are incredible things. Their simplicity belies their amazing seaworthiness. No other seagoing vessel can be rolled 360 degrees or pitch-poled end-over-end with no damage whatsoever. Some paddlers do this just for fun! A recreational kayaker can have an awesome paddle in weather that sends many yachts running for shelter. Ant had always said a well-built kayak is limited not by the modest dimensions of the craft, but by the imagination and skill of the person sitting in the cockpit.

Contemporary sea kayaks trace their origins back to the native people of Alaska, Northern Canada and Greenland, who saw the need to develop a fast, seaworthy craft to hunt seals and walrus. Archaeological evidence indicates that kayaks date back more than 4000 years.

During our first encounter with the New South Wales Sea Kayak Club, we realised that some of the older members dated back almost as far, and it seemed to be a great passion of these old sea dogs to debate the definition of a sea kayak. Several points were agreed upon in the never ending discussions: if you're facing backwards, you're not in a kayak; if you're using a single-bladed oar or paddle, you're not in a kayak; if you're sitting forward in a long (ranging from 3 metres to 5.5 metres), narrow (53 cm up to 90 cm), seaworthy craft with a covered deck and you propel the craft using a double-bladed paddle (i.e. one blade at each end of a long shaft), you are in a kayak. That's a definition at its most simplistic. And from the definition debate comes the type debate. Of course the traditional skins stretched over whalebone framework have long been replaced by plywood, plastic, fibreglass, and for the more serious paddler, the carbon-kevlar composites. Brand rivalry among the paddlers always leads to contentious, although usually light-hearted, discussion. Mirage, Pittarak, Nadgee, Greenlander, Baidarka, Arctic Raider – to name but a few of the many different makes on the market – all have their loyalists, who claim their kayak goes faster, handles better, rolls more easily. Personally, I figured it had more to do with the paddler's skill than the boat itself.

Neither of us knew all that much about kayaks back then, but I guess I could take the blame for Andrew's initial introduction to sea kayaking. A number of years back, I'd done a sea kayaking trip around the Bay of Islands in the north island of New Zealand. Paddling, I thought, would be a very levelling thing for Ant and me to do together. Compared to climbing, kayaking would be a breeze, and a tad less intimidating. After all, you're just sitting there, right? And if you fall, well, you just get wet.

In 1997 we were living in Glenbrook, a beautiful village in the lower Blue Mountains, only an hour from Sydney and the coast. We hired a couple of kayaks from the Spit, near Manly. The limitations of the hire were that we could only paddle west of the Spit Bridge, so we headed into Middle Cove. Being a strong swimmer, I had the advantage on this predominantly upper body activity. When we eventually learnt how to paddle properly, though, we realised that the paddling action actually requires effort by the majority of the body. But at that time I took great delight in having to stop regularly to wait for Ant to catch up. Sweet payback for all those gruelling days of sweat and strain on the cliffs.

The tides turned, so to speak, when we ventured into the ocean for the first time. Ant bought himself an old second hand Pittarak. I borrowed one from Greg James, one of Ant's good climbing buddies, and we headed down the south coast to my brother's beach house at Culburra. The flat water of Middle Harbour suited me, but here, the rough swells of the ocean held far more interest to a man who has an aversion to the mundane. He was in his element. I, on the other hand, was in the water when my cockpit filled with water (Greg forgot to give me his spray skirt), and I turned to use the hand pump on the rear deck just as a big wave splashed over me. It was a good thing, really. My first capsize at sea, and all that happened was that I got wet. I was much more relaxed after that and we had an excellent paddle down the coast. That is, until we came to the surf landing back at the beach house. Ant somehow managed to execute a perfect surf landing on his first ever attempt, while I . . . well, let's not go into that!

On their previous visit to Patagonia, Ant and Carsten von Berkhan had caught a glimpse of some very promising unclimbed peaks in the remote Chilean fiordlands. Thus, another climbing expedition to Patagonia was planned. This time, included in the vital luggage for the expedition were kayaks to access the mountains via the fiords, and girlfriends – the tall, flaxen-haired German beauty, Anke Claus, and me.

Kayaking in the remote fiords of Patagonia, reputedly the windiest place on earth, would be a vastly different experience to the relative safety of the populated New South Wales coast, so we needed to acquire more skills to be able to cope with the conditions. In early December of 1997 we moved into the house that Ant had just bought a few streets away from the place we were renting in Glenbrook. The following day we left my poor old mum and dad to unpack a houseful of boxes while we headed down the south coast to join the New South Wales Sea Kayak Club, and to learn how to eskimo-roll a kayak. Then, on Christmas Day, we lugged heavy backpacks and duffle bags full of climbing and paddling gear up to the station to catch the train to the airport.

Ant realised he'd left the tap running to top up the pool, so he ran back home to turn it off. I had one eye on my watch and one on the stairs, waiting for him to return. The train was due at 9.18 am and it was now 9.15. Ant liked cutting it fine. At 9.16 am the train pulled into the station. I had the luggage ready to throw on board, but there was no sign of Ant. If we missed the train, we'd miss the plane. At 9.17 the guard asked if I was boarding because the train was about to depart. I told him that there was one minute to go *and* it was Christmas Day. *Please.* The train pulled out a minute early (a first, I'm sure, for Cityrail) and Ant sprinted down the stairs five seconds later.

Déjà vu. He missed his flight to South America back in 1996, too. Ah, no. Not this time. Carsten wouldn't see the humour in it this time. We took a ridiculously expensive taxi ride to the airport and made our Aerolineas Argentinas flight with time to spare.

Patagonia was amazing. Our home for the next six weeks was beneath an overhanging rock at the base of a cliff in the Fiordo de las Montañas. The previous day a fishing trawler from Puerto Natales had dropped four people, four kayaks, and a mountain of expedition supplies off at a tiny island at the mouth of the fiord. The Chileano fishermen thought we were crazy, being dumped in the wilderness to climb a mountain that we couldn't see for the fog.

The kayaks were treacherously overloaded as we paddled up the windswept fiord to find a suitable base camp. The ground literally floated beneath us, such was the amount of rainfall in this region. Nothing was dry. No ground was solid. It was like walking on a trampoline. Moss grew over dead moss, building layer upon layer of soft, springy valley floor. Solid ground was perhaps metres below. The colours, though, were spectacular. Every shade of rich, deep green, sprinkled with carpets of vibrant-coloured wildflowers. And the bees – I've never seen anything like them. Enormous, fat things, their thorax and abdomen covered in thick, silky orange fur. I wanted to reach out and pat them.

The first night's camp was uncomfortable to say the least. It was as if we had pitched our tents in a shallow pool. At dawn we were up, scouting the region for more substantial ground. By the end of the day the best thing we could find, in the next valley, was a narrow overhang, with a sloping rock floor and just enough room for two tents. A nearby glacial stream we used for bathing. The challenge was to strip, dunk, dry and dress before we turned blue.

1998

On New Year's Eve, the weather cleared and we saw, for the first time, the distant peaks of Dedos del Diablo (fingers of the devil), the mountains the boys had come to climb. The first day of 1998 was spent trekking through the ruggedly undulating terrain to the base of these mountains. With heavily laden packs we traversed to the next valley, crossed a river, made a very steep ascent to a glacier and climbed rock and moraine before we reached a magnificent high lake, the colour of sapphires sparkling in the sunlight. Figuring we were the first people to set eyes on this beautiful lake, Ant christened it *Lago Victoria*. On its bank, we set up the climbers' high camp. Carsten and Ant climbed the first few pitches that day, to scope out the route. They were disappointed that they hadn't taken bivvy bags on the climb. Bivvy bags – lightweight, compact, waterproof cocoons used in lieu of a tent – would have allowed them to sleep en route and summit the next day. The weather was perfect.

But not for long. Climbing became impossible for the next few weeks due to the constant rain and snow, so we spent many days in the kayaks, exploring the neighbouring fiords, paddling past glaciers stretching down to sea level, around huge icebergs and getting caught in strong katabatic downdraughts. One day when Ant and I were out paddling – Carsten and Anke wisely chose to stay in bed and catch up on some reading – the wind picked up dramatically when we were a long way from home. We were hit constantly by roaring katabatic blasts as we pushed hard to make the mouth of our fiord and battle our way back to camp. With many near capsizes, it was nerve-racking. It was at about this time that I began to suspect that life with Ant might have a downside. Perhaps silver did not in fact line every cloud. In that instant, the clouds were very dark and ominous. We were both frozen, our fingers numb despite wearing glove-like things called pogies that wrap around your hands and the paddle shaft. When you're that cold, judgment can become impaired. Accidents can happen. A capsize here would be life-threatening.

As luck would have it, through the whitecaps and spray we noticed a moored yacht. A little dog barked a welcome, alerting the owners, who kindly invited us aboard for a warm cup of tea. Too wild for them to be out, they said. It was 40 knots [75 km/h], gusting up to 50 [90 km/h]. This lovely Danish couple had seen their children grow up and leave home, so they sold the house, bought a yacht, packed the dog and hadn't been home for seven years.

When the wind eventually eased, they generously loaded our kayaks with eggs, chocolate, fruit and vegies, and waved us farewell. A pod of dolphins escorted us up the Fiordo de las Montañas to our home. Carsten cooked up a gourmet feast that night.

The weather cleared at last, and the boys made a successful first ascent of the highest of the devil's three fingers, Cerro La Paz. Anke and I sat on a high ridge opposite, watching through binoculars as condors swooped past the climbers. The wingspans of these mighty giants dwarfed both men. We climbed a couple of smaller peaks in the region and, just as the guys were ready for an assault on the other fingers, the weather came in again. Some say the weather is unpredictable in Patagonia. Quite the contrary. You can guarantee it will be icy cold and raining or snowing. Still, we left Fiordo de las Montañas satisfied, and with a newfound love of kayaking. And that was a very good thing. So I thought.

Still, through the coming months we continued to climb, and week after week we drove south to the 300-metre sheer limestone cliffs of Bungonia Gorge, near Goulburn. Ant put up a new seven-pitch route that autumn and named it *Evolution*, which was significantly pre-emptive of his evolutionary transition from one adventurous domain to another. For it was *Evolution* that led to a gravity-defying moment that all but put paid to his climbing days.

I was at home one weekend in May applying myself to my studies when the phone rang. It was Vera Wong, Ant's climbing partner. Andrew has had an accident, she said. So much for my assignment. I ran around the corner to our neighbours and close friends' place. Shane and Lian Woonton, without hesitation, drove me the two hours to Bungonia only to have the National Parks officer refuse me access down the gorge. I had head torches, food, water, a sleeping bag. The ambulance officers had difficulty enough getting down there in the dark. I knew the path into the gorge like the back of my hand, I told him, but still he refused. He did, however, allow me access to the two-way radio.

I spoke first to the barely lucid patient and then with the paramedics, who advised me of his injuries – a smashed patella and associated damage, blood loss, shock and mild hypothermia as a result of being stuck down the bottom of the freezing gorge, unable to move. He spent the night in the gorge with the paramedics and Vera, and was airlifted to Nepean Hospital the following morning. I heard the chopper fly over our house, in fact. And I'm sure my lecturer thought it was a lame excuse for an extension on my assignment when I told him my boyfriend had fallen off a cliff. 'The dog ate it' would probably have had more credibility.

I've always been drawn to challenges at the sharp end of what is possible, initially with climbing and mountaineering, and more recently with sea kayaking. My climbing life provided over a decade of intense experiences filled with joy, hardship, struggle, and deep satisfaction. I lost several friends to the mountains, and frostbite took bits of others. Climbing is an extremely unforgiving pastime. One stunning autumn day in Bungonia Gorge, New South Wales, while climbing with Vera Wong, I had a long and unplanned encounter with gravity. As with many accidents, there were several contributing factors, and when combined those factors caused an outcome that was devastating and would change my life forever.

So it was that kayaking became a bigger part of who I am. The change was not immediate; I continued to deny that my smashed knee could mean the end to my climbing life. Mountaineering is what drove my life for so many years. To turn away from all that so quickly was unthinkable. Acceptance came slowly and over a period of years. I continued to go rockclimbing on weekends and had one more expedition to Pakistan. On this trip I watched two of my best friends come within a hair's breadth of losing their lives right in front of me.

Kayaking slowly took a bigger hold on me as I discovered the intimate pleasures that it offered, and the fact that it didn't stress my damaged knee. I found it interesting that there were many challenges left to the ambitious paddler. There were many 'unclimbed peaks' still waiting to be done. In kayaking terms, this took the form of achieving circumnavigations of challenging islands (or even continents) that had not previously been done by paddle-powered craft. The most significant 'first' that had been done in many years was Paul Caffyn's circumnavigation of the mainland of Australia. With no less than three sections of cliff-lined coast in Australia that each offered no landings for almost 200 kilometres, Caffyn pulled off a spectacular achievement in 1984 that is still revered and admired today.

[This epic has only just been successfully repeated in 2009 by German wonder woman, Freya Hoffmeister.]

After Ant's Bungonia accident, climbing was out of the question for a while, as were most other weight-bearing activities. I nursed him back to health, and kayaking became our very enthusiastic focus. Shane and Lian had just imported plans from the USA to build a marine ply hard-chined kayak – the Chesapeake. We borrowed the plans and turned our garage into a mini kayak factory. We made two kayaks. Mine, being the second, was much lighter and better finished than the first. Ant christened his the 'sea slug', and soon afterwards sold it to Arthur.

He had phoned Arthur with some other important news. 'Guess what?' he almost shouted down the phone.

'No idea!' Artie replied.

'We're getting married!'

Silence.

Seconds passed.

'Hello, hello. Artie. You there, mate?'

'Er, just picked myself up off the floor! Never thought I'd see the day!'

We finished my kayak and Ant thought it would make an excellent engagement present, in lieu of a diamond. His mother would have nothing of that. So, thanks to my beautiful almost-mother-in-law, I got the diamond too. I've never taken it off and now, on the finger next to it, sits the gold wedding band I gave Ant. The two rings, together forever.

Andrew's mother had great hopes that he would give up that dangerous pastime of climbing after the Bungonia accident, and then of course, when he was to become a responsible married man, he would undoubtedly do away with such recklessness. I, unfortunately, was not at all the right woman to be discouraging his adventurous spirit. Rather, I was intrigued, awed and in total admiration of his passion for adventure and I was, by that stage, firmly caught up in the adrenaline of life with my Ant. We had shared many a hair-raising experience, but with him, I didn't question my ultimate safety. I had a strong belief that all would work out, no matter how hazardous a situation I found myself in. He had an overt self-assurance. Not arrogance. In no way could he be described as arrogant. But he exuded quiet confidence that led to my indelible faith in his abilities. He was my Superman. Often very Clark Kent – modest, mild, humble, but always Superman.

The 1998 Sydney to Hobart yacht race was a disaster. Six men lost their lives to the sea. It was at that time that we were driving south to paddle from Mallacoota, just south of the New South Wales border, to Eden. I felt sick by the time we arrived in Mallacoota. All we'd heard on the news on the drive down were horrific reports of huge seas and tragedies. But Ant said the forecast was improving and we'd be fine, so I believed him.

By late afternoon we were on the water and paddling out towards Gabo Island. We camped the night with about a million very noisy fairy penguins on the tiny island just south of Gabo. The weather was mild, so we didn't bother erecting the tent. I woke at one stage during the night to find a little face inches from mine, just staring at me, probably wondering what we were doing on his island. We paddled over to Gabo Island the following morning, walked up to the lighthouse, chatted with the lighthouse keeper about the yacht race, and then continued north.

I thought I was going to die as we headed out around the Iron Prince – a reef that breaks six kilometres out to sea in the right (or wrong, whichever way you like to look at it) conditions. And this was after I insisted we break camp in the dark in order to beat the big winds and rougher sea conditions. All to no avail. But dolphins came to the rescue again. They guided us around the corner and into Nadgee Beach, which was breaking across the river mouth. I refused to go in there, through the monstrous surf. An old wreck lurks beneath the surface near the southern end of the beach, waiting for unsuspecting boats or kayaks. We had no idea where it might be, with the surf whipping up a fury. I wasn't about to risk being impaled by a rusting steel girder, so we paddled on to Merrica River, a further 17 kilometres north. That was when we heard an incredible noise and then the water in front of us became a horizontal waterfall, frothing and boiling around us, fish leaping out of the water in all directions. Hate to think what was underneath. Now would definitely not be a good time to capsize.

Later, as we rounded Green Cape, we saw a pod of killer whales in close to the cliffs. Huge fins protruded high out of the water. Ant told me they were dead, so I wouldn't worry, which was very thoughtful of him. We had already seen several large sharks that morning, and I felt that I'd exceeded my quota of hair-raising moments on this trip.

I pushed through my comfort zone, with a bit of prodding, substantially extending its boundaries, and then we amused ourselves with talk of grander adventures on the long drive home.

Vera had planted the seed of an idea. The Nangmah Valley in the Karakoram ranges of Pakistan has numerous unclimbed peaks just under 6000 metres. No climbing permit is needed for mountains under 6000 metres. 'Reckon the knee can handle one more big climbing trip?' he asked. 'Yeah,' he answered his own question with a grin. We let the seed germinate.

CHAPTER 6

Pakistan 1999

Flying into Lahore in the evening was quite unlike flying into any other large city. There was a different, almost ethereal glow to the earth beneath us. Not the abundant light of Sydney. Here soft, wavering, mysterious lights flickered and waned like a billion fireflies buzzing about this city. It reflected the warmth and exhilaration and mystery I felt every time I looked into my Ant's eyes. Andrew, the enigma. Deeply loving, caring, gentle, humble. Yet driven, passionate, pragmatic, determined, audacious.

We landed and made our way through the mad bustle, weathered old faces shouting and clawing at us from every direction, 'Come, come, taxi for you'. As we drove, squashed, nursing luggage in our laps, I saw the city, too, was a paradox. Squalid tents, with kerosene lamps flickering and grubby children yelling; next door, a mansion, electric lights blazing, Mercedes parked behind the security fence. We passed colourful buses in the street, cows and motorbikes with entire families on board

– father driving, three older kids straddled behind him, mother with babe in arms balancing on the handlebars. A constant chorus of car horns honking and chickens scurrying across the road. Dark alleys and brightly lit golden arches of McDonald's, vendors pulling rusty old carts stacked high with watermelons past neon Coca-Cola signs. That was Lahore.

From Lahore to Islamabad, from Islamabad to Skardu, gateway to the Karakoram Himalayas. Eight more hours in a jeep, and we journeyed into the Hushe Valley, and the tiny mountain village of Kande. Our expedition party consisted of six climbers and three hikers. I was one of the latter. Vera Wong, one of Australia's leading female alpine climbers of the day, and Kiwi Ned Norton were climbing with Ant. Chris Mason, Paul Weber and Mick Haffner made up the other team.

Life is fragile in the mountains, every moment precious. You never know when it'll be your last. The trekkers – Kiwi Dan Druce, Arthur and I – had left the climbers' base camp and headed further up the Hushe Valley with a host of porters. Porters to carry our gear and food, plus extra porters to carry food for the porters! We crossed the swollen Hushe River single file. I wondered, as my foot broke through a rotten plank, how long this rickety old bridge had been standing. Too long, apparently. As the last of our porters stretched his foot out to reach the safety of solid ground, the bridge collapsed, and was swallowed by the raging torrent. Women laden with bundles of sticks twice their size approached the far bank. They were left with no choice but to walk a further 20 kilometres upstream to the next crossing, just to bring their heavy burdens home to their waiting families, so they could start a fire and prepare a meal. Life's not only fragile, it's tough.

I trekked with Artie and Dan through the rugged ranges of the Karakoram for three weeks, where we caught glimpses of K2 and Broad Peak in our travels, but I left them to head back up the spectacular Nangmah Valley to the climbers' base camp. At 4300 metres, it was sitting on the last patch of grass before the snowline. Chris, Paul and Mick were there. They told me of a near-disaster with Ant's team which resulted in the change of climbing objective. Handing me a pair of binoculars, they pointed to a distant needle-like rock spire towering above a ridge on the far side of the valley. Ant, Vera and Ned had summitted two days ago. They'd been gone seven days, and they took provisions for only five. They'll make their descent tonight, the guys assured me. No option really – they've run out of food.

I sat up all night, wrapped in many layers of thermals, down jacket and sleeping bag, with tent flap open, binoculars in hand, watching three tiny dots of light making painstakingly slow progress down that distant couloir, a steep gully on the mountainside. Early the following morning the sun crept over the snow-shrouded mountains and hit the peak. They should have been down by now. It was harder to find the little dots in the daylight. Ah, there they are! Dark dots now against the dirty white backdrop of the couloir.

Crack! It sounded like a shot gun. Avalanche. The dots disappeared amidst billowing clouds of white powder. I screamed. My heart leapt up to my throat. As the echo and dust of the avalanche receded, I continued to stare at the spot where the dots had been. I scanned the width and length of the couloir through my binoculars. No easy task, considering the way my hands were shaking. Chris wanted a look. No. I needed those binoculars. A lone black dot appeared. Then another. I exhaled deeply. Finally, I could make out all three tiny figures in the shadow of a rock buttress. The danger had not passed, though. Two more avalanches showered them with snow and rock debris as they crossed the face of the couloir.

They would be exhausted, and very hungry. Chris, Paul, Mick and I loaded a pack with food and trekked across the glacier to meet them at the base of the mountain. I slipped on a rock and fell up to my waist as we crossed a stream of glacial melt along the way. It was late afternoon by the time we met up with the exhausted climbers. I threw my arms around Ant, then broke our embrace to hand him a muesli bar. 'Oh, I don't like that flavour,' he said. 'What else have you got?'

Australian Geographic later awarded Vera, Andrew and Ned a Spirit of Adventure medal for the first ascent of the 5400 metre peak, Mt Jo in Pakistan.

Ant recounted the near-death experience during the earlier attempt on their initial objective, Amin Brakk. They were climbing a smaller reconnaissance peak and something didn't feel right for Andrew that day. He had experienced a similar sensation of unease, a sixth sense if you like, the previous year in Bungonia Gorge. He ignored the voice of reason that day and fell 30 metres when a handhold pulled loose, ripping two sets of protection from the rock, smashing his knee against the cliff face, and jerking his climbing partner, Vera, from her belay. Reconstructive surgery and twelve solid months of physiotherapy later, here he was, faced with that ominous feeling again. He would not ignore it this time. You respect the mountains. He backed off the climb, and watched from the saddle below as Vera and Ned continued their assault on this peak by themselves. That subconscious unease marked the beginning of the end of a fulfilling life of climbing.

We were climbing a virgin peak in the Nangmah Valley, a hidden treasure of unclimbed peaks and world-class rock faces that is now quite well known in the climbing world. Vera Wong was leading up a winding, corniced ridge (a steep ridge with an overhanging ledge of snow on the windward side) with vertical cliffs plummeting hundreds of metres on either side to the glaciers below. Ned Norton followed carefully in her footsteps, taking what he thought was a safe line a respectful distance away from the edge of the cornice.

Suddenly there was a huge explosion. Avalanche! I looked up to see Ned in total free fall, sky-surfing an enormous ledge of snow straight down the cliff that formed one side of the mountain. I was speechless and unable to move. I watched in awe and fear as he reached terminal velocity. Tied to the other end of Ned's rope was Vera. She was ripped from her belay stance and tore down the mountain at the same pace as Ned. When you see something like this happen before your eyes, you quickly realise that there are some forces in nature over which we have no control. This was one of those situations. As this accident unfolded before my eyes, time slowed down and seconds became minutes, minutes became hours in my head. I was a disbelieving spectator watching two of my best friends die in the most spectacular and horrific accident I could imagine, but it was real.

Vera was being torn down the *other* side of the mountain. In seconds the rope would break. Both Vera and Ned would plummet to their deaths on opposite sides of the mountain. Three more seconds and each body would lie motionless on a different glacier, hundreds of metres below. One second passes. The rope pulls tight. Ned is quietly bouncing in mid-air, suspended on one end of the rope. Another second. The huge slab of snow that was a corniced ridge two seconds ago continues its free fall to the glacier below, exploding on impact as tonnes of snow and debris cause sonic booms that reverberate around the mountains with the sound of indescribable power. One more second. Vera is at the edge of a very steep snow slope, just metres from the cliff on the other side of the mountain. Neither body moves. The rope holds tight.

All three lived to tell the tale, however others were not so lucky. We didn't know until we returned to Skardu that the mountains had claimed the life of a Kiwi climber in the next valley while we were there. The mountains show no mercy, they demand the utmost respect.

And with this experience in the mountains – watching Ant almost engulfed by an avalanche, and hearing of Ned and Vera's near-tragedy, I was beginning to wonder if the words of someone back in Bathurst might not, in some way, be true. 'He will always choose the mountains over you' is what the man had said. Maybe, maybe not, but the mountains almost chose Andrew. The sea, after our collective experiences, was beginning to show far greater appeal. Those fibreglass, or in my case marine ply, cocoons beckoned us down an apparently less death-defying path.

We had flown into Skardu. Everyone had cheered when the pilot touched down safely and taxied down the runway. Perhaps a safe landing was a rare occurrence. We decided to take a bus back to Islamabad. If I thought the mountains were hazardous, they were nothing compared to the maniacal bus driving. The road from Skardu was roughly etched into the steep mountainside, the dark, angry Indus River thundered 200 metres below. I watched anxiously from my seat near the front of the bus as the driver spoke animatedly to the men directly behind him. Both hands were gesticulating wildly. How was he steering? He was turned completely in his seat to face the men. Ant held my hand tight as a small whimper escaped my lips.

I yelled at the driver as the bus skidded and slipped, sending a shower of rubble down into the raging depths of the Indus.

He smiled a wide, toothless grin and laughed, 'No worry, no worry!' Another bus approached from the opposite direction. And the driver laughed again as he saw the look of horror on my face. Artie's knuckles had turned white from gripping the seat so tightly. His face was an even paler shade. This ridiculously narrow winding road surely could not accommodate both vehicles. Neither bus slowed as they scraped each other's paintwork in passing. The trip became a constant of my whimpering and the driver's 'no worry' for another twelve excruciating hours.

We survived the mountains *and* the bus trip. Now the bazaars in the monsoon rains in Lahore. Ant had eaten something at the bus exchange in Rawalpindi that neither Artie nor I would dare touch. Consequently, he wasn't his usual chipper self as we waded through the alleys, knee deep in water and whatever else floated by. We passed marijuana growing head-high in every vacant patch of earth, marvelled at craftsmen creating masterpieces from stone, bartered for carpets and fine silk fabric for my wedding dress.

On the eleventh day of December that year, I became Mrs McAuley, and the happiest person alive. Our kayaks accompanied us on our honeymoon, and we spent a glorious month paddling up the east coast of Tasmania, then the south coast, and exploring the many tributaries of Macquarie Harbour in the west. As we sat on a deserted beach on Schouten Island just south of Freycinet Peninsula, eating our crumbled Christmas cake, for it was Christmas Day, the sun reflected in my beautiful husband's eyes. He stared out across the Tasman Sea to our east, then drew his gaze back to the kayaks beached on the sand. A kayak. An ocean.

We were aware of the legendary Paul Caffyn's attempt some years back to paddle his kayak from Fortescue Bay, where we had ourselves just paddled from, across the Tasman Sea to New Zealand. He had made two attempts, in fact, the first in 1987 and then two years later in 1989. Both attempts were made in a double with a paddling partner. He did consider going solo in 1989 when his paddling partner pulled the pin, but decided against it – the boat was just too heavy.

The possibilities are endless, Ant said, with that sparkle in his eye. Thus, on our honeymoon, an embryo of a plan was conceived. He had discovered new 'mountains' to climb.

CHAPTER 7

2000–2001

I am drawn to ocean crossings rather than to circumnavigations. The commitment that a big crossing draws from you is intense. With no engine or sail to rely upon, the buck stops with you. A circumnavigation will normally offer some form of landing at reasonably regular intervals. With a long crossing the difference is obvious: there's nowhere to pull over if you start feeling a little queasy, or if you have to go to the toilet for a number two. While it is tough and dangerous, there is a tremendous sense of achievement in completing a long and difficult crossing, particularly in such an unlikely and frail-looking craft as a sea kayak.

Bass Strait is something of a Holy Grail amongst Australian sea kayakers. As with several others before me, I was drawn to this place as the ultimate testing ground – something of an Australian sea kayakers' 'Everest'. The route that kayakers use in Bass Strait is almost without exception the 'Eastern Route', the chain of islands along the eastern side of Bass Strait that, in the last ice age, formed the land bridge between mainland Australia and Tasmania.

I crossed this route in early 2000 with my good friend and rock-climbing partner, Greg James. We had some difficult conditions but on the whole had a great time and this trip had left me salivating for more. The sea kayaking bug had bitten.

Almost immediately upon his return from his first Bass Strait crossing, Andrew began speculating about what was *really* possible in a sea kayak. Lengthy discussions ensued, that spark of an idea that was conceived on our honeymoon was ignited, and I knew then that one day Andrew would do what others believed impossible – he would cross the Tasman Sea in a kayak.

Andrew was no stranger to the ocean. He and his younger brother Mike had a long association with big waves and gnarly surf. They spent their childhood on surfboards. As an adult, Mike moved to Perth, but Ant would make excuses to take business trips to Western Australia to visit 'bro', where Mike relished the opportunity to 'get him way out of his comfort zone up the North-West or down to Margaret River, into some solid WA juice' [big waves]. With surfing comes a deeper understanding of the ocean environment and all she can conjure up.

In 2001, our good mate Ben Eastwood invited Andrew on a kayaking trip up the Cape York Peninsula and across Torres Strait to Saibai Island just 6 kilometres off the coast of Papua New Guinea, a journey totalling over 1000 kilometres of paddling. When I flew to Cairns to meet Ant off the plane from Saibai Island, his account of the trip was punctuated with numerous close encounters with sharks, plus a terrifying crocodile tale.

Terror gripped me as the tent was whipped from under my sleeping mat. The deadly saltwater croc lashed and attacked the tent again. I was helpless, naked and wrapped inside my silk inner sheet – they are surprisingly hard to get out of when you need to in a hurry! My mind was a blur. Amazingly, the tent fabric had not yet torn. I screamed again, wondering through my panic what was taking Ben so long to wake up and get off his bum to help.

We arrived on Bird Island in Shelbourne Bay after almost 700 kilometres of paddling. It was the only viable landing spot after a long 42 kilometre day in our kayaks. To our west across the bay lay Macarthur Island, where a fellow paddler, Arunas Pilka, was attacked by a big saltie two years earlier. In a story that is now legend amongst sea kayakers, David Winkworth had then raced into the water and wrestled with the beast, freeing Arunas and dragging him to shore before initiating a rescue that saved Arunas's life. There was no way we were camping there!

Saltwater crocodiles are territorial animals. The one that attacked Arunas was almost certainly still there and we did not want to tempt fate. So it was somewhat ironic that when we landed on our 'safer' alternative – Bird Island – after a long, hard day's paddling the first thing we saw was a huge croc slide. The tide was dropping and the slide finished less than a metre from the water's edge. In our estimation, this had the monster croc sunning itself on our beach less than an hour before our arrival. I had no desire to play heroics with these animals, and was humbled by the fact that we were definitely not at the top of the food chain up here!

Later that evening, we built a large bonfire to scare off any intruders and fell into a nervous, fitful sleep with our tents pitched just a few metres from one another. Then, at about 2.30 am, the world was turned upside down as I was jolted from my sleep by this terrifying attack.

Suddenly, everything stopped moving. Unbelievably, I heard a cackle from outside the tent. It was Ben, giggling like a madman. 'Don't worry, mate, it's only me!' he said, between bursts of laughter.

It was lucky we hadn't brought weapons of any sort to defend ourselves against crocs. If we had, I reckon I might have used them on Ben right there and then. This was probably the single most terrifying moment I have had in a long history of outdoor adventuring. When you are faced with anticipated danger and you have room to move and take calculated action, there is at least some level of control and opportunity to influence the outcome.

It's difficult to describe the feeling of helplessness I had during those seconds when I was unable to struggle out of my sleeping-sheet, absolutely certain that a big saltwater croc was ripping my tent apart and was literally inches from doing the same to me. Good one, Ben!

2003

Ant's next big sea kayaking trips were along the wild west coast of Tasmania with Paul Loker and Laurie Geoghegan and, directly afterwards, the western side of Bass Strait via King Island, solo. Andrew told the boys that he couldn't afford the ticket for the ferry back to the mainland after their west coast jaunt, so he would just have to paddle home via King Island.

He phoned to assure me that he was on solid ground on the mainland. I could hear what I assumed to be surf in the background. It was, in fact, the sound of the ocean pounding against the hull of the kayak. He had underestimated the time he thought it would take to paddle the 100 kilometres from King Island and he still had a few hours of paddling before he reached the safety of land. I was pregnant at the time and with the pregnancy came a certain apprehension. My concern for the welfare of my husband expanded in unison with my belly. A little white lie to put my mind at ease. God, I love that man.

CHAPTER 8

2003

It was something we'd thought about and discussed for years. Would we, should we have children? I had never experienced that sudden primal urge that many women feel – the need to procreate. I loved children – loved playing with them, always a big kid at heart, but frankly the thought of holding a fragile baby terrified me. But I was approaching 40. My biological clock was ticking, as they say, so our discussions became more fervent. And although in many ways we were both not quite ready for that monumental leap, who is, really? We both agreed that our later lives might feel lacking without children and perhaps grandchildren to dote on. The bond Andrew and I both share with our respective parents is a precious thing indeed. And the utter joy my parents experience in playing the grandparent role in the lives of my sister's and brother's kids is enviable.

Then again, despite the government's assertion that we needed to double the population of Australia in the next

20 years, we were adamant that the world was already overpopulated and under-resourced. Should we burden the planet with an extra soul of our making? Yet, as many couples do when contemplating this life-changing decision, we imagined the pleasure of teaching our children to swim, to climb, to love and protect nature, to make a positive impact on our world. Nothing could be more fulfilling or more worthwhile.

I had miscarried after just eight weeks back in 2001, yet the emotional bond I had already developed with the tiny foetus was intense. I was devastated. I think it was difficult for Ant to understand the intensity of my feelings of loss. The pregnancy to him was, at that very early stage, too abstract. Eighteen months later, though, when he placed his hand on my heavily swollen belly and felt the tiniest of kicks, he could genuinely appreciate the raw emotion that comes with the miracle of a new life.

The birth was long and excruciating. I won't bore you with details. Visit any mothers' group gathering if you're interested in that sort of thing. Never have I known such pure love and devotion until that day at the end of May 2003 when my husband held my hand, mopped my sweaty brow, massaged my back and whispered words of encouragement through the seemingly endless long hours of labour.

And then, when he stood over me, peeking over the flimsy privacy screen, I looked up at him and saw a mixture of fascination and horror as the surgeon sliced open my belly and pulled our son out. Try as he might, the little fellow couldn't make it out on his own. His tiny head was shaped like a cone from his efforts.

Together we had written a birth plan, as most couples who attend antenatal classes do, and it is testament to Andrew's character that he encouraged me to modify it when I had written, 'I refuse to use pethidine; under no circumstances am I to have an epidural; under no circumstances will I agree to a caesarean' – the list of my unreasonable restrictions went on. Ant's ability to respond and adapt to circumstances beyond our control was, thankfully, far greater than mine. He knew that I would regard it as failure if I couldn't adhere to my birthing plan. He, in his enviable wisdom, knew that things often don't go as planned and success is achieved only through an ability to modify and improvise. Thank God he was there. At least I didn't use the pethidine.

The nurse handed Ant the scissors to cut the umbilical cord and he took our little angel and held him in those strong callused hands with almost impossible tenderness. And the tears of pure, utter joy instantly erased the agony of that horrendous labour. Life's greatest adventure was just beginning.

I think many mothers would agree that giving birth, and instantly becoming responsible for someone else's life other than your own, makes you somewhat risk-averse. Even for the most adventure-driven women, an overpowering nurturing instinct comes to the fore with childbirth. I felt an overwhelming need for safety and security when Finlay was born. I was a nervous wreck driving home from the hospital with our newborn baby in the car. The 20 minute trip was heavily punctuated with 'Slow down' and 'Be careful', much to Ant's annoyance, I'm sure.

Of course the early stages of fatherhood must be difficult for any man, not to mention the woman. No matter how ready you think you are, *nothing* can prepare you for the absolute upheaval a newborn brings to the household. As we adjusted to our new life of sleeplessness, feeding, wailing, nappy changing, projectile poos and vomits, it occurred to me that perhaps the reason everyone extols the utter delights of parenthood is because they want others to experience that same indefinable level of suffering. It's a shock, I think, for the male to suddenly have attention diverted from him to the new little person and, as much as all the parental literature advises to maintain a healthy balance of attention on father and baby, it's not so easy in practice. The baby's demands must be met, thus the baby receives more attention. The husband returns from the office expecting a hearty meal and gets cheese on toast. Gone from his bed is the sex goddess – in her place, the dowdy wife with bags under her eyes and flannelette pyjamas. And the simple biological fact that men don't have breasts doesn't help the new dad to feel involved. Sure, he can help with bathing and changing, but often the mum exhibits an unreasonable overprotectiveness. Yep, those early days are tough on the poor ol' dad.

But Ant surprised me with his adaptability. He effortlessly swapped the paddle for the nappies, and then back to the paddle. It was a juggling act and, as with anything, he became good at it with practice. He commuted to work via kayak down the Parramatta River (after driving from Glenbrook to Parramatta) so training time would impact less on baby time. He dodged ferries under the Harbour Bridge and pulled up at the Man o' War steps next to the Opera House, slung the kayak over his shoulder, and marched up past the Toaster to his work in the Coca Cola Amatil office at Circular Quay. One day he arrived home from work wetter than usual. 'The kayak's leaking,' he said. The CEO of CCA backed his BMW into it in the carpark.

And so, I guess it seemed like a pretty good time, while our new baby was too young and I was too nervous to get involved in any hair-raising family adventures, for Ant to persist with his solo paddling challenges. With both eastern and western routes across Bass Strait ticked off, the next obvious venture was straight across the middle – a direct, non-stop crossing of some 230 kilometres from Tidal River in Victoria to Boat Harbour, Tasmania. No-one had ever attempted a direct crossing of Bass Strait before. The new father made it in 35 hours of non-stop paddling, with several interesting hallucinations and one capsize due to 'falling asleep at the wheel'. It was easier than the night feeding routine, he said. Not that you'd know, I replied.

To my eternal regret, I have a vivid imagination. After crossing the western side of Bass Strait in January 2003 I imagined that much more was possible. Although the 100 kilometre ocean crossing from King Island to Apollo Bay had felt pretty 'out there' and committing, I couldn't help but think this was just the beginning of an exploration into what is possible in a kayak. I had paddled 100 kilometres in a day and not a drop of water leaked into the hatches. If you have faith in your boat, why not keep paddling? Night paddling had never bothered me too much, in fact I quite like it.

However, I do like my sleep! I asked around and did a bit of research to find out whether anyone had successfully slept in an unmodified kayak at sea before. There was very little information available. After considerable thought, I felt that there were advantages to paddling right through the night rather than trying to sleep. For one, you wouldn't be kidding yourself that you'd get a decent bit of kip when it was pretty clear that this was unlikely. Also, by continuing to paddle you are likely to stay warmer with the body heat generated by paddling. You will also get off the water more quickly. This is important because the longer you are out there on the water, the more exposed you are to changes in the weather, adverse currents, and the movement of your kayak on the ocean, which can be tiring after 24 hours or so.

Aside from seeing what my kayak could do, I was also keen to explore the boundaries of my own endurance. I didn't have to look too far to find a suitable crossing to aim for. Bass Strait had never, as far as my friends and I knew, been crossed in a direct line by kayak. Almost all previous crossings had used the islands of the eastern side of the Strait, and just a couple of people had been successful on the western route via King Island. Although island-hopping either side of Bass Strait is a more reasonable proposition, both these routes are nonetheless serious paddles in themselves. With no previously recorded direct crossings of the Strait, there was an opportunity to explore the unknown that I couldn't resist.

There were so many questions: Could it be done? (I thought so.) How long would it take? What is the best route? How will tidal drift and ocean currents affect me? What is the best time of year? What sort of conditions will I need? Should I try to sleep during the night or paddle non-stop? How fit will I need to be? How will my body hold up? Who should I tell?

It was the unknowns that made this trip attractive. I loved the exploratory aspects. Obviously Bass Strait is well charted and there is no true 'exploring' left to be done in this part of the world, however for sea kayakers this was something new. No-one knew how long this trip would take or even if it could be done. It's a bit like a first ascent, which in climbing terms is always more attractive than repeating someone else's route.

I set off on the long drive from my Blue Mountains home in late November 2003. After an overnight camp at Canning River and a speeding fine courtesy of the Victoria Police, I arrived at Tidal River on Wilsons Promontory looking forward to the big adventure. I paddled around to Oberon Bay a couple of kilometres south for a quiet night's sleep on the beach.

The forecast was still good, although not absolutely perfect: there would be light beam-on easterlies turning north-east later in the day.

A perfect forecast would have been light northerlies the whole time, however the weather systems move quickly through Bass Strait and I reasoned that if you wait for perfect conditions down here you won't get much paddling done. The wind was forecast to gradually become more favourable later the next day.

Everything felt right, so I was fired up and ready to go. The paddle was on! Early the next morning I struggled down the beach with my loaded kayak. The tide was dropping and it was a long carry to the water's edge. Wilsons Promontory has stunning scenery and I savoured the last of the mainland that I would see for a while. I set off with a certain amount of trepidation.

A seal colony in the Anser Group of islands provided some light entertainment. Hundreds of these magnificent creatures were occupying a large cave and every available rock. They were making a huge racket and their grunting and barking echoed and was magnified by the cave. It was actually quite intimidating and, as I did not wish to disturb them, I paddled on. Besides, I had paddled just a few kilometres and still had a long way to go!

As expected, the wind was from my port beam most of the day, slowly swinging to the stern quarter as the day wore on. It was light initially but reached about 15 knots [28 km/h] with plenty of whitecaps by about 11 am. Curtis Island is a very steep and dramatic piece of rock that was visible in the distance. It provided a benchmark for my progress. It certainly was helpful to have something to measure my progress by, and a lot more interesting than looking at an unbroken horizon. By late afternoon the island had disappeared in the distance behind me and I felt very, very alone.

There had been one trawler pass by during the day but they hadn't noticed this lone paddler on their patch of ocean, which was fine by me. I checked my progress after 12 hours paddling and I had done about 90 kilometres. This was good progress, but I knew I would slow down as the effects of fatigue and sleep deprivation kicked in. I fuelled up regularly all day rather than have the usual three big meals.

As the sun went down, I stayed focused on paddling and I had no intention of stopping for sleep. As this trip was shortly after the new moon, I had just a thin sickle in the sky that would illuminate the night for a few hours before setting. With eyes well adjusted to the night this was enough light, however it was very dark when that moon went down! I had been hoping for a full moon for more light but in my mind the good forecast took precedence over the state of the moon. The stars were spectacular and it was exhilarating to be out in such a committing position on a beautiful night.

There was an exciting moment when I felt the need to pee late in the night. I deployed a drogue and sponsons in order to remain stable enough on what had become a fairly choppy sea and a very dark night.

[A drogue, or sea anchor, is typically an open-ended cone made of cloth, with lines that run to the bow to keep the kayak facing into the wind and waves when the paddler is at rest. Sponsons add extra stability by acting as mini-outriggers. These are usually inflatable for portability, and attach to the kayak on each side of the cockpit.]

Everything is harder at night. With the wind in my face as I deployed the drogue off the bow, the sea seemed quite wild in the dark, it was totally different to having the wind and seas from behind. The lack of visual cues makes an enormous difference to how you perceive the weather and conditions around you! You have to rely on your other senses and this can take some getting used to, especially after all day and half a night on the water.

With no moon, I was still reasonably happy to plod along, trying to maintain the pace and look after my body. There was a real low point between about 2 am and 5 am. I was feeling like a bit of kip and started nodding off to sleep while still paddling.

This is a lot like dropping off to sleep at the wheel of the car while still driving. I fought the urge as best I could but there comes a point where the heaviness of your eyelids is irresistible, and I nodded off and capsized. I woke up just as my head hit the water. A face full of Bass Strait made sure I was wide awake by the time I found myself upside down and staring at the cold black depths below. I rolled back up again and paddled hard for the next half hour or so to warm up, and then settled back into a steady rhythm.

Eventually dawn broke and I found myself somewhat weary but still plugging on.

An hour or so later I saw a jagged mountain range on the horizon in the far south. You beauty! Tassie really is out there after all! (You begin to doubt even obvious truths when you've been at sea for some time.) It took another couple of hours until I realised I was looking at a jagged bank of storm clouds off to the south. This was somewhat deflating, even though I had known it was far too early to see the mainland.

Around this time, my mind started playing tricks on me. A few times I felt I was passing close to a bridge pylon, although I was still 80 kilometres from land. The wrap-around style of hat I was wearing cast shadows on the side of my face and I ducked quickly to one side several times to ensure I didn't hit these imaginary obstacles. Later, the bank of clouds off to the south seemed to be moving towards me as though painted on a huge mobile background movie set. Eventually the world returned to normal and all the while I just kept plugging away, drawing inexorably closer to Tassie.

Towards mid-afternoon Table Cape came into view, and a bulk carrier passed by – firm evidence there were people out there to the south! I put total faith in my compass and hours later Boat Harbour, nestled close to Rocky Cape National Park, came into view. Needless to say the final kilometres in to shore were painfully slow. I finally pulled in to the beach, unsure of exactly where to land as I wanted a quiet, uninterrupted night's sleep that night. In the end I went straight to the surf club, as I could see some boatsheds that looked like a good place to doss for the night.

As I pulled up to the beach, I got out of my kayak in waist-deep water, which was good because – with the water supporting me – I didn't fall over straight away! One of the locals rushed down to help me, or so I thought. 'Sorry mate, we don't take boat people here!', he remarked dryly. After enquiring where I had come from, he offered me a bed for the night at his dairy farm a few kilometres away.

Boat Harbour is a small place and it didn't take long for the word about my trip to spread. Someone called the media and later that evening a newspaper photographer turned up. The ABC also got hold of me at the farmhouse.

Tassie hospitality was fantastic, as always, and I didn't have to try too hard to get a lift to Devonport for the ferry home the next day. Everything had fallen into place and the trip I had planned and dreamed about for over a year had finally been pulled off.

After returning home from that trip, he pulled out the *Times Atlas of the World* – I sometimes regret giving him that gift for his thirty-fifth birthday – and a tape measure.

'Have a look at this,' he beckoned, and I reluctantly turned my back on the washing up. 'The Gulf of Carpentaria. It's only 5 centimetres on the map!'

'Oh!'

Andrew, the quiet achiever. One thing that struck me and seriously impressed me about Ant was his modesty. He had done things that others wouldn't dream of, yet he wasn't one to blow his own trumpet. And he certainly didn't like to make broad public announcements of his adventurous intentions, especially as they became more and more challenging. He preferred to just do it, and talk about it when he'd 'bagged his peak'.

The Hawkesbury Classic is an annual highlight on many paddlers' calendars. On the night of the full moon each October, hundreds of paddlers race for 111 kilometres down the Hawkesbury River. My job as landcrew in 2003 simply involved doing a car shuffle leaving a car at the finish line and waving him off at the start – so I could take our little baby home to bed and let Ant drive himself home in the morning after paddling all night. They have an annual award for the best landcrew. I thought I'd be in hot contention for my efforts that year!

After winning the Open LRec1 division (long recreational kayak) in 10 hours 4 minutes, his paddling buddies congratulated him on his efforts. 'Oh, that was just a training run!' A subtle hint – he didn't elaborate that he was warming up for his assault on Bass Strait. After Christmas, while he was in peak paddling condition, he won his class in the Murray River Marathon, the world's longest annual canoe race of 404 kilometres, paddled over five days. Again, baby Finlay and I did a splendid job as landcrew.

Again, he said, 'Oh, yeah, that was a training run, too!'

And so it was – for the Gulf of Carpentaria crossing – seven days at sea in a kayak.

2004

All day and for much of each night, for the best part of seven days, I was paddling until my arms could stand it no longer and my eyelids became unbearably heavy. Exhausted, I would deploy my homemade sea anchor from the bow of my kayak. This would slow my drift and hold the nose of my vessel into the wind – a much more stable position than beam-on to the weather, which is dangerously vulnerable to capsize.

SOLO

I'd started this epic journey in the Torres Strait, paddling from Horn Island across to Pajinka, the local name for the tip of Cape York, where I'd met with some of the Injinoo indigenous community and received valuable advice on tides, currents and how to find water in the area.

Then I paddled down the west coast of Cape York. Near the township of Seisia a shark thought my rudder looked rather tasty and had a solid nibble at it, bending it dramatically and giving me a bloody big fright.

As I approached Injinoo I had my first encounter with a crocodile: a large salty eyeing me off from only 15–20 metres away. It's quite a humbling experience to suddenly realise that you are nowhere near the top of the food chain.

I reached Duyfken Point after some 33 kilometres of hard paddling and rested for three days to prepare myself for the big crossing to Yirrkala, near Nhulunbuy in eastern Arnhem Land. Then, with a good deal of trepidation, I launched my kayak in late August (2004) with a 20 knot [37 km/h] sou'easterly trade wind blowing.

Ahead of me, the nearest land lay more than 500 kilometres away. I estimated it would take 5–7 days, during which time I could never leave the 5.7 metre kayak.

I'd removed the front bulkhead so I could slip down inside it and sleep lying flat on the hull. To suggest this is claustrophobic is an understatement in the extreme. On a rough ocean it's torture. Squeezing into my kayak in this manner was so tight that I could fit only one arm down by my side; the other had to be crossed over my chest, Egyptian mummy style. Rolling over was impossible. I was really locked in tight.

[Andrew's home-made outriggers consisted of foam rectangles, approximately 600 × 300 × 150 mm, attached to a length of aluminium tubing. The outriggers would sit on the rear deck during paddling hours, and then be slotted into attachments at the sides of the cockpit to sit perpendicular to the kayak, providing stabilisation for the craft during the non-paddling periods.]

With the wind up around 20 knots [37 km/h] on the first couple of nights, breaking waves would regularly wash over the kayak. In anticipation of this I'd fashioned a cockpit cover from waterproof fabric, but I had to leave an airhole for breathing. On the roughest nights, buckets of salt water would wash through this hole straight into my face. It's near impossible to sleep while being tossed around inside a kayak with litres of water being splashed into your face every few minutes and the noise of ocean slapping on the closed-cell foam outriggers like a gunshot going off every few seconds.

As if all this was not enough, sitting and sleeping in tropical salt water took a terrible toll on my skin. It's impossible to stay dry in this environment. By day four of the crossing, I'd developed a nasty skin infection and salt sores that made every movement excruciating. The obvious cure was a freshwater shower, a change of clothes and a long sleep under a tree!

The paddle was not without rich rewards, however. I will long remember the pod of dolphins following alongside the kayak under a full moon on a silky smooth sea. Equally memorable was the tiger shark as long as my kayak, its body as thick as a 44-gallon [200-litre] drum, surfacing within metres to check me out and disappearing just as quickly.

I saw an incredible array of sea snakes of different colours and sizes, hundreds of kilometres from land. There was also magic in a moment early one morning when I saw deep, deep below me two small sharks circling my kayak, both as mesmerised by me as I was by them. I will remember forever those final paddle strokes towards land, the certainty that I had made it and the sense of victory for having safely pulled off a tough paddle.

Most of all I'll remember those first shaky steps on solid ground that somehow kept moving, and my relief at collapsing for that rest under a tree.

The Australian Geographic Society awarded Andrew their coveted Adventurer of the Year medal for his 2004 monumental kayaking voyage across the Gulf. He made landfall in Nhulunbuy on the north-east coast of Arnhem Land after six and a half gruelling days at sea. Another hurdle successfully negotiated. The Tasman Sea was looking more probable than possible now.

The awards ceremony was held in the Botanical Gardens in Sydney in September 2005. Ant's parents came down from Brisbane for the occasion and it was afterwards, as we dined at the café in the gardens, that he broke the news about his Tasman goal. Should we, shouldn't we, tell them? We had debated this for some months. They'll need to know eventually. Better tell them so they can get used to the idea. Their reaction . . . silence, and a furtive glance from one to the other. Then, after some thought, my father-in-law told his son that he would have his full support.

Andrew's mother, who never shortened his name and whom he lovingly referred to as 'Marsie', expressed her pride in him. She thought it was wonderful that he had such drive and determination, and such grand ambitions, even though the stress of his adventures caused her great angst. 'You'll do it,' she told him, 'because you always achieve what you set out to do. I know how meticulous you are in planning your expeditions.' I think it would be fair to say, though, that the magnitude of this expedition was far greater than they could have imagined.

We had a regular Sunday night dinner with some Glenbrook friends. Mark and Teena Windsor had moved to Sydney not long after we did. They tried the inner west for a while, until we convinced them that Glenbrook was the place to be. When you're from the country, the Blue Mountains is a far friendlier place to live than the big smoke. Neil and Pam Crabb and their two girls were locals, and Ant knew Neil through climbing. Everyone seems to know everyone in the climbing community. They quickly became part of our close-knit Glenbrook circle of friends, and so it was that one Sunday dinner evolved into a regular event.

And it was at one such dinner that Ant spilled the beans about his intentions with the Tasman. We were discussing our annual Easter get-together for the following year. 'Well I may not be able to make it next year,' Ant commented.

'Why not?' Mark asked. 'What are you up to?'

I said, 'Should we tell them?'

Ant looked at me and replied, 'Well, it seems like we already have. Guys, I've got my eye on another big kayak trip for April next year. I've been thinking about the Tasman.'

'Aha . . . that doesn't surprise me. I thought you'd have a crack at that sometime.'

'Oh really?' Ant said. 'Am I that transparent?!' It was becoming obvious to those who knew him best where these other trips were leading, knowing that Paul Caffyn had attempted the very same not once, but twice.

Mark commented, 'It's a noble objective. Very worthwhile.'

Neil, ever the analyst, said, 'When I saw you with that book, Andy, *Speck on the Sea*, I just thought, "In the hands of anyone else, that would be an interesting read. Letting Andy read that book, though, is bloody dangerous! He'll just get some big ideas, and then he'll go and act on them!"'

CHAPTER 9

2006

And act he did, and it was an admirable performance. This was a year of enterprise. A year of fruition. With that huge milestone, the big 'forty', looming just around the next calendar year for Ant, there was an almost palpable sense that he needed to fit everything in while he was still physically able. We had joked about a 'mid-life crisis', but deep in the recesses of his mind I think Ant was very much aware that he would eventually have to stop taxing his body to such extremes. And of course fatherhood . . .

Not yet, though. Andrew and his kayak had a date with Antarctica in February. Two months off work gave him the time – with two companions, Stuart Trueman and Laurie Geogeghan – to charter a yacht from South America to drop them off at the Argentinian scientific base at Hope Bay on the tip of the Antarctic Peninsula. From there, they would paddle over 800 kilometres along the Peninsula to the Antarctic Circle, a latitude of 66°33' south.

For 35 days, the three men endured sub-freezing temperatures, blizzards, horrific katabatic winds and some of the most incredibly beautiful scenery you could ever imagine paddling through. They encountered leopard seals and whales, slept with noisy and smelly colonies of elephant seals and woke on occasion to find Gentoo penguins sleeping in their kayaks. They attempted, often without success, to paddle through brash ice so thick that you could almost walk on it. They became iced in, snowed on, worn out, but returned with stories, photos and film footage to turn me green with envy.

Andrew's father Peter turned 70 while he was down south. The very best of presents came for Poppa (as he'd become at the birth of Finlay, his first grandchild) when he received a birthday phone call from the frozen continent. The sheer excitement and joy in his son's voice as it crackled down the line from the bottom of the world was something he'll never forget.

Ant, I'd noticed, had an inclination towards, well, I wouldn't exactly say melancholy, but something just short of it – restlessness perhaps – upon return from an expedition. That awkward transitory period of fitting back into conventional life after incredibly intimate experiences with the natural environment and his own psyche was always challenging. You know, re-establishing the work routine, meeting deadlines, mowing the lawn. I used to feel it too, when I accompanied him on his adventures. When you're out in the wilderness, there are no trivial concerns. All that matters are the basics of survival – food, shelter, safety. Nothing more. Just that sense of being pitched against the elements – I loved that. Now, with the responsibility of our precious little person, I felt more a degree of envy that he still had the freedom to go off exploring, while I had an overbearing nurturing instinct to stay safe at home caring for our beautiful child.

There was no hint of melancholy after Antarctica. His return yacht voyage across the Drake Passage was filled not only with copious seasickness, but also many hours of contemplating his next two adventures. And what incredible adventures they promised to be. A traverse of the Antarctic continent using kites and sleds was in the pipeline. Ant was teaming up with Ben Deacon and Pat Spiers for what they called the Icebird project, which they hoped would be a groundbreaking journey, focusing on the global warming issue by awakening awareness of the potential of wind power as a viable alternative energy source.

And, of course, the Tasman was waiting patiently, turbulently, relentlessly, for Andrew McAuley's assault. It was simply a matter of timing, weather windows and finances as to which adventure came first. The boys were hoping to attempt the Antarctic traverse this summer, although their attempts to drum up the very substantial financial support was making this trip look less and less likely for the 2006–2007 season. Therefore, the Tasman was likely to be next.

And so it was that I picked up from the airport one very excited individual, high on the adrenaline of his Antarctic paddle and intoxicated by the thought of the upcoming adventures.

CHAPTER 10

It's an often-explored question. What makes an adventurer? What sustains the recklessness of childhood and hones it into a more sophisticated form? A mutant gene, perhaps? That was Ant's explanation when Finlay, dressed in his little Superman costume, asked his dad why Superman was so 'super'. 'What does mutant mean?' asked Finlay. 'And Dad, he's not wearing jeans!'

Base jumping legend Dr Glenn Singleman discovered a certain amount of truth to that theory. The thrill gene, he calls it. Some have the blue eyes gene, some the tall gene, the premature balding gene. And a small percentage of the population were born with that mutant, the thrill gene.

This D4DR gene, as it's scientifically known, is more prominent in people who like taking risks. Extreme thrill seekers may have eleven copies of the gene, whereas the risk-averse might have one or two. This gene is resistant to the 'feel good' neurotransmitter dopamine, meaning that while some of us would get a thrill out of jumping in the deep end of the local pool, those with multiple D4DRs need to take that 'jump into the deep end' metaphor to the extreme.

I wouldn't necessarily categorise Andrew as a thrill seeker, in fact throughout his adventurous life he took pains to minimise risk, but it's all relative. Many of the cliff faces he dragged me up over the years brought me to tears, while he was in his element. And the fundamental traits of the D4DR gene indicating a higher tolerance to risk can be advantageous, especially when facing the types of challenges Andrew set himself. The less likely you are to be deterred by uncertainty, the greater likelihood of success. And certainly, to date, it had worked in Ant's favour.

Paddling the eastern route of Bass Strait, for example, would be a prohibitive risk to many, yet a perfectly reasonable undertaking for others, as evidenced by the hundreds of kayakers who have successfully made the crossing. Then, of those hundreds, only two — first Ant, then Stu Trueman several years later — have considered a direct, non-stop crossing within the realms of minimal risk. Everyday life is full of risks. In the words of the estimable Bilbo Baggins, 'It's a dangerous business, going out your door.'

Part of the drive is undoubtedly genetic, although psychology plays its part, and arguably the greater part. In saying that, psychological make-up is largely genetic too, I expect. During the preparation phase of the Tasman Solo project, Andrew took part in a personal development profile analysis with one of his sponsors, John Walker of Walker Wilson Associates in Sydney. The 'QO2™' profile measures the energy people put into seeing either the opportunities or the obstacles in life. As the literature accompanying the test indicates, 'the QO2™ taps into the fifth dimension of the human psyche. This fifth scale is widely used in the area of clinical psychology to distinguish between normal and abnormal behaviour.' While this profile analysis is typically applied to the working environment, the resulting profile is applicable to all aspects of life, from choice of vocation to vacation. I can think of few others in the world who would want to spend their holidays paddling a kayak across the Tasman Sea.

The Opportunities–Obstacles scale (O2) measures where people focus their energies. At one extreme are those who tend to focus their energy on 'seeing opportunities' – the optimists. People who score strongly towards this end of the scale are typically brimming with enthusiasm and tend to have a positive effect on those around them. However, there is a downside. If too much energy is expended in seeking opportunities, there may be insufficient reserves to focus on potential obstacles. This is known as 'Pollyanna-ism'. Eleanor Porter created the character Pollyanna in her book of the same name – the little girl whose behaviour is often described as a naïve form of optimism. She believes that no matter what happens, things will always turn out for the best. There are never any obstacles, only opportunities. In the working environment, managers who fit this end of the scale can cause major problems. Their enthusiasm can cloud judgements, leading to poor decision-making. The extreme of the other end of the scale is known as 'Eeyore-ism', after A.A. Milne's eternally pessimistic old donkey in the classic tale *Winnie-the-Pooh*.

The Opportunities–Obstacles Quotient (QO2™) is defined as 'the ratio of the energy you put into seeing opportunities to the ratio of the energy you put into seeing obstacles', a measure that quantifies a person's position on the Opportunities–Obstacles scale.

Not surprisingly, Andrew's overall QO2™ value put him at the extreme end of the scale towards 'Pollyanna-ism'. His Moving Towards Goals (MTG) Energy, was 100 per cent, MTG Energy being 'a form of psychic energy – the energy that gives us the determination, enthusiasm and resilience to formulate and achieve goals in life'. Andrew's individual report stated:

> You will expend a considerable amount of energy in trying to achieve the goal that you set for yourself. When problems arise which seem likely to prevent you from attaining your goals, you are likely to push even harder to get where you want to go. You are not the sort of person to give up easily. You are likely to set yourself challenging goals that will stretch your capabilities, as you are usually confident in your own abilities.

He scored 94 per cent on the Multi-Pathways subscale (when obstacles arise he is likely to put effort into finding a way around them, indicating good improvising and problem solving skills), 95 per cent for Optimism and gained a Hope Index of 97. According to the report,

> one of the differences between optimists and high-hope people is that the optimist may have a generalised expectation that things will work out whereas the person with high hopes will also look for alternative pathways when blocked from a goal.

Andrew's profile summary read:

> You are likely to approach your goals in a positive emotional state, with a sense of challenge and a focus on

success. You are enough of a realist to know that plenty of setbacks will occur, but you are likely to treat these as challenges and not failures.

Yep. That's Ant in a nutshell. The qualities summarised in the report I've witnessed on countless challenging occasions over the years, not the least of which was the birth of our son.

There is no question of Ant not being cognisant of the challenges of the Tasman Solo Expedition, and he was only too aware of the price of failure. Could his high QO2™ score, verging on 'Pollyanna-ism', be enough to pull him through?

In delving into the psychology of the 'why', adventurer Greg Mortimer, a member of the first Australian expedition to climb Everest without oxygen, comments: 'Everest and the Poles have been achieved but now adventurers are going off and having adventures in their own head space.' That ultimate dimension of the challenge is obvious in Jon Muir's account after his successful south to north crossing of the Australian continent on foot in 2001:

> Nothing I've done before has been as hard as this, so that's been fantastic for me because I got to go places on this trip. And I'm not talking about landscape – I'm talking about places in my mind and body that I strove towards for years and never reached.

That, indeed, would be the challenge of Andrew's journey.

How did he grapple with the idea when he knew that this expedition would stretch his comfort zone beyond anything he had ever attempted? He once confided to a friend that the thought of not doing the trip was far worse than the thought of doing it and failing. A vast range of complex emotions pervaded his thought processes and preparation. In discussing the inherent risks of adventure with our good friend and medical consultant for the Tasman expedition, Richard Stiles, Ant stated with great profundity:

I find it interesting when someone is lost in the outdoors, people often say that they died 'doing what they loved', as though this somehow makes it better. Well, perhaps it is better than dying crossing the road on the way to work, but it still doesn't make it 'worth it', in my opinion. No adventure is worth dying for, or losing your fingers and toes for. The bottom line is that life is more precious than any of these things. The paradox is that some of us need to put it at risk to really understand that, and to feel the intensity of this gift we have. Living it all from an armchair through the eyes of others doesn't quite do it.

From this conversation, and his own curious choice of interests, Richard explored the notion:

In this light, our experience of life only has meaning because it also involves death. The two rely on each other – and are meaningless without the other. We can only know light if we have also some conception of darkness. From this perspective, risk activities can provide us with one avenue to experience something of the totality underlying living and dying. However, as Andy describes, the unsettling price of seeking this totality, of experiencing the immense and potent wonder that is life, is the real risk that we might lose it altogether – and that is an outcome that most of us don't really want! In this sense, I wonder if this is one of the greatest paradoxes of them all – we love life, or are engrossed by it, but to experience its full potency some of us feel the need to hold it in a way that we may lose it, to hold it as an open question.

The trip scares me. I am trying to work out the best time to do it, by analysing every weather map for each month during the last five years. There is no pattern. You can get any weather in any month. Some of the weather maps scare me to the core. The most frightening are the deep, deep low pressure systems that scream westwards across the Southern Ocean like crazy, back-spinning bowling balls hurled by the devil. These systems can be as low as 950 hectopascals (15 September 2001), creating 'Perfect Storm' type waves with terrifying regularity. I dearly hope I don't see one of these systems in the Tasman Sea. However, I know the chances are a lot better than even that I will.

This begs the question, why should I do this anyway? Why not just flag it and give the project away? It's a difficult question. I have a lot to lose. I have a beautiful wife with whom I share the deepest respect and love. I have a wonderful baby boy, parents and siblings who are very, very important to me and whom I love with all my soul. Why risk it all? The risk is more than mine. While I risk losing my life, I also know that losing me will cause all of them pain and suffering that I have no right to inflict.

It's clear to me that many of my expeditions are selfish endeavours. I refer to those that I classify as the more risky trips; those where I stand a good chance of losing my life. In considering the expeditions I have done, the crossing of the Tasman Sea stands tall as the riskiest and the most selfish of them all.

But then, what would Captain Cook's family have said? Or Shackleton's? Or Christopher Columbus's? Or Edmund Hillary's?

While I was not off to discover new land, the drive and motivation behind my expeditions is essentially the same. It is a journey of personal discovery, an extreme test of endurance and of the inner spirit. By risking death, and doing so in a very careful and calculated manner, I live a life of intensity and deep satisfaction.

Paddling across the Gulf of Carpentaria is one thing. The Tasman, and below the 40th parallel, is something else entirely. The distance from Fortescue Bay on the east coast of Tasmania to Milford Sound, New Zealand, is over three times the length, water temperature a good 15 degrees cooler. Then there are the seas. Sure, the tropical waters of the Gulf can conjure up some wind and waves, but nothing compared to the tempestuous Tasman. It doesn't bear thinking about.

And why paddle below the 40th parallel south? It's a question many have asked. The weather and sea conditions are notoriously unfavourable at this latitude. In his words, 'It's in the Roaring Forties and it's gonna be a heck of a trip!' And, the idea of the trip is attracting him like a magnet.

It's a funny thing. It has attracted me, that's true yeah. It has. Okay, so why has it attracted me? Why has the Tasman Sea drawn me to it? And why have I chosen to cross below 40 degrees south? For me, the Tasman – it's known as a rough ocean and to cross north of 40 degrees somehow to me seems to be missing the whole point of the Tasman and I know that sounds ridiculous but that's just how it feels to me.

If you cross from Tassie to the South Island of New Zealand, you've really experienced the Tasman Sea, you've really, really done something that experiences the guts of what the Tasman is all about. But you have to be very, very careful, you know, and it worries me. I'm scared. I'm scared about this trip.

Yeah, it's a funny thing for me too. Funny in that when the first embryo of an idea was forming, it did indeed seem like a heck of an idea. As time drew inexorably on, and the field tests were being ticked off one by one – Cape York and Torres Strait, Bass Strait western route, Bass Strait direct, the Gulf of Carpentaria, Antarctica – and the trip was taking a stronger and more definite form, I began to feel increasingly anxious. And it was a dilemma. I had a choice – give Ant my unconditional support, or put a stop to it. But did I have that right? Some have said it was selfish of him to do this trip, but would it not be selfish of me to stop him? Is it not incredibly selfish to prevent someone you love more than anything from pursuing his dreams? Would it not be selfish to stifle his inherent need to explore? When someone is so passionate and determined and driven to achieve seemingly impossible goals, how can you stifle that?

Richard Stiles often addressed me as Queen Victoria – a title he perhaps felt I deserved for my altruism in allowing my husband to 'escape' on so many adventures. His wife and also expedition doctor Sharnie Wu, however, said in jest that I was giving wifedom a bad name. Perhaps she thought that I exhibited Queen Victoria's less admirable qualities of total devotion to her husband, Prince Albert, in submitting completely to his will. I assure you that was not the case, but Richard argued that his wife should take some lessons from me in allowing a husband to become less shackled.

It was by no means submission. It's just that, at the risk of sounding repetitive, I say again I had an unshakable faith in the man. If he thought it was possible to paddle a sea kayak across the Tasman Sea, I believed him. If he thought he could make it, he would. I believed that. I *had* to believe that.

The ocean is a force far more powerful than us. If it decides to unleash its fury, there is no stopping it. Every year, around the world, an alarming number of container ships are lost to the sea. If one of these behemoths weighing millions of tonnes cannot survive the savage sea, what chance do I have in a 21-foot [6.4 metre] sea kayak?

Every time I see my little boy Finlay, and he says, 'It's my Daddy!' with all the excitement that three-year-olds have, I feel almost physically ill with guilt that I am even contemplating this trip. To those that wonder at the irresponsibility of it all, what can I say? We who are drawn to expeditions try feebly to justify our passion. Expeditions are a guiding light for me, a driving force. They are as essential to me as life itself. Regularly during media interviews I explain how we adventurers are not adrenaline junkies in the reckless sense. We do not needlessly take risks without carefully minimising every possibility that something might go wrong. Sure, risks must be taken at times. However these are carefully calculated and, through meticulous research, preparation and training, we reduce those risks to a level that is acceptable (to us at least).

Having said all that, though, sometimes nature throws a wild-card. There are parts of this planet that are not meant for mankind. Those places are often the most alluring and dangerous of them all. The Tasman Sea is certainly not meant for a man in a sea kayak. The ocean can throw anything at you, and in the Tasman, south of the 40th parallel, it most likely will. So, is it reckless of me to attempt this crossing? With a child and a wife to support, does it make me even more irresponsible? There are many who will answer yes to both.

I have spent a lifetime pursuing adventurous dreams in the wildest places on the planet. For the most part, I believe that even as a father I have been responsible and done justice to the duties that every father and husband must perform. But I have to think hard about this trip across the Tasman, the wildness and unpredictability of the ocean there, and the ferocity of what can be unleashed. The answers to all those questions that must be asked make me feel ill and heavy with unbearable guilt. Can I justify doing this trip, as a father, a husband, and the sole breadwinner for my family? Is it fair? There is only one answer, and it nags at me incessantly, hauntingly.

It is no.

CHAPTER 11

Over the years, Ant had spent quite a bit of time out on the water with the rather cerebral Richard Stiles, either on their surfboards or in their kayaks. During a lull in the surf one day, Richard spoke some very confronting words. Of course it wasn't something Ant ever felt he could, or should, discuss with me.

'You need to consider Finlay, man. Since Ringo [Richard's dog] died, it made me realise that it's really not those who die who suffer most. It's those who are left behind. A friend of mine lost both his parents when he was young, maybe when he was 18, and it's caused a scar that he has had to work through for the rest of his life. If you die on this trip it could have profound consequences for Finlay. It's different when you have kids, I really think it is.

When you're 21, 22, and you have no chosen life partner, you are freer to go on adventures. It will still hurt people if you die, there's no doubt. You have a relationship with your parents and any siblings, but those are different, I think, because you did not choose to enter into such bonds. And I think that creates a different moral sense of obligation in terms of your freedoms. But in your life now you do have two critical people that you did choose to enter into a relationship with, and these people need you. You need to consider Vicki and Finlay in your choice, Andy, and especially think how they would cope if you don't come home. When you have people depending on you, especially critically depending on you, like Vicki and Finlay – and you die – then you could really scar them. They will likely find a way through but you need to consider this, I think. There really is this responsibility that you didn't have before.'

The enormous challenge of the task, the importance of not letting ego get in the way, and the cruel impact on those around me if I don't come back. All these factors weigh heavily on my mind. I study historical weather maps and conditions carefully. Mid-spring conditions had been my target up until this point, for a few different reasons.

Undeniably, one reason was because I wanted to be first across the Tasman. It is overstating it only a little to say that in the adventuring world, to be first is everything. Despite our will to help our fellow adventurers, and the co-operative, tightly-knit nature of the adventuring community, it is so. Human competitiveness tarnishes the purity of our goals even in this noble realm. I would like to say that I can leave competitiveness and ego behind altogether, and I know I would be a better person if I could. I do my best to live with more altruistic and unaffected intentions, however there is a niggling need to be first, driven by traces of competitiveness that I cannot let go.

As I pored endlessly over weather maps and sought to determine the best time of year for the crossing, a few things became obvious. First, springtime was likely to be more windy than summer, with a greater chance of strong wind conditions that would be dangerous to me and my kayak. It also became apparent that December, of all the months I studied, was the most favourable. As the Icebird project [the Antarctic traverse] was slated for this coming summer (November 2006–February 2007), I could either try to fit it in before Icebird or after. With windy conditions from a favourable direction, I began to consider early spring as the time to go. After all, I was looking for wind assistance anyway, I reasoned.

Sometime around May, when Ben and Pat returned from Greenland [where they did heavyweight field testing of the prototype Icebird sleds in extreme conditions] we agreed that the 2006–2007 season was unrealistic for Icebird due to the enormous funding requirements. We hadn't really made a start on raising the funds required as yet. Deferring Icebird opened the door up for me to do the Tasman anytime I wanted. This was good. I was still focused on a spring-time crossing.

However the importance of coming back in one piece weighed heavily on my mind. Every time my little Finlay called 'Daddy!' with excitement and joy, it tore at my heart. I seriously considered giving the Tasman project away, as it just seemed too risky and dangerous. I spent a lot of time soul-searching during this period, and I was really torn between a desire to pull off this trip – surely the most bold and audacious thing I was ever likely to do in my life – and the responsibility to be there for those who needed me.

The trees were bare and a chill was in the air. Winter arrived all too quickly. The decrease in temperature was inversely proportional to the sense of anticipation in our household. It was foolishly wishful thinking on my part that Ant might just reconsider his need to paddle across the Tasman. Instead, he was throwing more and more time and energy into the project.

11 June 06

Today I went paddling on Botany Bay to test the kites and a new drogue that Mick MacRobb sent me. I also had a riding sail mounted to the rear of the boat, and wanted to test how well it kept my bow pointed into the wind.

It is blowing 30–40 knots [55–75 km/h] from the south-southwest. I consider tackling the open ocean for my afternoon of gear testing. Without having to think too hard about it, I decide that it's too dangerous out there. I know that I must be prepared for 30–40 knots out in the Tasman, and the paradox is not lost on me. I paddle out on the bay and feel the strength of the wind grabbing my paddle and tearing it from my hands. I get into position and deploy the sea anchor I want to test. Everything is hard in this wind. My hands are freezing and I fumble with the ropes. The magnitude of the task I have set myself in the Tasman finally dawns upon me.

Sometimes I wish it would dawn upon Vicki too. I wish she would plead with me not to do it, for the love of her and for our son. I could gracefully exit then, saying that I'd love to paddle the Tasman, but respect for my family prevents me from doing this expedition – it's just too dangerous. My friends and family would understand, and respect me for my selflessness in choosing to stay at home. They know my love for expeditions. I would save face, and probably my life, by sitting this one out.

But there is no such reprieve. Vicki remains supportive of the Tasman expedition. I wonder if she realises that I may not come back. It is by far the most dangerous thing I have ever contemplated, and the risk of not returning home is very high. I'm frightened. One day Vicki asks me whether I am scared. 'Yes,' I reply. 'Very.'

I'm actually wondering if Andrew has any depth of understanding as to how difficult this is for me. This is such a deep dilemma. Damned if I do. Damned if I don't. I know him well enough to know that even if I pleaded with him not to go, he would go anyway, and then how would I feel? How would I resolve things with myself if I didn't give him my full support? And then, of course, to give him my assurance that I'm happy for him to leave us, his wife and beautiful little boy, who is becoming more like his dad every day, is a lie. But it's a lie I need to let him believe. He needs to believe in himself, and so do I. There is no doubt in my mind that this is an outrageously risky undertaking, by far the most extreme of all his adventurous pursuits to date. But, as I've said, I have that unshakable faith. And the possibility of him not coming back? I cannot bring myself to contemplate such thoughts. It couldn't happen. It won't happen. I know it won't happen. Am I a fool for holding such firm belief?

CHAPTER 12

Doubt is never a good thing on an expedition, and this is all the more true when a good part of your chances of survival depend upon your belief in yourself. I have always believed that expedition success depends for the most part on self-belief and determination. The struggle that appears to be physical is so often really a mental struggle. I quickly realised that I would never pull off the Tasman trip if I didn't believe that I could do it. I visualised life-threatening struggles on the ocean, and wondered if I had the strength to do it. I am ashamed of my weakness. Surely I am made of sterner stuff than that? I transport myself to a time much later in life, looking back on this moment and the chance I had to cross the Tasman. How will I feel if I don't go for it now? Will I be comfortable in deciding not to do this?

And if I do go for it and pull it off? I knew that if I crossed the Tasman safely, I could die a happy man, deeply satisfied that I had done something truly bold and significant for the world of sea kayaking. I knew that, although there would be other expeditions, nothing would approach the genuine risk and danger associated with crossing the Tasman. It was important to me to do this.

While many would look at me with admiration for pulling off a difficult and dangerous feat of endurance, I suspected that many others would question my sanity. I'm sure still others would shake their heads in disgust and marvel at my stupidity. 'How irresponsible,' they would mutter. 'He has a wife and a young child as well!'

While it didn't matter to me much what other people thought, sometimes it's hard not to listen. (In truth I always listen, and then choose whether to ignore or absorb what someone says to me once I have heard them out.) I suspect that it was the latter group of people who would challenge my own beliefs to the core.

Ant's little sister Juliet had inherited her mother's grace and beauty, and her worrisome concern over Ant's choice of hobbies. In early June she sent her brother a clipping from *The Weekend Australian Magazine* about British explorer David Hempleman-Adams. The opening paragraph read, 'For me, exploring is a compulsion. It's a need to make my mark, and to prove to myself that when I'm up against all nature can throw at me, I can survive.'

The story went on to recount Hempleman-Adams' near-disaster on a solo expedition to the geometric North Pole – a new route negotiating glaciers and waterfalls and pulling his own sled. 'No companions, no dogs, no supplies airlifted in. I suppose I was mad, but I had to do it.' Some days into the journey, Hempleman-Adams received word that his journalist friend Terry Lloyd had died. The effect of this news was profound:

> I started thinking about all the loved ones who'd died, all the friends who'd been killed on trips. I completely lost it.

I started thinking about my wife and children, which I never do when I'm away – I cut them out completely. But I couldn't stop it. I found myself obsessing over how they'd feel if anything happened to me. And for what? A stupid challenge. Terry also had a family but at least he died doing his job. Here was I, actually seeking danger.

His loss of focus resulted in a broken ankle – a life-threatening predicament when he was 80 kilometres on foot over extreme terrain from where a plane could reach him. For the last five days until the plane arrived he lived on tea, pieces of chocolate and thoughts of his wife and family, and Terry.

The envelope from Juliet contained just this one page, and a scrawled Post-it note: 'Hey Ant, thought you might be interested – it might even change your life!! Yeah right, here's hoping!! J xx'

I could fully appreciate where Juliet was coming from, but I must admit I was surprised when Ant told me of his former climbing partner Vera's reaction to his Tasman project. An accomplished rockclimber and mountaineer, Vera Wong is now mother of two beautiful girls and she no longer harbours the desire to tempt fate on big rock walls or big mountains. She was shocked, and frankly appalled, when Ant revealed his Tasman plans to her. She seriously could not comprehend how, being a parent, he could undertake such an inherently risky adventure. This, coming from one of the toughest women I'd ever met? Motherhood had mellowed her.

'You're crazy, man!' she said to him. 'I've been down in the Southern Ocean and it was terrifying. When we went down to Heard Island we had waves breaking way over the bridge of the ship. The bridge was 60 feet [18 metres] high. I just think the Southern Ocean is so powerful, you'll be bobbing around like a cork getting blown whichever way the wind goes.'

Vera's negativity disturbed me. For such a petite figure, she had always seemed larger than life. Her skill and confidence on rock and ice was something to behold. And for her to be calling Ant crazy was unexpected. Of course, it was understandable for those with a lower tolerance for danger to be terrified, but I thought Vera would be, if not supportive, at least understanding. I told Ant to shut the negativity from his mind and he agreed, of course. He was far better at that than I am. Yet deep down, I couldn't help but wonder if the negatives would worm their way into his otherwise incredibly optimistic outlook.

CHAPTER 13

I guess I'm really drawn to journeys like this, you know. It's a real personal challenge.

There's a great deal of satisfaction in coming up with an adventure that's unlikely and it's improbable, but working through all the different scenarios that you've gotta work through to do a trip like this safely and in a responsible sort of manner is tremendously satisfying and I just love to do this kind of thing. I'm just drawn to extending my own personal limits and showing that these kinds of trips can be done safely and responsibly and encouraging other people to get out and challenge themselves as well.

For about a month I'm going to be living in the kayak. Every day I've gotta paddle a long way, and then I've gotta live – I've gotta eat, I've gotta sleep, you know I've gotta do all the basic things like go to the toilet. I've gotta have enough water. I've gotta have access to food, and there are all these little complex problems that you've gotta deal with and work out how you're going to do without any assistance whatsoever. So each of those has involved a lot of innovation because there are not many people who have done this sort of thing in the world, and there's really been no-one I can turn to for help and advice.

So many questions, so many hurdles to overcome. But, first things first. The trip could not be done without a kayak. Soon after his return from Antarctica, Ant began a stream of serious conversations with Paul Hewitson, owner of Mirage Sea Kayaks in Gosford, on the central coast of New South Wales. Many lengthy phone calls ensued. It's pretty hard, actually, to have anything other than a lengthy call to Paul. They tossed up a few options and Ant tested Paul's dad's kayak, a Mirage 22 (too small), a double, the Mirage 730 (too big), and then considered reworking something that would be just right. He was after the smallest possible boat he could fit all his gear into. And, from the purist's perspective, he wanted something easily recognised as an off-the-shelf kayak, with minimal modifications. Not an ocean liner.

It wasn't until mid-June that Andrew engaged Paul in a pivotal conversation:

'What did you have in mind for this boat, Andrew?' asked Paul. What he was driving at was who was going to pay for it?

'You know what I had in mind!' I replied.

'Tell me. What did you have in mind?'

Somewhat tentatively I said, 'Well, I was hoping that you might supply the boat, in return for the publicity that a trip like this will generate.'

'This could go either way, you know. It could be good publicity for us, or it could be very bad if you don't make it. What if you have to get rescued? The publicity around this is a double-edged sword. It might be good, it might not.'

'Yeah.' There wasn't much else to say about that. He was right.

Chris, one of Paul's employees, called out, 'Maybe we should put Mirage logos on top of the boat and Pittarak on the bottom!' Pittarak is one of Paul's competitors in Australia's sea kayak market.

'Now, let's look at the cost of this. It's a lot of mucking around to make a boat like that. I'll have to go up to the factory at Macksville for a week to supervise it, like I did for your last boat.' Paul had built me an expedition-model fibreglass/Kevlar 580 for the Antarctica expedition.

'Let's look at the orders I've got here. There's about 30 boats per page here, and I've got nearly three pages of orders to fill.' He showed me the order book to prove the point. It was overflowing.

'I've got my ring hanging out here. We're flat-stick. We're so busy at the moment it's got to the point that I'm sick of it. Now if I take a couple of the boys off the job for a week to make your kayak, there's an opportunity cost there. It would actually be easier if we weren't so busy, then we wouldn't have that opportunity cost.'

'This is sounding grim,' I thought to myself.

Paul continued, 'So if you take into account that opportunity cost, I've got all this forgone income, and then there's the cost of the boat itself, and wages that week, and so on. It all adds up to thousands and thousands of dollars, you know.'

He fired an unexpected question at me: 'Do you expect to profit from this?'

I was a little taken aback. 'Well no, not really,' I replied. 'You know I do some public speaking work, but I'm doing that already. I have got a contract to write a book about the trip . . .'

'Who's that with?'

'Pan Macmillan.' I continued, 'Writers' wages are effectively below the poverty line, though. And I'm quitting my job to do this.'

'Quitting your job?' Paul's voice rose an octave. 'Why?'

'Well, I'm out of holidays.'

'Hmmm. Where are you getting the money for this, then?'

'I'm drawing on our mortgage.'

'Geez! What does your wife think?'

'Well funny enough, she supports it. I don't think she's given much thought to how dangerous this really is.'

'Hmmm. How did you get the holidays for Antarctica?'

'I had paid leave for that. I got a bit lucky there. But I've already had two months off this year, there's no way they'll give me another two months off.'

'Why are you doing this? Why is it so important to you?' The question of why has been asked of explorers and adventurers from time immemorial. When people ask it of me, I feel clumsy and struggle for words. How do you answer this age-old question in just a few brief words? This time was no different, and I fumbled for words that were, as always, inadequate.

'That question is quite difficult to answer. I'm not sure that I can tell you why. I'm just drawn to doing this sort of thing. I have been my whole life. I've got a long history of doing stuff like this, and so it is consistent with what I've done in the past.'

'So you don't think you'll profit from this? I'm surprised, because I'm wondering why you're giving up so much.'

'Well, Paul, it's not always about money. If I pull this trip off, when I'm an old man, I'll look back on this and I'll be able to feel very happy that I've done a worthwhile thing.' I realised immediately that many others would not consider it worthwhile at all, but rather foolhardy and dangerous. 'Well, it's something that I consider worthwhile anyway.'

I knew deep down that I could be happy with my life if I succeeded in doing a really significant, pioneering trip like this. I don't know why I place so much value on this. It's a character trait (flaw?) that has seen me spend a lifetime in mountain base camps around the world, waiting for weather and that opportunity to climb. In kayaking I saw lots of opportunity to do things that had not been done, and I was drawn to that opportunity, like a moth to a flame.

'You've talked a bit about the investment that you'd be making. It might help to know that the investment I'm making myself in this is greater than yours by a factor of many times over.' I chose to overlook the fact that I might pay the ultimate price and not come back at all.

'If you want to talk about forgone income, well, I'm quitting my job for this. I'll be living below the poverty line on writers' wages while I write this book. And I still have to feed the family.'

'Yeah, I know,' Paul replied. 'That's why I'm wondering why you're doing it. I thought you'd surely be looking to profit from it somewhere along the line.'

'Nah, not really.'

Paul's a businessman and businessmen are driven by profit. This is what makes our capitalist society go around. It's not necessarily a bad thing – profit drives innovation, and competition keeps the whole system efficient. At least, that's what the economists will have us believe.

But Paul's also a family man, a human and a good bloke. He knew as much as anyone that there was more to life than profit, balance sheets and money, and I think he empathised with my motives (which were, primarily, self-satisfaction).

He also displayed a spirit of friendly rivalry with his next comment. 'I must admit, some of this is a Pittarak versus Mirage thing, you know. And I want to see Mirage get there first!'

At this point I finally had a glimmer of hope that he might supply the kayak for me.

Nothing ever happens too quickly with Paul, though, and it is sometimes hard to get a straight answer from him.

'When were you hoping to have this kayak, Andrew?' he asked.

'By the end of July, if possible. Do you reckon that's possible?'

'It's not out of the question.' Not a very definitive reply.

Eventually, I called Paul after a couple of weeks with some great news that we'd recovered our kayaks from South America at last. He had expressed interest in having the kayak at the shop in Gosford so they could display this Antarctic veteran for customers to see.

The conversation turned to the Tasman project.

'About that boat, Andrew.'

'Yes . . . ?'

'Well, we're prepared to assist you. We'll do the boat, though I still have to work out a few details about it – like how to raise the deck, for example.'

'Awesome, Paul! I'm stoked . . .'

'No worries, Andrew. We'll get there soon. I just have to go to Victoria to sort out this mob who are selling Mirage imitations, and then do that repair job between Melbourne and Adelaide. I reckon we'll get to your boat in early August.'

'Sounds good to me.' I rang off and let out a whoop for joy. It was late to be getting the boat, but I thought I could manage. I just had to focus really hard on fitting the kayak out quickly when it was ready, and then get it on the water for testing as soon as possible. I wasn't really sure what I would do if it handled poorly. It had a high chance of being a pig of a boat, actually, but I needed the extra volume to be able to live in it for a month or more. It was at the same time both a scary and an exciting thought.

CHAPTER 14

They say a bloke's shed is his refuge. You know, a place to escape his nagging wife. Well, Ant's shed was more than that. It was his creative suite, his contemplative place, his workshop for assembling the many pieces of puzzle to allow this trip to happen. Finlay would hang out with Daddy in the shed on Saturday mornings, in his Bob the Builder hard hat, while I was at my yoga class. It was male bonding time.

While the kayak was still in question, another critical and even more challenging item was the pod or capsule or whatever you'd like to call it. I called it the life-support. Without it, the journey would not be possible. It was obvious to Andrew after crossing the Gulf of Carpentaria that his little Gore-Tex curtain set-up would be entirely inadequate for this trip. To contemplate a month-long crossing of the Tasman Sea in a conventional sea kayak meant devising a solid shell of some sort to lock out the elements. Together we roughed up various design options of an airtight, watertight 'thing' that could be retracted during paddling hours, then simply locked over the cockpit coaming to provide a haven for sleeping and riding out storms. It needed to have enough height to allow the paddler to sit up and enough volume to make it self-righting in the event of capsize. Several prototypes were designed and built in the shed, under Finlay's watchful eye, the first of which lies somewhere on the bottom of Wollongong Harbour.

It was late July when the first prototype of the 'bubble of life' was ready for testing. This bubble was made to fit the *Raider-X*, the kayak that went across the Gulf of Carpentaria, since the Tasman kayak was not yet in existence, but the theory had to be tested on something. The result was a fibreglass sheet construction, formed to a dome shape the size of the cockpit (80 cm × 45 cm for the *Raider-X*) and sitting approximately half a metre high. After preliminary trials in the pool and down on the Nepean River, it was ready for some 'real' tests in the surf. We took it down to our close friends John and Jedda's at Wollongong.

John Totenhofer, Jed Lemmon, Ant and I had recently returned from a paddling trip along the coast of Hinchinbrook Island, and the Family Islands and past all the rich people holidaying on Dunk Island, where riffraff like us weren't even allowed to land, and on to Mission Beach in north Queensland. It was to some extent amends for all his other distractions, but at the same time, we loved going on adventures together. While there's no doubt he loved the extreme challenges, he equally loved quality time with family and friends. He was a rare entity.

After a pleasant night reminiscing over our brilliant holiday, the boys were up early for some surfing action in their whitewater kayaks. Another Wollongong paddler, Matt Turner, joined them.

Bellambi reef is going off. There are some screamers coming through at about six feet, barrelling hard over the reef. If you make a mistake, the whitewater will crush you against the rock wall of the harbour. It's a committing place for a Sunday morning paddle.

Matt excels in these conditions, taking off deeper and scoring more waves than John and I do. He has a longer boat that gives him more speed to catch those hard-to-get waves, and fins for directional stability, but even without these advantages I suspect he'd still do better than us. He has an innate talent for kayak-surfing.

We all catch a few goodies. I eat it on one, and get swept along upside down towards the rock wall. It's scary, and the power of the wave won't let me go until the last minute. I narrowly avoid being smashed, and sprint for the channel before the next wall of whitewater gets me.

Soon afterwards, I find myself in the 'sweet spot', right on top of the bommie that triggers these waves to break. A thick, corduroy line of swell approaches. It accelerates as it hits the bommie, doubling in size. There is only one thing to do. I turn and paddle my hardest. It has me. It's a late, late take-off. I am free-falling.

The wave hurls forward into a thick, powerful, roaring barrel. The guys are in the channel paddling out, eyes wide and cheering. I scream, hoot and holler as I thump down to the bottom of the wave. Edging hard, I shoot across the wave at breakneck speed. I'm in the pocket, and it is at once terrifying and exhilarating. There is a roaring wall of whitewater just inches behind me, and the green face of a barrel above. Without fins, my short, stubby playboat has trouble holding its line high on the face. Or maybe it's me that is having trouble and not the boat at all. Now I am deep inside the tube. It is raw, powerful and loud, but at the same time it is a peaceful place. There's nowhere I'd rather be. I'm trying for more speed, but can't find it.

The inevitable happens. I'm too high now, way beyond vertical. I am taken over the falls, following the curl in an impossible arc.

I slam face-first into the concrete-hard water several metres in front of the wave. Now the roaring, furious steamroller comes. Tonnes of whitewater mash me and crush me, rolling me towards that rock wall. The only place to be is locked inside my boat. With me in it, and the sprayskirt sealed tight, the kayak will float and, I hope, offer protection. If I panic and wet exit the kayak, I am in all sorts of trouble. 'Stay calm, and stick with it,' I tell myself.

I burst to the surface, upside down. Quick, an eskimo roll! It is hard in this aerated water, but I come up, my lungs heaving. Somehow, the wall of whitewater has left me behind. I briefly ponder my good fortune as it smashes against the groyne, sending spray tens of metres into the air. The sprint to the channel is now becoming familiar, though it is a little more desperate this time. I reach safety and turn seaward again, meeting up with the boys out the back. I am grinning from ear to ear, and so are they.

'What a cracker, mate!!'

'You were free-falling on that take-off, you know!!'

'Woohoo!' I yell.

The adrenaline is still coursing through my veins. This is too good. I feel like the luckiest bloke in the world. The surf is free, it's beautiful, and good friends are priceless. If I had all the money in the world there's still no place I'd rather be. How good is this!

Later, we test the pod on the *Raider-X*. We're in the channel next to a groyne. There's a reef underfoot and a current running directly out to sea. It's not a great place to be testing the kayak, but we are here now, and the girls are on the beach with Finlay, so we're not about to move somewhere else.

I paddle out, just beyond the breakers. John swims out with me, to keep an eye on things and to right the kayak if I go upside down and don't come up again.

I deploy the sea anchor, and paddle back into the breaker zone, waiting for the rode line [the rope between the kayak and the sea anchor] to come tight. It does. I let a few breakers hit me, to see the effect. I notice a few things. Firstly, when I'm hit by a wave, the sea anchor holds my head to sea quite well. But it's not all good. The worrying thing is that I bounce around on the end of the rode line like a rubber band. As I am hit by a wave, the stretch in the rope takes most of the shock. That's good. But the rope is so elastic that I am slung back towards the sea anchor like a catapult after the wave passes. When this happens, the rode line goes slack and I turn beam-on to the seas. That is a very bad, dangerous position to be in.

It's time to take this a little further. I tuck down inside the kayak and seal the hood on top of the cockpit. The hood is critical to my safety and to the success of this project. It is my own innovation. I moulded a fibreglass shell with a double seal that I will store on the back deck of the kayak during the day. At night, I will snuggle down inside the kayak and seal the hood over the cockpit. The idea is that this will keep the weather out and provide me with some self-righting momentum as well. Because there is volume up high, effectively an air pocket, the boat shouldn't be able to stay upside down. At worst, it should stay on its side if hit by a big wave. Then, I hope, the next big wave to come along should right me.

Well, this is what we're here to test. In fact, the initial testing that I did on the river with Vicki showed us that the hood was not buoyant enough on its own. I had anticipated this last year sometime, and had some inflatable buoyancy 'bubbles' made up to resolve the problem. With the big one strapped to the back, I had a system that was self-righting – on flat water at least. Did it work in the surf? We were about to find out.

Tucked down inside my kayak, I actually felt quite comfortable. Everyone else who tried it said it was scary and claustrophobic. In the surf, it was. I waited. A big one hit me. I was slammed around, and capsized almost immediately. Suddenly, I was upright again! It works!

Jedda, Finlay and I had a great vantage point out along the rock wall, quite close to the boys. I was quite concerned that he was too close to the rock wall. This really wasn't a very good spot for the testing because they were in between a rocky reef on one side and a rock groyne on the other. With the surf coming through, they were bound to hit something, but I figured they knew what they were doing.

A huge wave came through and slammed into the kayak. Ant, enclosed in his little bubble, was tossed violently and was thrown completely upside down. The amazing thing was, he came straight back up again! His system worked and it was a confidence-booster to see it in the surf that day. But the wave washed him closer to the rock wall and as he was being tossed around, he missed it by inches. It would have looked great on film, but of course we'd left the video camera at home that day. Bummer!

Wave after wave pounded the kayak. It was amazing how much punishment this system could take. I sincerely hoped Ant wouldn't come across waves like this in the Tasman, but I had to be kidding myself to think that he wouldn't see this, and much, much worse, so he had to be prepared for it. That was precisely the reason he was testing this gear in the surf.

The area we were in had an undertow heading out to sea. We were using a sea anchor, and this acted as a drag device under the water, and took us out to sea in the direction of the current. So after a while we drifted beyond the surf zone. John tapped on the hull to bring me up. Elated, I emerged from the cockpit, a little wet but excited about our success. 'Stoked, mate! That was unreal!'

'Yep, works pretty good, hey?' replied John with a grin on his face.

I lifted the hood up and put it on the front deck. John was a little cold now – it was winter in Wollongong – so he clambered up onto the rear deck and asked me to paddle in. This caused some instability, and with all this weight up high, I capsized. Bad one! We brought the kayak back upright and I paddled her in, swamped with water now, with John hanging on to the back. 'You got the bubble, mate?' 'Yep, no worries,' replied John.

I was yelling from the rock wall: 'THE HOOD, THE BUBBLE! THE THING! WHATEVER YOU CALL IT! WHERE IS IT?'
I heard Ant call, 'Hey John, you got that hood, right?'
'Yeah, mate.'
When the boys made it back to shore I ran down to them screaming, 'Where's the hood?'
'Oh, shit, the hood . . . I thought you meant this . . .' John was holding up the outrigger that Ant had used on the Gulf trip.
'OH, NO!' was Ant's frustrated reply. What could we do? The water was so murky after the rain all week, not to mention freezing. Ant donned his wetsuit. I didn't have one with me, but I went for a swim anyway. Ant said it was character-building. I could think of a few other choice names for it! We did at least have snorkelling masks, and we spent the next freezing hour scouring the murky bottom, to no avail.

A lot of work had gone into that hood. And even though it was only a prototype, it had the yacht ventilator on it, which came all the way from Holland. This was critical to the project. Ant was very fortunate to receive sponsorship from Air-Only Ventilators, and their product proved to be very good. He didn't want to lose it.

I took full responsibility for the loss. It was clearly my problem – I had not devised a foolproof system for the storage of the hood, and so when I capsized out there, it went straight to the bottom. It was like a dish. Upside down, it had some buoyancy, but on its side, it filled with water almost instantly and went to the bottom so fast we hadn't noticed it. There was a big lesson there.

John suggested stainless steel pivot arms to allow the hood to be stored on the rear deck and then moved over the cockpit while always being attached to the kayak. I resolved to ensure that *everything* important like that would always be attached to the kayak. This was basic stuff and I should already have known it, but sometimes we get complacent. I had been reminded, and was extremely grateful that the reminder took place in a test environment rather than out in the real deal.

Within a week, I had a new hood made up in the garage at home, and the stainless steel pivot arms welded together by a local metalworker. I made this hood bigger [sitting approximately 60 centimetres high], with more vertical sides to give more of a self-righting effect. The idea was to get rid of the inflatable bladder on the back deck. I felt that relying on this was dangerous. It was too vulnerable to big waves sweeping the deck and ripping it to shreds. By making the canopy bigger, I had a solid fibreglass structure that was stronger and better able to handle big waves washing over the boat. I felt a lot safer with this set-up.

Early August

We're down in Wollongong again with John Tot and Jedda. These guys have been fantastic in helping me test the boat and critiquing the ideas I had for doing this safely in huge seas. Time is the most valuable commodity we have, and they gave theirs freely. I value their friendship enormously.

I paddle out into the surf with the new canopy and John swimming beside me. John's there to capsize me and bring me up if the hood doesn't work. We're on the edge of the breakers. I tuck down under and clamp the hood tight on top of the cockpit. I yell to John from inside the boat: 'OK, mate!' He shoves the boat hard and over we go. Bang! She bounces upright immediately. 'Righto, mate, do it again!' She's up again in an instant. 'And again!' There's no doubt now. She just keeps coming up. There's so much volume up high that the kayak simply can't stay upside down. This is great! It WORKS!

A week later

Rose Bay. Vicki is with me. We decide to do some more testing. It's flat water but I want to test the self-righting capability a little more thoroughly. I'm concerned that with the testing done last week, I may have been 'bouncing' upright with the momentum of being shoved over fairly hard. What happens if the kayak is gently laid over on its side, with no momentum pushing the canopy deeper and providing a return 'bounce' effect as it rises to the surface and helps to right the boat? It's impossible for the kayak to stay upside down, but will it be in equilibrium on its side, slowly taking in water through the rubber seals?

I'm inside the kayak. Vicki lays me over gently. I stay there, in equilibrium as I had feared. I'm not coming back up again. I gently bounce the canopy *deeper* into the water. This is counter-intuitive. I want the kayak to come upright, I should be trying to roll it higher out of the water, not deeper, surely?! As I roll it deeper, the positive buoyancy sends the canopy up out of the water. She rises, slowly but surely, shaking the water free and my trusty kayak is upright again. It WORKS! We test it again and again, each time with the same result. The key is the wider, more vertical sides of the canopy. This gives more buoyancy out wide, which is critical to the self-righting movement of the system.

Bondi Beach, later the same day

I am keen to test this on the ocean now, and today's a rough day. The forecast is 20–30 knots [37–55 km/h]. It would be a mild day for the Tasman, probably a good weather day actually. Up here in Sydney, though, it's rough and windy. There aren't many beachgoers on the busiest beach in Sydney today. I walk up to the North Bondi Surf Club, to tell the lifeguards what I'm up to in case I strike trouble. The front doors of the clubhouse are shut tight to keep the wind out. I enter through a side door and find a clubbie. 'No worries, mate,' he says with a wry grin when I explain what I'm doing. 'We get all sorts of weirdos here,' he's thinking to himself. 'We'll keep an eye on ya,' he says.

I have the canopy bolted down to the rear deck, and a flotation bag up in the bow fully inflated with air. My big fear is that if I come out of the kayak, it will fill with water, and with no front bulkhead [the front bulkhead of the *Raider-X* was removed for the Gulf of Carpentaria crossing to facilitate lying down for sleeping], the boat will be unmanageable in a big sea. I could get into a lot of trouble very quickly if I come out.

I paddle out into the strong wind. It's rough, with a lot of clapotis [rebound waves] coming off Ben Buckler headland. I deploy my sea anchor and watch for a while to see how it performs. It's not good. The wind is hitting 25 knots [46 km/h] and there are breaking waves hitting the kayak periodically, with a big swell rolling underneath it all. The rode line goes tight and the kayak bounces towards the anchor. The line goes slack, the kayak is then completely unstable and turns beam-on to the weather. She doesn't go over, but it's a vulnerable position and I don't feel safe.

Shit. This is a mild day compared to what I have to face on the big crossing, yet I can't handle it. I am despondent. What do I do?

I sit and watch for 30 minutes or more. I'm drifting with the weather and surface currents. Before too long I am close to Ben Buckler. The waves are steeper here. A mountain of angry water approaches, standing up steeply as it feels the ocean floor beneath. It is impossibly steep, then it breaks. I'm drenched, face and head wet, wind howling fiercely into my face. Oh, shit. I am not meant to be here.

It's very tempting to turn to shore with my tail between my legs. But what then? I've invested a lot into this dream of mine. I can't give in too easily. I retrieve the sea anchor and move camp, back towards the middle of the bay, and away from the dangerous headland.

I deploy the sea anchor again. This time, mustering all my willpower, I force myself down into the kayak. This is the most vulnerable moment of the procedure. There is an unavoidable period of exposure as I take the sprayskirt off, wriggle deep inside the kayak and lie flat on the cockpit floor. If a wave breaks over the kayak at this moment, as they often do, the boat will fill with water and become dangerously unstable. As fast as I can do it, I pull the hood over the cockpit. If I can clamp it tight before the next wave comes, I'll be safe from the pounding sea.

It doesn't fit. What's wrong?

I realise now that earlier today a wave caught me broadside and moved the whole hood sideways out of position. Now it doesn't line up with the cockpit properly. I'm in a mild state of panic, fumbling with the clamps and trying to force the hood down. A wave breaks over the boat. The hood sheds most of the water, though I still get a mild flood inside. The front clamp is stuck and won't budge. Finally I'm able to close the others and they set the hood into a better position so that I can close the front one also. *Whew, I'm safe!*

Now I lie flat on the hull, listening to the pounding seas and howling wind outside. I'm aware that the rode line to the sea anchor will be slack a lot of the time, and the boat could easily broach and capsize. I can't see what's happening outside, so I'm relatively oblivious to it all. Surprisingly it's a quiet ride inside. Despite the bouncing around with no outriggers, this seems to be working pretty well.

I'm aware that the surface currents will be taking me closer to Ben Buckler headland, where the waves are breaking heavily over a shallow rock shelf. I don't want to be anywhere near there. I decide to time my little jaunt 'down below', to ensure that I stay there long enough for this to be an adequate test, but also to ensure I'm *not* there long enough to drift into Ben Buckler. I also have concerns about the oxygen supply inside the kayak. Since losing the last ventilator, I have decided not to fit my remaining one to this hood for fear of losing it, so I need to survive on the oxygen inside the kayak. Five minutes should be long enough, I decide. In the end I stay for seven. I emerge from the kayak, fitting the sprayskirt as quickly as I can.

I am ecstatic. It works! I feel the elation of someone who has invested an enormous part of themselves, while being often unsure of the final outcome. It WORKS! I am so excited. I wonder briefly whether others, who dare less and risk less in their lives, ever feel the pure joy that I feel now. I'm sure that many do know this feeling, but I fear that many more do not.

It takes risk and an uncertain outcome and a huge personal investment to reach this point. It is precisely because we risk failure that the taste of success is so sweet and joyous.

It's interesting to observe that the joy of success does not necessarily have to come at a cost to others. This is in contrast to competitive sports, for example, where for every winner there are 'losers'. While we celebrate in the reflected glory of those winners if they are 'our' team or representing our country, the 'losers' often wallow in deep disappointment at the outcome. We, and the media, tend to focus only on the glory of the winners. While there's no doubting the excitement of the home team pulling off an unlikely victory, I have long been attracted to the non-competitive sports where no losers are required.

My feeling of elation lasted all week. There is deep satisfaction in seeing a project like this come together. There is no doubt for me that a large part of the joy in any expedition includes the preparation stages, training, innovation, thinking difficult problems through and coming to a solution. There's no money in it, but these challenges are a driving force for me.

CHAPTER 15

One of the most important things that any successful adventurer will do is assess every risk to his team's wellbeing very carefully and take every step possible to minimise these risks. I am no different. None of us likes to rely upon luck or chance. A competent adventurer prefers to rely on skill, careful training and preparation. However the Tasman, I soon realised, could dish up anything. It is a melting-pot of weather systems. Low pressure systems come screaming up from the Southern Ocean and unleash their fury here. Many have died in vessels much safer, and larger, than a sea kayak.

In 1968 Robin Knox-Johnston became the first man to sail alone and non-stop around the world, being the only finisher in the Sunday Times Golden Globe race. He says that the waves of the Southern Ocean are the largest to be found anywhere in the world. The monsters he saw in this part of the world were 25 metres high. He describes seeing one of these terrifying behemoths rearing up into a wall half a mile astern. It began breaking at its crest and by the time its true proportions were clear it was too late to seek shelter below.

He climbed the rigging and hung on as the stern reared up and the wave crashed over the boat. For what seemed like an eternity there was nothing in sight but two masts and boiling water. Finally, *Suhaili* shook herself free of the maelstrom and re-appeared.

It's a chilling description of the power of the Southern Ocean. I knew, deep down, that I was really rolling the dice on this one. Gambling with Lady Luck is a very dangerous game, and I fervently hoped it would not be a fatal attraction.

I gave this expedition months of deep thought, oscillating between the equally difficult decisions of whether to go or not to go. It is a double-edged sword and I feel a little as though I am damned if I do and damned if I don't. If I go, I might easily become another statistic, 'lost at sea', never to be seen again. This will cause immeasurable pain and hardship to those around me, to say nothing of the life-long impact to a small child having to grow up without a father. The price of failure is far too high. If I don't go, I may be damned to live a life of unrealised potential. I will die dissatisfied with my life, wondering what might have been, and taking this question to my grave. It is certainly a selfish view, however it is one with which all those with audacious goals and high levels of ambition will be familiar.

I decided to believe I could do it. To truly, deeply believe it – and go for it.

Once I decide to do something, I become very focused, so much so that I tend to ignore other aspects of my life. I am not alone in this affliction. Tim Macartney-Snape describes this condition as the 'mono-mania' that consumes him before a mountaineering expedition. While some will say that focus and determination are admirable qualities, they are also very selfish. As a husband and a father, in the lead-up to an expedition you tend to be there, but not really there. Even if you are present, your mind is often elsewhere, planning, thinking things through, organising. Although

I knew it was selfish, I reasoned that my life depended upon proper preparation. It was less selfish to do this thing properly than to miss something and not come back at all. I was acutely aware, all through this preparation phase, that I might not come back. Aside from the impact on those around me, this would have been failure, and I'm not in the habit of failing.

This project was becoming so all-consuming that one day I actually phoned Ant at work to make an appointment to see him when he came home. I must admit that a part of me harboured resentment. He was spending more and more time on the project, less and less time with Finlay and me. I needed a better balance. I was verging towards 'Eeyore-ism' – a dangerous place to go. Yet my more logical side reasoned that the time was essential, critical to the success of the trip. Keep the end in sight, I said to myself.

His focus was singular and you could say obsessive. There simply weren't enough hours in the day to fit in all the planning and preparation for this trip, not to mention work. The hour-long train commute to the city for work (when he didn't drive and paddle) became valuable 'Tasman' time – time to collate the plethora of research data pertaining to weather, tides and currents, safety equipment, medical supplies and dietary requirements and all manner of other necessities. So engrossed was he that more than once we had to chase the train up to Katoomba to retrieve his wallet, book, even his new paddle that he had left on the train in his single-minded state.

It seemed the only way to get to talk to him was to phone him, although more often than not I'd get an engaged signal. His phone was becoming like an obscure growth on his ear. And more often than not it was Paul Hewitson on the other end. It was fascinating how totally and absolutely Paul had immersed himself into this project. He seemed almost as obsessive about it as Ant. I guess it was a difficult decision for him to become involved in the first place, but once committed, he was wholly committed.

It was our turn to host Sunday dinner, so I was cooking and entertaining our guests while Ant was just 'finishing off a quick couple of things' in the garage. I sent Neil Crabb's oldest daughter Becky out to tell him that dinner was on the table. 'He said he'll be in in a minute,' Becky reported. Half an hour later, I sent Becky back out with a reminder call. An hour after that, Ant entered the house as we were finishing the washing up. He was genuinely startled to see that we'd eaten without him. 'I thought Bec was only joking when she told me dinner was ready!' It was, by this time, getting on towards 9 o'clock. But then he was virtually overflowing with contagious enthusiasm for this project. We just couldn't help but be swept up in it, although I have to admit that my enthusiasm was heavily laced with apprehension.

A couple of Sundays later we had more guests for dinner. Ben Deacon, who was working with Ant on filming this trip, brought a friend – a highly accomplished yachtsman – to our place, on the pretext of teaching the friend the finer points of filming. When Jonathan Bogais was introduced to me, he spoke so little, and so softly, that I detected only the slightest hint of an accent. Being typically Australian, I called him John, which I soon realised was a mistake. No-one ever called him John. When the menfolk adjourned to the garage to admire and film Ant's work, I told Ben's girlfriend Urs that I couldn't place the accent.

'You're kidding,' she said in disbelief.

Urs and I looked at each other and laughed when the men came inside to dinner and Jonathan was 'deescusseeng zee seetuaytzeeon' in the strongest and most unmistakable French accent.

The charismatic French yachtsman owns and operates a highly regarded sailing school in Sydney. He has sailed across the Tasman, and around the globe, many times and it was soon discovered that Jonathan's real purpose for coming to dinner was to meet this Andrew McAuley and assess his character. Rather than consider Ant a fool, Jonathan was impressed with his attitude and his courage, and so came on board as the meteorological consultant.

Jonathan recalls: 'I love adventure and this was something new to me. I'm a sailor. I'd never been in a sea kayak in my life before, so I was very curious. I found that it was strange, but he seemed so passionate about it that I became excited.

'Of course I didn't know at the time he planned to go in those latitudes (below 40°S). I thought he was going to do a passage between Sydney to Auckland, which is very comfortable because at those latitudes there's very little risk involved if you can plan the weather very well.

'When I finally discovered, and that was soon after, that he was planning to go in a much higher latitude, well that was different. I could see why immediately because of the distance – less distance to cover. But also the risk factor was much higher. But there were a number of elements that I could understand very quickly, and the very first one was that in those 30s latitudes there are bands of high pressure systems and it is very easy to be locked in one of these high pressure systems and have to face headwinds for a long time and often not go anywhere. While if you go further south, you are influenced by those big low pressure systems and therefore the risk of being stuck literally in a high is much more limited. So it's technically more challenging, more risky, but from a navigational perspective it makes a lot more sense.'

Andrew had a general knowledge of meteorology and had had several meetings with the experts at the Bureau of Meteorology to discuss weather conditions in the Tasman, but he needed to learn much, much more before he set out across a sea renowned for its harshness. So Jonathan 'trained' him. Andrew would paddle in to the Fish Markets at Glebe, where Jonathan's yacht was moored. There, the two men spent many hours over the coming months, 'deescusseeng' every aspect of weather forecasting and the types of weather systems and conditions Andrew would likely face in the Tasman Sea, below the fortieth parallel.

'Most of the training I did with him was very much psychological,' Jonathan explained. 'It was to prepare him for the worst. It was to prepare him for extreme conditions so that he could anticipate it first and react safely. I've been in those waters myself many, many times so I actually know the conditions. The difference being I had been there on much bigger vessels, yachts and so on. Andrew was going to go there in a kayak. So the first thing was to detach ourselves from the fact that he was in a kayak, to see if he could be there mentally, so that he could understand the elements, he could understand the sea.

'It was critical for him to be able to understand the environment he would live in for so many days so that he could anticipate any form of changes and that's what the training was about. When I started to talk to Andrew about the conditions, to describe the violence of the elements, we always looked at the worst, always. So sometimes we laughed and I would tell him, "Look, you may find 10-metre waves, how do you think you're going to feel about it? Visualise what it's like to have a wall of water coming towards you." Just beyond where we were doing the classes, there was an old building and the height of the wall was actually about 10 metres and I got him to look over there regularly and say this is what you're going to experience. Do you want to do it? And he kept saying yes, I do. He was excited. He was scared and he was excited. He was very much alive. He's someone who just would think of what he was going to experience in a very rational, yet very excitable way.'

The team for this solo voyage was coming together. We had the paddler; we had the kayak in the making, with Paul Hewitson agreeing to be the primary contact for emergency services. (Andrew felt Paul would be more level-headed in case of an emergency, although I do think he underestimated me.) We now had the meteorological consultant, who would send forecasts each day at 1700 hours; we had Ant's brother Mike as media liaison; Ben Deacon as the documentary producer/media man; Doctors Richard Stiles and Sharnie Wu as the medical consultants; and me as the – well, I don't exactly know what you'd call me.

On deciding to support this project, Paul stated, 'It was the project itself, but it was also about who was asking. I don't think there's anyone else who's capable of doing what you're setting out to do.'

'Well, thanks for your confidence in me,' Ant replied. 'I mean, this trip is fucking dangerous and I just want to make sure I come back in one piece.'

'I'm glad to hear you say that, Andrew. I'm glad to hear that you realise how dangerous this is. And you know, no-one's going to think any less of you if you don't do it. You might decide to draw a line in the sand and just say it's too risky, and if you do that's just fine, I reckon.'

I'm feeling a little more confident about the trip since talking to Paul Hewitson. He pointed out that 'the worst that can happen is that you call a rescue'. Actually I think the worst that can happen is a whole lot worse than that. I believe there really is a chance I could die on this trip. It's certainly the most dangerous thing I'll ever do. At least, that's what I think at the moment. I do have a habit of forgetting about the bad trips after they're finished and going on to plan something even more ambitious.

Paul says mountaineering is more dangerous. He has a point there, but inevitably such comparisons and analogies break down. Both are dangerous. Mountaineering can take you in an instant, if you slip and fall. Perhaps you are unroped, or perhaps the companion you are roped to will fall with you. Crevasses lie hidden in the snow. Exposure to rockfall or avalanche is sometimes unavoidable. One day, your number comes up and your luck has run out.

In sea kayaking, it is true that the danger is often less immediate. Coastal paddling is often regarded as being relatively safe. In some parts of the world, though, this does not hold true. Paddling along the Antarctic coastline, my friends and I very nearly lost our lives when a 50-knot [90 km/h] katabatic wind came up from nowhere. This caught us just a couple of kilometres offshore while crossing a bay. Bullets of wind drove huge walls of spray ahead of them, heralding some kind of meteorological fury about to be unleashed upon us.

So coastal paddling is safe? Not here it isn't. A sea kayaker cannot paddle into a 50-knot wind. Even the strongest paddler will struggle. We were being blown backwards at a frightening rate. Laurie screamed, 'I don't want to die! I am too young to die yet!' If I had been within a couple of metres of him, I would have heard the panic in his voice. He was 50 metres behind me, though, and the wind tore his words away and I heard nothing. Stuart was ahead of me. I lost sight of him in the fury of it all. Spray blinded me and my world was reduced to just a few metres ahead and either side. This is serious. I really could lose this battle. What now?

The wind had just a bit of north in it, so fortunately it was not dead offshore. Our only hope was to ferry-glide across it, and try to reach the safety of the southern side of the bay. We paddled desperately into the wind. Joinville Island, 20 kilometres behind, seemed to be getting closer and closer. I seriously considered turning around and running with the wind for Joinville. My pig of a boat would not let me turn, though, so even if I wanted to I could not do it. I have never before experienced the helplessness of paddling a kayak I could not control. Everything was wrong and I cursed myself for allowing this to happen. I cursed the kayak, the wind, the spray, I cursed everything. This was really wild, and now when I needed it most, my kayak would not respond.

I do know one thing. I know that if I can pull the Tasman off safely, and then go on to write a book about it, I can look back and be happy with my life. I'd be deeply satisfied with the achievement. I know also that failure is not an option. I must make it, and I will. Hannes Lindemann said the same thing when he crossed the Atlantic. [The German doctor set out from the Canary Islands on 25 October 1955 in his home-made dugout canoe *Liberia II*. After 65 days at sea, he made landfall at Christiansted, Saint Croix.] The power of positive thinking is not to be underestimated. However, it is not positive thinking alone that gets you across a wild and dangerous ocean. Careful planning, meticulous attention to detail, the assistance of the best people . . . there are a whole host of elements that need to come together. A good deal of luck also helps.

CHAPTER 16

When you're enduring something unpleasant, like suffering through an exceedingly boring lecture or working in the school canteen, time has a habit of slowing to a crawl. You look at the clock, and it's only two minutes past the last time you checked. When great projects are on the horizon, time waits for no man. The months since Ant's return from Antarctica became a blur of planning, excitement, stress, action, anxiety...

As we shook off the remnants of winter and stepped into spring, the blossoms bloomed, new buds on the trees miraculously turned into leaves, the sweet and almost too subtle scent of freesias filled the air, and an urgency to bring this long-planned venture to fruition became almost overwhelming. Well, I say *almost* – it absolutely *was* overwhelming for me, but I just let myself get swept along in the frenzy.

An increasingly agitated air pervaded our household as we awaited the kayak. Paul had a challenge on his hands. Given the parameters of the design brief (the smallest possible kayak that would fit Andrew and all his supplies for a month or more at sea), his solution was a modified double, shortened to 6.4 metres and reworked to fit only one cockpit, and reinforced with Kevlar. The height of the fore deck was the defining measurement. It needed to be raised to clear the width of Ant's hips so he could roll over in the cockpit for sleeping and accessing the rear hatch (unlike a standard kayak where the rear hatch is on the aft deck, this hatch opened into the cockpit). The rest of the deck was built around that all-important hip measurement.

At the end of August, a very anxious Ant phoned Paul. 'How's the kayak looking?'

'Getting there,' Paul told him.

Early September, another phone call to Gosford. 'Is it ready yet?'

'Not quite.'

Mid September. 'Ready?'

'Almost.'

As it happened, the kayak wasn't quite finished by the October long weekend, but Ant drove up to Gosford to collect it regardless. Paul's a perfectionist, and he was reluctant to let the kayak out of his workshop before buffing and polishing the gelcoat. Basically, what he took was a bare shell. No deck lines, no pump, no seat, although that was no bother – Ant preferred his home-made seat – a plastic bag filled with beanbag beans. Time was now very much against us and Ant could not waste the opportunity to test the kayak on the 'boyz' annual south coast long weekend paddle. By all accounts, his obsession with the project was such that he talked of nothing else for five days. He reported with great excitement, upon his return from down south, that the kayak performed admirably. It handled much better than he had anticipated – not the 'pig' he thought it might have been. The raised cockpit gave him what he felt to be 'adequate' living space. It's all relative, of course. He was ecstatic.

Then back it went to Gosford for finishing off. The electric bilge pump was fitted, along with a manual foot pump; deck lines were added; an electrical system was installed for charging batteries. A five-watt flexible solar panel was mounted on the rear deck, with 2 × 3 amp sealed gel cell batteries with diodes fitted to prevent reverse charging at night. These were housed in a waterproof box inside the rear bulkhead, accessible only from the hatch inside the cockpit. Andrew would be able to isolate one battery while charging accessories – phone, beacon etc. – leaving the dedicated bilge pump battery fully charged. The bilge pump was set up with a deck mounted switch for operation while paddling and another switch mounted inside the kayak for use when holed up inside the cockpit canopy during bad weather or at night. Both batteries could be fully charged from flat in approximately 20 hours.

The days became a blur. How many times did Ant ask me if I was OK with this? I've lost count, but my answer never varied. I needed him to be confident that he had my support. And on the many occasions when he asked how I thought we'd manage when he quit his job for this project, I always replied, 'We'll manage. We'll be OK.' But it was a nerve-racking day when he handed in his resignation from his job of the past ten years with Coca Cola Amatil as a network analyst.

That day was one of mixed emotions for me – fear, anxiety, a tinge of excitement. Who knew what the future might hold? This Tasman project had been looming for some time now, but suddenly it had just leapt upon us and there now seemed to be a great urgency. So much to do and so little time. The estimated departure of late November was suddenly too close. With one month's notice, we'd have one more pay cheque, and then only two weeks for all the last-minute preparations before we headed down to Tasmania for 'take-off'.

Suddenly it was too scary. Too real.

Coca Cola Amatil Friday, 6 October 2006

My boss, Steve, rejected my application for long service leave (to which I was entitled). I outlined the importance of this trip to me and pushed the issue as hard as I reasonably could, taking it to his superior as well. However, as I expected, it was all to no avail.

A couple of hours later, I was ready to hand in my resignation. The decision was easy in the sense that I was committed to the expedition and the book-writing project. So I wrote out my letter and banged on the boss's door. Taking a deep breath as I sat down, I looked at him and paused, before blurting it out: 'I've decided to leave.'

At this point I began to realise what a big step I was taking here. With a wife and young child to support, and a mortgage to pay off, I certainly felt the pressure. I am the sole breadwinner in our household, and we don't have the luxury of going for extended periods with no income, without creating significant impact.

Steve's jaw dropped. 'Er, I'm lost for words. This is a surprise.' We chatted about the decision, and he was very supportive, offering to treat my resignation as tentative until I'd thought it through properly. I began to lose it. I had thought that I'd be cool, calm and collected, but I was not. Tears were soon streaming down my face and I felt rather pathetic.

In my mid-twenties, I'd regularly take up work for a while, with full intentions of chucking it in when the next climbing expedition came along. At that age, I'd found it liberating and exciting to leave work and head off on another great adventure. I had thought that

I might find the same feeling repeated this time around. However, I was disappointed. I found the experience stressful and emotionally taxing – far from the liberating experience of years earlier. I realised that this was a reflection of my age and increased responsibilities. I wondered whether I was being irresponsible and selfish, again, by doing this.

Glenbrook Saturday, 7 October 2006

The phone rings. It's my sister Juliet. She's ringing to see how I feel after leaving my job yesterday.

'Sister!'
'Hey, Ant, how are you going?'
'Yeah, pretty good.'
'You feeling OK after yesterday?'
'Yeah, not too bad. There's plenty going on here at the moment though.'
'Is there? What's happening?'
'Well, I need about a week to tell you about it all.'
'Are you feeling OK about the whole job thing?'
'Yeah, that's pretty much settled down, sis, you know. I mean it's pretty daunting going into no income, but what the hell!'
'Yeah, I know, Ant, but have you got a bit more acceptance that it really is happening?'
'Just don't look back, all forward.'
'Yeah, she'll be right mate!'

Thursday, 12 October

I called my sister.
'Ant, how are ya?'
'Yeah, awesome, sis!'

'Oh, that's great to hear. So you're feeling good about leaving work now?'

'Yeah, much better now. Actually I'm pretty excited about it all. This is all stuff that I've wanted to do for a long time, so I might as well leap into it. Gotta be careful of what you wish for sometimes!'

Saturday, 14 October

Juliet emailed Ant, expressing her thoughts and fears of the imminent crossing:

You first told me about this trip maybe two years ago. When a trip such as this is so far out, it is still very 'conceptual' and therefore easy to ignore! If I'm honest, I think I believed that I would be able to talk you out of it, scare you off it!! (yeah, right!!) Thus, I sent that article about the English bloke who crossed the Arctic Circle but found out a mate had died, questioned why the hell he did this stuff when he's got a family, etc and STOPPED DOING IT!!! That obviously fell on deaf ears.

As the time got closer, probably about six months ago and it was obviously a reality, I found Dad wanting to talk to me about it. By this stage you had briefed us all a bit more, preparations were fully under way and it became clear Nov/Dec was approaching faster than any of us liked. I actually kinda shut it out then. Didn't want to talk about it. Didn't want to think about it. Cut Dad off when he raised it. Usual-type answer was – 'There's no point analysing it; he's doing it and that's that.' I guess deep down I didn't see the point in reinforcing our fears to each other. Nothing productive in that! And that's what would have happened. And I think our relative ignorance in what this really entails, the preparation you actually put in and your ability, only made our little Queensland imaginations run riot and certainly did not instil any comfort.

Then a couple of months ago, I had a good chat to Vic about it and that changed my outlook a bit. Speaking to someone so close to it all but obviously still with her sanity intact (not to attempt it!) was like the perfect intermediary for me. I totally respected Vic's view and place as someone far less ignorant than myself, and yet who could relate to my fears and foreboding. Vic shed some light on exactly how thorough the preparation is (not that I ever doubted it, but it helps to hear it from a third party), how consumed you are and have been by it for some time and the general vibe in the kayaking community. I guess I saw it as a more balanced and objective perspective and I have to say, I derived a lot of comfort from this chat. So much so that I could talk/think about it again!

And now, here we are about 10 days out. I can't deny the feelings of dread have been creeping steadily back over the last week or so. Those early mornings when the birds start stirring have seen me wide-eyed and staring and imagining all sorts of deep blue horrors. So I decided to try and quantify it a little in terms I could understand. Let's say it takes 30 days, give or take. I was thinking, that's 90 meals I have to try to choo-choo train into Olivia's mouth (whatever it takes!) and clean the resulting 3 metre diameter of rejected food. It's probably twice that number in terms of breastfeeds for Caitlin. And if I really want to bring it home, that's HUNDREDS of nappy changes between the two of them!!!! All while you paddle, paddle, paddle, stroke, stroke, stroke . . . on and on and on. That's crazy shit man. There's no two ways about it. And I think MY month will be a marathon!!!

Friday, 20 October

My last day at work . . . Steve said to me, 'I think that people really envy you. They envy the passion that you have for your activities, and they envy the courage you have to follow your dreams.'

'Do you mean you think that others wouldn't be prepared to leave their job to follow a dream like this? Or that others don't hold the same passion for something?'

'Both,' he answered, 'and I speak for myself there as well. I think most of us don't feel as passionately as you do about whatever it is that they have. I also think they don't have the courage to take that monumental step to leave their job, and follow a path of uncertainty the way you have, in pursuit of a dream. Especially when you have a wife, a child and a mortgage!'

'Yeah, it's a big step alright.'

'How does it feel?'

'I feel like I'm standing on the edge of a cliff and I'm just about to step over the edge. It's pretty full-on. I feel a mixture of fear and trepidation at the future, and excitement at launching into a new project. It's the start of a new chapter in life. One door closes, another opens. I'm looking forward to it. It's a project of enormous personal importance to me. You have to be happy with your life, and I know that if I look back on my life and I know that I had this opportunity and didn't take it, I'd be unhappy. It's not a financial decision – we'll be financially worse off. It's just something that I value and not everything in life has a monetary value attached to it.'

Thursday, 26 October

Vicki's in tears.

'Are you worried about me?'

She nodded, unable to speak for a moment. 'I just want it to be finished so I know you're safe and you've made it to the other side,' she sobbed.

Then I realised that finally it had hit her. This is a bloody dangerous trip, there's no two ways about it. She's scared, very scared. She does support what I'm doing, but she's scared. So am I.

I had a call from Bill Alexiou-Hucker [director of Global Product Supply Management (GPSM)]. Graeme Evenden from work had been speaking to him on my behalf. Bill stated, 'I'm just really impressed by anyone who has the drive and commitment to leave their job and follow their dream. Most people just keep working in the same old job all their life. That kind of passion is just fantastic. It should be supported. I'm told you need some cash to get all this off the ground. How does five grand sound?'

'Sounds fantastic, Bill. That's very generous of you. Thank you so much for your support!' I was flattered by his enthusiasm for what I was doing. This is unreal! I'm on a roll.

This kind of support helps Vicki through the dark times of doubt. She was also flattered by the support and enthusiasm of people. *Australian Geographic* came through a couple of days ago, and also Dick Smith himself, and this was just fantastic. She was ecstatic and blown away by the enthusiasm out there.

Friday, 27 October

I'm chasing up a Flash for the Hawkesbury Classic. I am overwhelmed by the incredible kindness of the kayaking community. Several offers of a kayak came through and in the end I got a Flash to race with.

Yahoo!!! I have been a little stiff in the lower back lately, so I am wary of the fact that I may seize up on the night (I sincerely hope not). I'd like to do a sub-10 hour time if I can. I don't expect to win though, because I am up against kayaking supermen the Slade brothers.

Monday, 5 November

Came second in the Hawkesbury to Jason Slade. I did 10:09, I would have liked to do sub-10hrs but it was not to be. I wasn't feeling so 'flash' on the night, and struggled a little. Paul Hewitson pointed out that with so much on my mind lately this was the reason I didn't tear it up. I think he's right, actually.

Wednesday, 8 November

I have so many things to do. I have to fit the yacht ventilator to the Bubble of Life, fit a hatch to it also, work out a method for raising and lowering the cage that protects the rudder, call Alby McCracken regarding the sea anchor rode line, follow up on Power Bars, send Gore an invoice for sponsorship, call *Australian Geographic*, get some fabric for the cockpit change bag, etc. etc. The list goes on. I was joking to someone the other day that I used to work eight hours a day and get paid quite well. Now I work 16 hours a day and don't get paid anything! But I am enjoying it immensely.

Saturday, 18 November

I had a call from Jeff, of *Paddling Life* magazine in the US: 'I know the North Atlantic has been crossed, someone's paddled from California to Hawaii, and stuff like that. But this is the most hairball kayaking trip that anyone's ever done.'

'I haven't done it yet,' I thought to myself.

'This is really out there. That's a rough piece of ocean, mate. What is the motivation for doing this trip?'

'Well, I guess I am just drawn to ocean crossings. It's been a natural progression for me. I started on the eastern side of Bass Strait, which has a 60 kilometre crossing, and then went to the western side, where there's a 100 kilometre crossing and an 80 kilometre crossing. Then I crossed the middle of Bass Strait, which is 220 kilometres of open ocean.'

'Yeah, but these are not in the same league as the Tasman Sea.'

'Well, that's true. I've also paddled across the Gulf of Carpentaria, which involved seven days in my kayak. While this was in tropical waters with stable weather patterns, it gave me a chance to live in my kayak for a week at sea. At the start of this year I went to Antarctica. We sailed there and then paddled about 850 kilometres to the Antarctic Circle. This is some of the harshest and most inhospitable coastline in the world, and sailing down there also gave me some insight into what the Southern Ocean can do.'

'Right. But what about this trip? Tell me about the kayak.'

Stu [Trueman] came around for a look at the kayak. He jumped in and we tested the self-righting ability in the pool. He was impressed. 'That looks bloody good, mate. You've done a great job there. Tickety-boo!'

Paul Hewitson called.

'There's a few people who've asked me about it. And I tell them: "I don't know if anyone can paddle across the Tasman. But I know if anyone can, he can." I've been where you are. You get mentally tired as well as physically. You need to be well rested for this. One thing I've learnt in life is that you only know where things start. You never know where it's going to end up. You could make some money out of this.'

'What motivates me, Paul?'

'You're not motivated by money. It's a personal challenge for you. It's the next logical step, and it's another feather in your cap.'

Gages called. 'See you when you get back, if you don't *die*, that is!!!'

We'd had lengthy discussions about bringing Finlay to Tasmania to wave Daddy off. In the end it was decided that he should stay at home. It was essential for Andrew to have a good night's uninterrupted sleep prior to departure. God only knows when his next decent sleep would be. Absolute focus on the task ahead was necessary, and an exuberant Finlay might prove a distraction. Mum and Dad (AKA Grandma and Donnie) were more than happy to look after Finlay for the week. They picked him up on Tuesday, 21 November. They needed to be in Queensland late the following week for a golf tournament, but I assured them that I would be home before then. Andrew was expecting to depart on the 25th.

21 November

Farewell to Finlay. We had a few minutes before Don and Lorraine drove off with Finlay. Finlay said, 'Will you play on the see-saw with me, Daddy?'

'Of course I will, little munchkin!'

'Mummy plays on the see-saw with me. Lets go really really high!'

'Yeah, OK, let's go really high!'

And then the time came. There was no putting it off any longer. I love you Finlay. I love you too, Daddy. I hugged him, and held him tight. He returned the hug.

It brought me to tears. This was hard. Would I ever see him again? Was this trip worth the risk? Right now, I don't think so.

Vicki was crying too.

Right now I feel like I'm on the edge of a big cliff. I'm about to take a leap, and I'm either going to fly or I'm going to plummet like a stone to the bottom. I don't know which. I think I'll fly, at least for a while, but it's a risk, it's a big risk. I'm scared.

22 November

Paul: I think what motivates you is the personal achievement. It's another feather in your cap.

Later he said: I think you want to be known as the greatest paddler of all time.

Me: Well, my first priority is to get across in one piece. That's number one.

Juliet was near to tears saying goodbye on the phone today. I really think I won't put my family through this again. It's too hard on everybody. It's selfish to some extent, although when I see the inspiration it brings to people I can see the upside. However, these people are not affected if I die out there. My family and those closest to me are irrevocably affected.

And of that phone call, Juliet recalls:

'I just had to ring Andrew to say goodbye before his trip. In all honesty, I actually didn't want to call him. I know I have been avoiding that for a few days now. Since he left home to drive to Tassie, it has meant the whole thing is actually real, it's happening.

'I guess I have gone back into shutdown mode more than I realised. To ring meant to say goodbye. Somehow if I didn't call, I wouldn't have to say goodbye (he wouldn't go?). Anyway,

I almost just sent an SMS, but of course I called. Only a quick call, not much to say, after all. Naturally I felt quite emotional but was trying not to get that across – the last thing he needs is a blubbering sister on the other end of the line. Doesn't do anybody any good. A couple of chokes which I'm sure he heard and that was that.

'I'm scared shitless.'

Never again will I risk bringing them the pain and heartache that my premature death would bring (at least, that's the way I feel at the moment!). I've already brought them stress and worry simply by contemplating this trip, and then following through with it. I love them all too much to take on a risk of this magnitude again. Above all, Finlay, my beautiful little boy, is far too important to me. If there's one good side to risking it all and facing the very real possibility of death, it is that the experience brings into ultra-sharp focus the things that matter most to me in this life. Above all, the most important to me is my family, followed closely by my friends. I don't ever want to risk losing them again.

CHAPTER 17

I lay there the night before our long journey south to Tasmania, staring up at the ceiling, spotted a mossie and then watched Ant leap up and dance all over the bed, long arms flailing, until he squashed it. I asked how he was feeling, and he answered in honesty, 'I am scared. It's a big ocean out there, and I have an enormous amount of respect for the Tasman Sea and for what the ocean can do. Sometimes I really think that a certain amount of fear keeps you alive. It's important and it's nothing to be ashamed of at all.'

I stared at his many handprints and mosquito remnants as tears welled in my eyes and I thought how strange it would be lying here alone when he was out there in the middle of the ocean. I'd be going about my daily routine, doing the things that normal people do. Simple things that we take for granted Ant was going to have an unbelievably challenging time with. Preparing dinner, lying in bed, even going to the toilet.

People seem to have a curious fascination with ablutions. Everyone wants to know (some are too polite to ask) how, when you can't even stand up in the thing, do you go to the toilet in a kayak? You can't pull over if you're out in the middle of a very rough ocean.

The fact is, when you're at such extreme levels of exertion, you don't need to 'go' as often. When your energy expenditure is greater than your energy input, the body tends to utilise more of what goes in. Thus, less solid stuff comes out. Nevertheless, the act, even though needing to be performed much less frequently, still requires thought. And so it was that a solution presented itself early one November morning. Ant came back from a bike ride in the bush with a wombat femur. The smooth, white, perfectly rounded end – the equivalent of the head of the trochanter on a human femur (I guess it has the same name on a wombat) would, he declared, be a perfect ablutionary aid (bum-wiper), along with a cut-off soft drink bottle.

During those last mad weeks prior to departure, I laboured over the sewing machine making and modifying many last-minute necessities. One such item was what Ant called a 'cockpit change bag'. Basically, it was an oversized sprayskirt that came right over the shoulders and fastened around the neck. This fitted over the cockpit coaming, so Ant could sit upright, remove his sprayskirt and do the things he needed to do and still keep the Tasman Sea out of his kayak. Sounds good in theory, but imagine, on a rough ocean, trying to get the cut-off drink bottle in the right spot and . . . ah, well, best not to imagine, really.

While we're on the subject, a problem that has been known to occur with athletes during extended periods of extreme exertion is the inability to urinate, even when the bladder is screaming to be emptied. The muscles are simply unable to relax enough. In the event that this should happen, Richard and Sharnie gave lessons in self-catheterisation and supplied the necessary equipment. I shudder at the thought. Ant had experienced the excruciating insertion of a catheter without anaesthetic when he had that big fall at Bungonia Gorge. The paramedic dropped and broke the only anaesthetic vial. Ant's body had suffered shock from his injuries and the agony of not being able to urinate was greater than the pain of inserting the catheter. I sincerely hoped he would not face this problem in the Tasman, but he needed to be prepared. Thanks to Richard and Sharnie, his extensive medical kit should cover most problems from infections, fever, seasickness, diarrhoea, sleeplessness . . . you name it.

Legend has it that the explorer Eric Shipton was once asked his opinion on food for a Himalayan expedition. Apparently Shipton thought for a bit and then replied, 'Well, I think there should be some.' Andrew thought so too, and the effort required to organise the food for this trip was enormous.

Our good friend Sharon Trueman, wife of Stu and practising dietitian, had calculated a balanced diet for the boys on their Antarctic trip, and she kindly offered some assistance with this one. The trickiest part of the food preparation was including enough fat. The daily calorie intake of an average 39-year-old male with moderate energy expenditure should not exceed 3000 calories. Ant would require a minimum of 6000 calories per day, consisting of 40 per cent fat, 15 per cent protein and 45 per cent carbohydrate. And whereas you might think it wouldn't be too difficult to include such a high intake of fat (some people seem to manage it with ease), it actually proved a real challenge.

I caught many puzzled stares in the supermarket queue when my trolley was loaded with twenty blocks of cheddar cheese, twenty jars of peanut butter, heaps of chocolate bars and packets of jellybeans and little else. I spent ages in the confectionery aisle (something to which I am not unaccustomed, I'll admit) weighing up the pros and cons of Snickers bars versus Mars bars versus the plain old block of Cadbury Dairy Milk chocolate. And then, in the canned fish aisle, looking for the flavoured tinned tuna with the highest fat content. Did you know, for instance, that the Safcol brand sandwich style tuna has 16.8 grams of fat per 100 grams, yet the Greenseas Spicy Chilli flavour has only 1.8? It may seem quite pedantic, but when you're trying to make a diet very high in fat yet low in protein, every choice can make a difference.

During our last couple of Sunday night dinners Neil Crabb and Mark Windsor took great delight in barbecuing kransky sausages for Ant, which must contain at least 99 per cent fat, and watching him force them down. From the time I'd met Ant, he had always had a problem with his weight – he had difficulty keeping any on his tall, lean frame. I had made a concerted effort since before Antarctica to increase the fat content of our meals. I made more lasagnas and pastas with rich cheesy sauces and even put butter on his sandwiches. We ate icecream every night. The only thing it increased though was the food bill. He remained lithe and lean.

When Ant was packing for the Antarctic expedition, he had all his gear laid out in the backyard, double-checking the inventory with Stu. They foolishly left the gear unattended for a few minutes and came back to find the entire stock of more than 30 Power Bars missing. The guys were very concerned about the Power Bars. I was more concerned for Noushka's stomach and intestines, and her general wellbeing, since

Ant threatened to make a fur coat out of her. She pooed foil wrappers for the next several days. Needless to say, Ant took greater care in packing his rations for this trip.

On the eve of our long drive south to catch the ferry to Tasmania we were up late, despite our intentions of a good and restful night's sleep (as if that were ever likely!), packing the rations into drybags, checking and double-checking all the gear, loading the car and feeling the ever-increasing weight of unspoken concerns.

Each two-day ration pack contained:
– 1 200g packet of Mountain bread
– 1 375g jar peanut butter
– 1 250g block Kraft cheddar cheese
– 1 'Back Country Cuisine' breakfast, two-person serve (150g) [Yoghurt and Muesli or Porridge Supreme]
– 2 'Back Country Cuisine' dinners, single serve (90g) [an assortment of flavours for variety – Spaghetti Bolognaise, Beef and Pasta Hotpot, Beef Stroganoff, Babotjie, Moroccan Lamb, Chicken Tikka Masala, Mexican Chicken]
– 1 'Back Country Cuisine' dessert, two-person serve (150g) [Apple Pie, Apricot Crumble, Fruit Salad Trifle, Strawberry Icecream Dessert (don't try this one!)]
– 2 Power Bars – Protein Plus (high protein bar) (65g)
– 2 Power Bars – Original performance Energy bar (65g)
– 2 slices of home-made (by Ant's mum) Christmas cake
– 2 Ensure Hospital powder sachets – vanilla flavour (53.4g)
– 2 Sustagen hospital formula – vanilla flavour (60g)
– 1 Snickers fun size bar (22g)
– 2 small snap-lock bags of mixed lollies – peanut M&Ms and jelly lollies (150g)

– 2 heat pads for cooking dinner (with the 'Mountain House' Mountain Oven flameless heating kit)

Twenty of these ration packs were loaded into the car, along with the following equipment which would be systematically packed into or onto the kayak for the groundbreaking voyage:

- Paddling equipment
  – 'Solution' carbon fibre split paddle (primary paddle)
  – 'Legend' carbon-fibre split paddle (spare paddle)
  – Seat for the kayak [a heavy duty garbage bag filled with polystyrene beanbag balls]
  – 'Seattle Sports' inflatable paddle floats with custom-made outriggers [ball-joint fishing pole mounts were bolted to the deck; flat rectangular blades were welded to poles which then clamped onto the ball-joint mount. The blades, with paddle floats attached, would sit on the fore deck during paddling then swivel out to sit perpendicular to the kayak for stability when at rest]
  – 2 sea anchors – 1 large (800mm long – home-made) and 1 small (340mm long)
  – Sail with rigging and kite (to aid paddling in case of injury or illness)
- Paddling clobber (i.e. attire)
  – 'Sharkskin' full-length paddling pants [Sharkskin is a tri-laminate fabric with light fleece lining, breathable windproof membrane and lycra outer]
  – 'Sharkskin' long-sleeved paddling top
  – Hooded cag [waterproof, breathable paddling jacket with neoprene closures around the neck and cuffs to keep the water out]
  – Type 2 PFD [personal flotation device]

- 'Kokatat' paddling shoes
- Legionnaires hat
- Sunglasses plus spare
- 'Kokotat' Expedition Dry Suit [to be worn when storm conditions were forecast]
- Communications equipment:
  - 'Motorola' Iridium satellite phone, model 9505A (primary sat phone)
  - 'Motorola' Iridium satellite phone, model 9500 (backup)
  - GPS tracking beacon [provided by Fastwave Communications]
  - 3 GPSs [Global Positioning System]
  - VHF marine radio (handheld waterproof) [for line-of-sight communication]
  - Waterproof casings, batteries and chargers for all communications equipment
- Safety equipment
  - 406 MHz GPS EPIRB (Emergency Position Indicating Radio Beacon) with Hex ID [hexadecimal identification: Hex ID is registered with the RCC (Rescue Co-ordination Centre) in Canberra, providing vessel and owner identification and ground crew contact numbers. If the EPIRB is activated, search and rescue authorities will immediately know who and what they are looking for.]
  - 2 'Skystreme' personal radar reflectors [to deploy at night to alert passing shipping of his presence]
  - Flares
  - Sea Marker dye
- Water supply
  - Katadyn 'Survivor-35' manual desalinator [15 minutes of pumping yields one litre of fresh drinking water]

- 5 10-litre 'MSR Dromedary' bladders [to carry 50 litres of fresh water at start of voyage]
- Medical kit containing:
  - 2 sterile Procedure Packs for catheterisation
  - 2 urinary drainage bags
  - Baclofen – muscle relaxant
  - Paracetamol tablets – analgesic (pain reliever)
  - Codalgin Forte tablets – analgesic (pain reliever)
  - Doxycycline tablets – antibiotic
  - Doxyhexal tablets – antibiotic
  - Keflex capsules – antibiotic
  - Dormizol tablets – sleeping tablet
  - Ibuprofen tablets – anti-inflammatory
  - Nurofen tablets – anti-inflammatory
  - Lomotil – dysentery/excessive bowel movement treatment
  - Senokot tablets – anti-constipant
  - Stemetil tablets – anti-nauseant suppositories
  - Stemzine tablets – anti-nauseant tablets
  - 1 100g jar of Vaseline petroleum jelly – lubricant
  - 2 50ml tubes of Lotil cream – barrier cream, salt sore preventative
  - Tape and dressings – blister/abrasion treatment
  - Emergency Space Blanket
- Repair kit containing:
  - pliers
  - Swiss Army knife
  - Phillips-head screwdriver
  - 5mm nylon cord (drogue line spare)
  - 4mm nylon cord
  - 1 tube 'Selleys Aqua Knead-It'
- Filming equipment
  - Pentax Optio waterproof digital camera

- 2 Sony DCR-HC96 Handycam digital video camera recorders (in Sony Sports Handycam waterproof casings)
- Video camera remote-control (in waterproof casing)
- Manfrotto extension pole for camera mounting
- Bullet lens camera mounted on monkey-grip tripod
- Mini DV Sony HDV/DV tapes
- Sony DV 60 minute tapes
- Spare clothing
  - Thermal long-sleeved top and pants
  - Polartec thermal balaclava
- Sundries
  - Mountain Hardware Lamina 20 synthetic sleeping bag
  - Paddling helmet [to be worn when sleeping to prevent being knocked unconscious in the event of a capsize]
  - Home-made proofed nylon cockpit change bag [like a spray skirt but comes up to the neck]
  - 'Mountain House' Mountain Oven flameless heating kit
  - Spork (spoon/knife/fork)
  - Head torch
  - Spare batteries and chargers for all electrical equipment
  - iPod
  - Toothbrush and toothpaste
  - Bailer [cut-off PET bottle]
  - Wombat femur

CHAPTER 18

22 November 2006

Our drive to Melbourne this morning was made somewhat more stressful by the small but vital matter of a passport. Every last item had been meticulously checked off the list and packed. Nothing could be forgotten. Every single thing on the list was essential. And every single thing on the list was, indeed, packed. Only problem was, the passport wasn't on the list.

Andrew was leaving the country with the intention of arriving in another country, so customs procedures must be adhered to. It was only when we pulled in to the petrol station at Narellan, about forty minutes from home, that he realised he'd forgotten his passport. Nothing for it but to turn around and go home to get it. An hour and a half wasted. Still, we should make the ten-hour drive with time to spare.

The wind was howling as we motored down the Hume, me at the wheel. Andrew had a few last-minute phone calls to make, and he had a bad habit of talking on the phone while driving. Not only is it illegal, but it seriously stressed me out, so I insisted on taking the wheel. From Ant's perspective: 'We hit the Hume Highway with my passport in my hot little hand and then we cruised down the Hume Highway and yeah, it was interesting, you know, a little bit of stress in the car. We both had the jitters, we were both a little bit nervous.'

The most crucial of Andrew's inventions, the 'bubble', was painted bright yellow the week before we left home. And the night before, amid the frenzy of the last-minute packing and checking, Andrew asked me to give it a personality, so I painted big cartoon eyes and a broad smiley mouth on it. He was ecstatic! He christened it 'Casper'. Why? No particular reason. He just thought 'Casper the cockpit canopy' sounded pretty cool. Casper, however, created a lot of wind resistance on the drive. Bushfires were ravaging southern New South Wales and Victoria. We drove through thick walls of smoke, with gale-force north-westerly winds buffeting the kayak around on the roof. I gripped the steering wheel tightly to prevent the car being blown off the road.

Where are all the signs to Port Melbourne when you need them? Andrew had taken the driver's seat a couple of hours out of Melbourne because all that spare time we had was blown away in the gale. As we approached the city via the ring road, not a sign was to be seen. We pulled over several times for directions, with the minutes ticking away, but nobody in Melbourne seemed to have any idea about anything. And we sure as hell didn't have the foggiest!

At last! Someone who knew his way around the city! We had 12 minutes before boarding closed on the *Spirit of Tasmania* and, according to our very helpful guide, it would take us 15 minutes to get there. I held my breath.

'I think we'll make it,' Andrew said, just as he turned down a one-way street – the wrong way. I hyperventilated.

Horns honked and tyres screeched. We ran a red light. My breathing returned to near normal when we pulled into the long drive leading up to the loading dock just as a burly man was pulling the barriers to a close. We smiled sheepishly. He rolled his eyes and let us through.

After dinner we went outside for some fresh air, my queasy stomach made all the more so by the ominous sight of the black water of Bass Strait beneath us. Oh God! Imagine a tiny, insignificant kayak out there in the middle of a cold, dark ocean, night after night, being tossed about in the unrelenting swells. I kept my thoughts to myself as we adjourned to our luxury cabin with a porthole. Andrew surprised me by paying extra to upgrade our cabin. What a thoughtful gesture. Anything, I guess he thought, to ease the mounting tension.

Our arrival in Tasmania was marred by a peach, which we failed to declare at quarantine. We had both forgotten about it, buried as it was at the bottom of the Esky. The beagle found it, though. One hundred dollars and two foul tempers later, we pulled out of the quarantine bay and hit the road.

We were merrily (actually not so merrily after the peach impeachment) driving along on our way to Fortescue Bay when the phone rang. It was Sergeant Paul Steane of Tasmanian Police Search and Rescue, asking us to drop in to Hobart for a visit.

'We weren't planning on going to Hobart,' Andrew stated. (Fortescue Bay is 100 kilometres, or 90 minutes drive from Hobart on the Tasman Peninsula, near Port Arthur.)

'Well, you are now!' Sergeant Steane replied.

We phoned Paul Hewitson, primary contact for the 'Tasman Solo' support team and salt of the earth. He had flown down to Hobart that morning and was in a hire car, heading east to Fortescue Bay. Andrew explained the call from the police, so Paul did a U-turn and headed back to meet us at the police station. Ben Deacon was also in Hobart with his film gear, awaiting our arrival and he too would meet us at the station. I'm sure he was thinking that a bit of drama would make a nice addition to the documentary. Little did he know that we were in store for far more drama than we could handle.

Apparently the police had been notified, by an undisclosed source, that Andrew McAuley was grossly unprepared for a crossing of the Tasman Sea by kayak and should not be allowed to proceed with his plans.

The interrogation lasted hours. I think the police initially thought Andrew had a screw loose. I mean, what sort of delusional madman would even conceive of such an idea to paddle a conventional sea kayak across the Tasman Sea, and what's more, below the 40th parallel? That's venturing into the Southern Ocean at that latitude. We did eventually manage to convince them that Andrew was not only a man of high intellect, but also of great talent in the world of climbing, mountaineering and expedition kayaking. He had planned meticulously for this trip, having made various record-breaking open water kayak crossings in the lead-up.

Inspector Ross Paine, the man in charge of Marine and Rescue Services, handed Andrew an official-looking piece of paper. '**DETENTION NOTICE**', it read in bold caps, below a MAST (Marine and Safety, Tasmania) letterhead. The craft was deemed unseaworthy. I couldn't help but admire my husband for the restraint he showed at that moment. He stiffened, exhaled and politely asked to speak with the CEO of MAST, Colin Finch – the gentleman whose signature adorned the bottom of the letter.

Mr Finch explained that the operations plan was unsatisfactory, which, apart from being contradictory to the information on the detention notice, was surprising since no-one had asked to see an operations plan to know if it was satisfactory or not.

'We won't impound the kayak,' Inspector Paine advised. 'However, we trust that you'll abide by this decision.'

Much has been written, and debated recently, about the spirit of free will and adventure. Everest was the centre of a storm of controversy in May 2006. Questions were raised and fingers pointed after the death of British climber David Sharp, when many other climbers passed his body on their summit bids. The following week, on 26 May, Lincoln Hall made history with his miraculous return from the dead on Everest, yet that elation was crushed by news of the death of prominent Australian climber Sue Fear on another Himalayan peak, Manaslu, days later.

When the Australian Geographic Society announced Andrew as the Adventurer of the Year in 2005, one woman felt compelled to voice her disapproval in the Society's journal. 'He was no hero,' she wrote, 'rather a damn stupid fool to undertake such a hazardous journey single-handed and in such a flimsy, easily capsizable kayak.

Andrew shared his adventure philosophy in a radio interview on 2UE after his successful Gulf crossing:

> There's a deep sense of satisfaction in conceiving an adventurous and unlikely objective such as crossing the Gulf. It engenders in you a sense of self-reliance. You need to make decisions under pressure and you need to take responsibility for your own actions out there. There's no-one else to blame. I think it could be argued that adventurous activities can strengthen one's character. If

you challenge yourself as an individual and if we all do this, then as a whole, as a society, we could become a better society.

These days there's an increasing trend to eliminating risk from every part of our lives, and creating more rules and regulations and so on, and what that does is it shifts responsibility away from the individual which is ultimately a disempowering thing to do. I think activity like this is good for the individual and therefore good for society as a whole.

What right do authorities have in stifling the spirit of adventure in the interests of safety? If individuals weren't willing to take risks, would we still believe we might sail off the edge of the world? Would Australia have been colonised? Would Neil Armstrong have taken 'one small step for man, one giant leap for mankind'?

Andrew, as with every other aspect of his preparation for this trip, was assiduous in his approach to seeking clearance from the relevant authorities. He had contacted AMSA (Australian Maritime Safety Authority) back in August with his intentions. They advised him at the time to copy his intentions to a vast list of authorities, including MAST, which he did. I thought it peculiar that MAST had been notified months ago, yet here they were, at the eleventh hour, expressing concerns that they'd had ample opportunity to do much earlier.

Paul, Ben, Ant and I adjourned to the pub across the road for a stiff drink. Actually, we settled for coffees, and a bottle of water for me since I drink neither alcohol nor caffeine. The conversation was heavily punctuated with profanities, and then Ant dropped a bombshell. He had called AMSA last week to confirm details of his trip. His contact there told him that he'd just received an interesting email, which he would 'forward for your amusement'. The email, from an unknown source, stated, 'We are aware of AM's attempt from Tasmania. We believe he is unprepared and seems to be leaving things to chance.'

The stress of the previous day's drive, and now this, gave me a splitting headache. Ben wangled us an invitation to dinner that night at a friend's place. I was reluctant to accept, since my head was about to explode, but Ant was keen since Ben's friend was fellow adventurer and filmmaker Wade Fairley. It was Thursday night, our first night in Tasmania, and we had intended camping at Fortescue Bay. Wade and his beautiful French girlfriend, Fred Olivier, graciously offered us accommodation at their place for as long as we needed to sort out this predicament.

Friday was to be spent packing the kayak. Now it would be spent in a meeting at MAST headquarters. At 9 am, we met with Colin Finch and Gwin Alway from MAST, as well as Sergeant Paul Steane from Police Search and Rescue. Paul and Ben were also in attendance. They grilled us for two solid hours.

'OK, run me through a day in the life of Andrew McAuley. You wake up in the morning and you want to take a dump. How you gonna take a dump?'

Andrew patiently explained the cockpit change bag and how it worked.

'It's blowing south-west. What do you do now? Which way do you go?'

'OK, you've eaten your food rations for day two. What do you do with all the left-over packaging?'

'Your satphone fails. What happens now?'

'The solar charger carks it.'

The barrage went on and on.

Paul Steane asked Andrew if he was a 'God-botherer'. I think if he'd answered 'Yes, the Lord will save me when I'm in trouble out there', they would have confiscated his kayak on the spot. I guess Sergeant Steane has seen it all. He has been in search and rescue for over 20 years. He is also a police diver, and an avid whitewater kayaker and adventurer.

After the meeting, we adjourned to the bay to put the kayak in the water. Paul Steane was keen to test Casper's alleged self-righting ability. He donned a wetsuit, slid down into the cockpit, pulled Casper the cockpit canopy overhead and locked himself in. Paul Hewitson and I watched nervously from the jetty. Imagine if it didn't work. It had, of course, worked in every test in every condition Andrew could thus far devise. Of course, the ultimate test was waiting to begin. But now, what if it failed? Andrew tipped the kayak, containing the police officer, over. I held my breath. Seconds passed. Andrew was turning a dreadful shade of grey. His teeth bit down on his bottom lip to form the letter 'f'. Paul and I exchanged a panicked glance. The white hull was still glaring up at us. The kayak failed to right.

'What were you doing in there?' Andrew demanded, as he manually pulled the kayak upright.

'I just let my body go limp and fell into the canopy,' Sergeant Steane replied.

'Well, for one, the cockpit will be packed so tight with gear that you wouldn't be able to do that. And secondly, I've slept in it, and my body simply won't fit in it like yours just did. Give it another go.'

Several 'goes' later, Sergeant Steane was satisfied that Casper was a workable invention.

Our hosts during our unexpected stay in Hobart proved to be not only generous, but also very helpful. Wade Fairley had many contacts at the Australian Antarctic Division, and we were lucky to enlist the help of Rob Easther to bring all our documentation up to standard. We spent a good portion of the weekend, and of Rob's valuable time, at his house, reviewing the Operations Plan, Communications Plan, Risk Assessment, and associated attachments.

First thing Monday morning we delivered the comprehensive documentation to Ross Paine. Later that afternoon, Inspector Paine handed Andrew another letter. As Andrew scanned through it, a smile spread across his face.

The first paragraph stated: 'MAST has decided to lift the detention notice on your vessel issued on 24 November 2006.'

A comment from AMSA also recorded in the letter read:

It is difficult to make a judgement about chances of success – this is very weather-dependent. All we really say is that a passage of such distance in such a small craft is high risk and I guess this is why he wishes to do it. He has previous experience and this pushes his envelope.

Colin Finch closed the letter with the following paragraph:

You are undoubtedly very experienced both as a kayaker and in undertaking difficult and hazardous voyages in remote locations. However, the voyage that you are proposing to undertake is extremely hazardous and cannot be endorsed by MAST. We urge you to reconsider the voyage.

Inspector Paine echoed the sentiments of that last paragraph and with fatherly concern implored us to drive back up to Devonport and catch the next ferry home.

'You're intelligent and articulate, and you're a man of principle. You will do this trip anyway, and they were reluctant to make you a lawbreaker by leaving the detention order on your kayak. Your detention order has been lifted, but I strongly advise you not to go,' he said sternly and in no uncertain terms.

'I want to tell you something else,' he continued. 'My son's in the army, and he's on the front line, he's not a pen-pusher. Right now I feel the same way about you as I feel about my son when he goes out to the front line.' These words he spoke with feeling and with genuine care. I had to fight back the tears. So, I noticed, did Ant.

I caught an early flight home the next morning. Ant had lost the favourable weather window he needed for the start of his voyage, and the next decent high pressure system was forecast for Saturday – five days away. Mum and Dad had their golf tournament to get to in Queensland, so I had no choice but to go home, get Finlay and fly back down here with him. Ant took the opportunity to drive up to Jeff Jennings' place at Bridport, up the top of Tassie.

Jeff is one of the tried and true tough Tasmanian sea kayakers, with a mountain of experience filming from his kayak. He had kindly agreed to lend his video gear to Andrew for this expedition. The pair spent a few days on the water testing the camera rigging and housing, while I was clocking up air miles.

CHAPTER 19

Fortescue Bay, Tasmania 2 December 2006 2.45 pm

I'm scared. More than scared. Terrified. Actually, I'm searching for an adjective to adequately capture my feelings, but I'm coming up short. Never in my life have I experienced emotions such as I have today. The final stages of packing were nerve-racking – for me at least, although I could sense that Andrew felt the same. To see the amount of gear, all essential for surviving a month at sea in a tiny kayak, piled up in drybags on the beach, I wondered how on earth it could all fit. Finlay had been running around wildly, burning energy as only a three-year-old can.

Now here I was, with the two people in this world I love more than my own life. One I was holding tight physically, the other I held to my heart figuratively, for that's all I could do now. Too late for anything else. I had to settle for waving goodbye, as my heart tore in two, wishing him safe travel across one of the roughest stretches of water in the world and praying that I would see him in New Zealand in a month's time.

* * *

The Immigration officials had been here this morning, dutifully stamping Andrew out of the country. Several media reps had been here too, intruding upon our very private final moments before my beautiful husband departed on a landmark kayaking voyage from Australia to New Zealand. Not long before that, Finlay, in his enthusiasm, had run up to his dad, stumbled and landed on the paddle. Andrew was carrying a spare, of course, but imagine if his most important piece of equipment was broken just before departure.

Finlay and I had arrived at Hobart airport the previous afternoon with Paul Hewitson, who had also gone home for a few days to check on his business and his family. We hired a car and drove directly to Fortescue Bay on Tasmania's east coast, where we found Andrew and his kayak on the beach, amidst a small crowd of onlookers. I gave him a hug and a bag full of goodies from the bakery back in Sorell, which he devoured in seconds.

We then spent the next couple of hours ferrying all the gear down to the beach and I watched Ant painstakingly pack everything into the allocated places. Twelve of the 20 two-day ration packs went into the rear hatch, which was accessed from inside the cockpit. Each ration pack had a length of cord attached and an identifying tape so that Ant could pack gear right into the pointy end of the stern, but still retrieve it by pulling on the cords. Along with the food went the bulk of the water, the Mountain Oven kit, desalinator, medical kit, tool kit, drysuit, spare clothes and back-up comms gear.

The remaining eight rations packs plus some of the water supply were stored in the front hatch. Accessing these supplies would be a risky business. It involved tethering himself to the kayak and swimming to the front hatch – strictly a calm weather activity. The benefits of this were the chance to rinse his salt and sweat encrusted body – something that would have helped alleviate the skin infections he incurred on the Gulf of Carpentaria crossing – and to stretch his legs. He anticipated doing this only a couple of times during the voyage, and in the earlier days. He could not risk running out of easily accessible supplies as he approached the less predictable conditions later in the trip.

All essential navigation, communications and safety equipment was stored (safely tethered) within easy reach inside the cockpit itself, along with one bladder of water, sleeping bag (in a drybag), head torch, stills camera and spare paddle. It was by no stretch of the imagination going to be a comfortable trip.

Finlay, momentarily distracted from his sandcastle construction, wandered over and opened one of the drybags and pulled something out while we were too busy to notice.

'Cake!' he squealed. 'Can I have it?'

'No! That's Marsie's special cake for Daddy. He needs it. In fact, he needs *everything* in there, so please don't touch!'

Andrew's beautiful mother had mailed one of her famous Christmas cakes, the highlight of the McAuley festive season, down from Queensland. I had cut it into exactly 40 pieces, individually wrapped the portions, and packed two in each rations bag.

With the cake came a special note. This I also packed in one of the food bags.

Dearest Andrew,
Hope this will give you strength for your long journey. It may be a moment to look forward to each long day!
I hope you can keep it dry. It does not need any salt!
Will speak to you soon. Good luck, darling. Our prayers are with you. Keep safe & don't lose the paddles!
Our love always,
Mum & Dad xoxo

The sky turned purple, then pink, then blazed orange and red, and purple again until the sun finally dropped below the horizon. We erected two tents near the beach – one for Ant, the other for Finlay and myself. A good night's sleep, remember. I hope it was good for Ant. I cried myself to sleep.

So, here we were. Early afternoon. We sat in Paul's hire car – a big, comfortable four-wheel drive – while we waited for the rain and wind to abate. Jonathan predicted a change early afternoon. Ant would sit patiently and wait for it. As we sat, Paul, Ben, Ant and I – Finlay was out playing in the rain with Ben's friend, Jono – the conversation was sparse. So much to say, yet so much that I couldn't say, like, *please* don't go; this is too hard for me; this is too dangerous for you. So we sat mostly in silence. An anxious, tense silence, punctuated with the occasional inane comment.

I prised Finlay's little arms from around my neck, handed him to Paul and ran. A narrow track followed the shoreline and I ran and ran, calling to Ant, although by now he was too far away to hear me. And he couldn't see me for the trees. The path headed away from shore and steepened. I climbed, frantic, then completely lost sight of the water. I collapsed. Hysterical screams escaped me and I wept.

Jeff Jennings was filming from the top of the cliff and a man came up the path to find him. Finlay followed with Jono. I stood, wiped my face and attempted to pull myself together. I took my precious boy in my arms and followed the man to the cliff's edge.

Paralysed, my eyes searching, probing. Where was he? There.

Long, lonely minutes passed as I stared out to sea. Finlay whispered, 'Love you, Daddy' and the clouds darkened overhead.

I was finding it more and more difficult to see the kayak, as it disappeared into the distance, lost amid the swell. The rhythm of the ocean, the cold wind blowing on my face, Finlay's arms wrapped tightly around my neck, the numbness in my chest – it was all too surreal.

With one final lingering gaze out to sea, I turned away, tears streaming, with a deep sense of foreboding.

CHAPTER 20

Tasman Sea, several nautical miles east of Fortescue Bay
2 December 2006

The wind howls and whips up a flurry of sea spray. The sea is littered with whitecaps.

Well, I'm just outside the heads of Fortescue Bay. I can see Cape Pillar down there, just past the Candlestick and the Totem Pole . . . The weather's a bit rougher out through the heads of the bay here, which is not unexpected . . . and the reality of the trip is starting to dawn on me. It's a big, big ocean, and I'm not gonna see land for a long time, which is . . . exciting in one sense, but it's also scary. All I really want to do is make it in one piece.

A large wave breaks across the bow, spraying up into his face. *It's a very, very heavy boat . . . and a big sea. But the conditions are moderate so . . . hopefully it won't be too bad.*

He turns to look back at the receding shoreline, but maintains his momentum.

It's just starting to rain . . . typical Tassie weather – four seasons in a day. Anyway – he sneaks another quick glance back over his right shoulder – *I'm feeling just a little bit better now after a very tearful farewell with my wife and my three-year-old boy.* He swallows hard. His zinc-lathered face distorts with the pain of that departure. *And now* . . . another wave breaks over the tiny craft, he braces . . . *I have to do everything within my power to make sure* . . . yet another wave – he lifts the paddle high to deflect the water . . . *that I get to New Zealand in one piece and I see them again. Because I love them both very much. They're my whole life* . . . He sniffs, chokes back a tear and bites his lower lip . . . *and this trip is really incidental.*

I'm looking forward, after this trip, to really taking it easy. Ha! I say that after every trip . . . *but this time I really mean it. I just want to kick back* . . . *enjoy some time with my wife and my little boy. I love them both. They're more important than anything. They're definitely more important than this trip.* He sighs. Bites his lip again. Sighs louder, grits his teeth and digs the paddle blade in harder, with more force, and pushes through that emotional barrier.

Dark clouds scurry across the sky. Grey engulfs the last of the blue patches.

Well! It'll be exciting to get there. Yep. It'll be exciting to get there. The wind howls. The sea is decidedly more choppy now, swells increasing. The kayak slices its way through the breaking waves. He glances left, glances right. The receding coastline seems to bob up and down, tip one way, then the other. A gull flies overhead, its lonely cry echoing the sentiments of the solo paddler. The gull's flight is effortless, as the paddler would wish his journey to be.

CHAPTER 21

Maria Island, Tasmania 4 December 2006 Late afternoon

Clear blue sky peeps through the backdrop of lush green eucalypts. The orange kayak is beached on the long stretch of white sand. A lone figure sits, resting on the cockpit coaming. He wears a black balaclava, peeled back from his face like a beanie, and a weary expression beneath the zinc-covered face. The thick layer has worn off in parts, exposing the tip of his nose and his lips. His eyes are puffy from lack of sleep.

Well, I'm here on Maria Island, after pulling the pin last night. I'm feeling a little bit better now, but I was pretty wasted when I got here this morning.

The wind was blowing around 30 knots [55 km/h] from the SW, and I had an upwind slog to reach the mainland. The swell was running at about 3 metres, with a 3 metre sea on top of it; 6 metre waves in the face for 80 kilometres of paddling is not everyone's idea of a holiday! I put my head down and got stuck into it. There was no choice. There was no way in hell I was going to call up the rescue authorities, even if I might consider them friends after working with them to get this trip approved through the proper channels. I knew that although headwinds can be soul-destroying, I would make progress into it, no matter how slow. The tough thing is stopping for a drink or a quick bite to eat. I would really have to be quick, for fear of letting the kayak lose all forward momentum and start that inevitable backwards drift.

Basically I decided that . . . well, I was very cold. Not so much . . . uncomfortable wasn't the problem. I was cold inside the cockpit when I went to sleep. His shoulders lift, then drop heavily in a sigh of resignation. He recites his monologue in a monotone and his eyes are dull, drenched with disappointment and exhaustion. *And there are a few reasons for that. It was very, very crowded inside the cockpit. I had 21 litres of water. I had a drysuit, a sleeping bag, two paddles, a hand pump, GPS, satphone, iPod. A whole stack of stuff. Food, spare clothes. I had too much stuff inside the cockpit and it made it very, very tight. There was no way in hell I could roll over.*

But the worst thing of all was that I couldn't use the hammocks properly to raise myself off the cockpit floor. So I was sleeping in cold water, and water conducts heat away from your body twenty times faster than air and it meant that I was very, very cold. I got to the point where I'd been shivering for about twenty hours — something like that — and I must have been mildly hypothermic. I mean, not sure I've ever had hypothermia so I can't confirm what it feels like, but it was hard going anyway. And I felt that if that's what the first night was like, the trip was not achievable if every night was like that. And while it's true I would have been able to clear some space from the cockpit, that wasn't the only problem. It's basically the fact that I couldn't keep the cockpit dry and that pushed the level of risk to a level that was beyond the boundaries of risk that I was happy to take.

So I decided to return to shore. I was about 80 kilometres off shore – something like that. I had a good tail wind behind me, and I had to paddle back into the wind to get back to shore, which was very, very hard going. It was about 30 knots [55 km/h] for a lot of it.

Fortescue Bay was almost impossibly far away by now. At sea, 80 kilometres is a long paddle when you are fresh and full of beans. When you've hardly slept and have hit the early stages of hypothermia, it's bloody tough. Add a 300 kilogram loaded kayak, a 30 knot headwind and huge Southern Ocean swells, and a genuine feat of human endurance is required. Things can get really exciting.

I inched my way forward towards Fortescue Bay. I resolved not to check the GPS too often, but rather just keep my head down and keep paddling – this was the only way I was going to get there, after all! Any interruption to paddling would simply slow my progress. Waves would regularly break into my face, the wind-driven spray making it hard to see. But I had no choice. The sooner I got there the better.

After three hours of slogging away, I decided to check my position – 10 kilometres closer! 'WHAT?!' I couldn't believe it. My grandmother could paddle faster than I was paddling. This really was soul-destroying.

I worked out later than an ocean current had been working against me, At the time, I didn't know this and thought that I was paddling like an old woman and that if this continued for too long, I simply wasn't going to make it.

Eventually, over many long, hard hours I made a dent in the mileage. I turned off the wind a little, to allow for better distance to be made. Over time I noticed a steep, dramatic island out to the north. It wasn't downwind, but with a beam-on course required it was a better option than my current plan.

I worked out that it was Maria Island. I had no charts of the Tasmanian coast with me – I'd had no plans to return to Tasmania! However, seven years earlier, Vicki and I had paddled the east coast of Tassie during our honeymoon. I have a good recollection of places I've been before and I was fairly comfortable that I could find my way around as I approached the coast.

I remembered Maria Island as having a narrow isthmus joining the northern and southern 'halves' of the island. I also remembered two steep and dramatic peaks – Mount Maria and 'Bishop and Clerk'. I couldn't make out these features from so far offshore, and mused that I might even be looking at the Freycinet Peninsula, with Great Oyster Bay behind making it look like an island. Either way, it didn't matter much – I just wanted to feel dry land beneath my feet. The geology of the two places is quite different and I'd soon know where I was as I drew closer.

Eventually I decided I could take a more direct line to Maria and I started to take the weather beam-on. This is an aspect that makes a kayak like mine quite vulnerable to capsize. The sea state was big and I'd regularly get surfed sideways by big monsters breaking on my kayak.

Big ocean swells. Big waves. I had a huge wave crash right over the boat. The cadence of his speech increases with excitement. His voice raises a pitch with a hint of enthusiasm. He becomes more animated now.

I kept a wary eye on these big mothers walling up as they approached me. Sometimes they'd wall up and break nearby, and sometimes they'd wall up and then fade away. It took some judgement and a good feel for the waves to know which ones to worry about and which ones to let pass without a second thought. Eventually the mother of all waves came along and gave me good cause for serious concern.

I was inside the tube and saw this thing breaking ... and ... I was quaking in my boots. I thought I was going to get rolled for sure. I leaned right into it, and popped through the other side of the tube, and it crashed down on the boat. Somehow ... I still don't know how, I didn't capsize. I think the bubble on the back actually helps a bit, 'cause when you get bashed by a wave, it's got that bit of buoyancy that helps stop you going over.

This huge wall of water approached and loomed up above me. A wave doubling or tripling effect was at work here, and I was in the path of this monster. I'd never seen anything like it. I was beam-on, and this thing just grew and grew, steeper and more terrifying than anything I'd ever seen. Suddenly this wave just threw outwards with all its force and I was inside the barrel. I hadn't thought it possible to get 'tubed', like a surfer, on the open ocean before, but I was about to be re-educated. You wouldn't think of this wave as being a proper tube-ride – it was more like a close-out. I was really scared. Loudly I yelled, 'Oh, fuuuck!' with the quivering voice of one who knows real fear. I thought I was gone. I threw myself into the face of this mother, bracing for all I was worth. Somehow, I punched through and out the other side. I shook the water off and yelled with exhilaration: 'YEAHH!'

But anyway, that was fairly mild Tasman Sea stuff too. That was 30 knots. I mean, 40–45 knots – I'd hate to think about it. It'd be tough. So I paddled back. Got back here about four in the morning, something like that, here on Maria Island. There's a current coming round the southern end of the island. Might have just been wind, I dunno. Then he drops back to a monotone. *But I really didn't have much left in the tank. I was pretty destroyed. Slept in the boat for a few hours. Got up at about ten, and I've just been refuelling all day today. It's about four o'clock now.*

Er, yeah. I'm still coming to terms with the fact that I've canned the trip that I've dreamt about for a long, long time. I've invested a lot of time and effort into it. Quit my job to do this trip. Argh, it's tough. It was a very hard decision . . . but I do think it was the right decision. A lump catches in his throat. He swallows hard. *And, well, I hope to come back. I hope to do it again. I hope to have another go. I'll refine a few things in the kayak. The basic problem is it's so bloody tight in that cockpit. I need a bit more room. I still do think it's achievable in a conventional kayak. I want to do it in a conventional sea kayak.* He pauses to consider. *It needs a bit more thought.*

I feel like I've probably let a lot of people down, actually. A lot of people put a lot of time and effort into this trip aside from me. My wife Vicki – she's done it pretty hard, and spent a lot of time stressing and worrying about all of this. She might be relieved, I dunno. But . . . Ben invested a lot of time, coming down filming and stuff, 'cause we're hoping to make an adventure doco out of it, and I think it'll be a classic if we can do it . . . Another trace of excitement registers in his voice now and in his eyes. *You know, maybe . . . these things take a couple of goes sometimes. When Børge Ousland crossed Antarctica for the first time, it took him two goes. He got frostbite the first time round. Also, Peter Bray took two goes to cross the Atlantic as well. Plenty of other examples, so it's a matter of looking at it again, and working out what can be done better. I'll use wind next time for sure.*

[There are a number of purists out there in the world of sea kayaking who feel that kayaking isn't kayaking if you use wind assistance devices such as sails or kites. Others find it exhilarating to attach a sail to their kayak and virtually fly downwind, racing down the faces of big waves. Whereas Andrew was not averse to the pleasures of hooting along the coast with a kite attached to his kayak, he did want to take the purist approach on this trip, as he had across Bass Strait and the Gulf of Carpentaria. He was adamant about the use of a conventional kayak for this crossing. That was part of the challenge. But he debated long and hard over the sail issue. It really came down to a matter of safety. The authorities from Marine and Safety Tasmania had insisted that a sail or kite be carried on board as a back-up. And his decision was to carry a sail but not use it, unless injury or emergency warranted it.]

It's so windy out there, it's just so windy, and it's so hard to paddle all the time. With a very heavy boat, it's very, very hard on your body, and wind makes you go a lot faster and therefore you can be a lot safer. You can finish the trip quicker. Get more miles done each day. Puts you further from land more quickly, but . . . I think next time I'll definitely use the wind. I don't think there's anything wrong with that. I think it's safer and I think it's smarter, actually.

Yeah, so . . . I'm gonna stay here tonight as well and just rest up a little bit. Fuel up a bit and get feeling semi-normal and paddle back to the mainland tomorrow, which isn't too far. I might try to reach Laurie Ford.

Fortunately we've got a car in Hobart, so I'll be able to go and get that. No clothes though. No wallet. No money. Nothing.

I was planning to go to New Zealand. I wasn't planning to be back here. It's tough.

He stares long and hard towards the water, a few metres in front of him, his eyes weary, tinged with disappointment.

CHAPTER 22

Maria Island, Tasmania 4 December 2006
A little bit later . . .

Still sitting on his kayak, now with a sleeping bag wrapped around his legs, he basks in the late afternoon sun. A line runs from the bow to tether the kayak to an exposed root of a eucalypt a few metres up the beach. Satellite phone in hand, he stares at it, fidgets, stares again for a long time, and sighs heavily.

Righty-oh. Gotta call Vicki. Let her know where I am.

He has difficulty getting a connection. A crow caws loudly overhead, as if to ask this pale-faced intruder what his purpose is on this island. A finch sings in chorus with the crow and Andrew rolls his eyes heavenward in frustration. The phone refuses to connect.

Not getting through at the moment, Iridium being what it is.

Minutes pass. He checks the phone and adjusts the aerial. Clears his throat. *Righty-oh. We'll try again.* He stares down at the sand beneath his feet. *It's ringing.* His expression blank, eyes dull.

Hello, gorgeous. It's me. His eyes light up. A smile appears, and broadens as he listens to the enthusiastic reply. *Good. How are you?*

We've always had an agreement that when he's on a trip, he won't call me. He always does, of course, and it's always a wonderful surprise to hear his voice hailing from some remote body of water. That's where I thought he was calling from, the water. My excitement bubbles over with the joy of hearing his voice. He sounds tired.

'Yeah, actually, I've pulled the pin. I'm . . . back at . . . I got into Maria Island just a short time ago.'

I burst into tears – overwhelmed with sheer relief on my part and yet tremendous disappointment for Ant. I know how much he's put into this trip. The dreams, the frustration, the excitement, the effort of everything that went into this project to get this far, and now . . .

'Yeah, because I was too cold sleeping in the kayak . . . and I was just shivering uncontrollably, you know, for hours and hours, and . . . I couldn't go on like that. It's too dangerous, so . . . I've pulled the pin. So it's a bit of a bummer . . . I just felt that it pushed me outside the boundaries of what I thought was an acceptable risk, you know. I always thought that I'd be warm inside the cockpit, not cold. And I was cold. And you're cold enough paddling. I paddled all night the first night and made some good ground but, oh, the position report you got, I was only 30 ks out or something, but then I kept paddling. And so I was a long way off and I . . . had to turn around and paddle into the wind.'

I comment on my concern about not getting a position in the daily sched the previous night.

'Yeah, I just kept paddling instead of mucking around, and it was hard enough actually just sending a message back, 'cause the weather was quite big, and so it was a pretty brief report back and it was quite hard to even do that, so I didn't want to muck around with the beacon.'

Listens as I express my concern for his welfare.

'It's disappointing, but . . . I'm fine. I was pretty shattered when I got here because I hadn't slept much and I was hallucinating and stuff by the time I got here, which was pretty wild . . . Whereas I was able to handle it there, in another ten days or so, I don't like to think how I would have been . . .' The crow concurs with a loud caw. 'So I just felt that it wasn't an acceptable risk for me . . . so I chucked it in.'

I tell him I'm so proud of him for making the right decision and I know it must have been a difficult one.

'Oh, thanks, gorgeous . . . I'm just gonna wait for the tide to come in . . . 'cause the boat's up high and I can't drag it out on my own, and then I'll paddle into Orford and I might try to chase up Laurie Ford. Hey listen, are there any clothes in the car or not?'

I'd taken the clothes home on the plane. I took home as much as I could fit – just left the camping stuff. I hadn't anticipated any need to leave smelly clothes in the car. I tell him I'll catch the first flight down in the morning, and bring some gear for him, and his wallet and some money.

'No, I'll just borrow some clothes from Grant [a friend in Hobart] or something. How are you, gorgeous? Are you OK?' His voice is warm, and deep with concern.

I go into a long spiel about not being able to sleep as I toss and turn in my comfortable and spacious bed, thinking of him out there in that claustrophobic and extremely space-challenged little pod.

'Well don't you worry.'

I've been nothing but worrying. Such a huge undertaking. It's just so very hard being stuck at home, unable to focus on anything but my beautiful Ant in that tiny kayak, in those huge seas.

'Yeah, OK, you've been a nervous wreck . . . well wait till you see the footage of me paddling out of Fortescue Bay. I wasn't a very happy chappy either.'

I reiterate my pride in his decision-making abilities and voice my concern for his wellbeing – more his mental health than physical. Sure, he must be exhausted. That will pass. But the disappointment . . .

'Yeah yeah, I'm fine, I'm fine, I'm fine . . . I'll have to go back and pick up the car and drop this camera gear off to Jeff and stuff, and . . . er . . . and we'll talk about whether or not I have another go at it.'

I can see that lopsided, sheepish little grin through the phone. So, it's not over. I guess I knew it wouldn't be. This is just another hurdle. He won't let it defeat him.

'We'll just talk about that, OK?'

I swallow hard. A shiver runs down my spine. OK.

'All right.'

A few hours on solid ground to think it over, and already he's planning a rematch. Not that it surprises me in the least.

I'm eager to hear more details of the epic turnaround.

'I was paddling all night to get back and I got back this morning. And the main reason was that I was too cold in the cockpit 'cause I was sleeping in water. I couldn't dry it out properly, and also the hammocks are a bit fucked. They need a bit of sorting out . . . I'm on solid land and I'm feeling the sand between my toes . . . OK, so you call Paul. Just put something pretty vague on the website about how I made good ground on the first night, or something . . . I'll turn the beacon on in a sec and I'll send you my report, which is gonna say Maria Island.'

I tell him about Laurie Ford's partner Elli emailing me and wishing Finlay and me well over the coming month, as well as sending a whole bunch of pics from the departure. I comment about how Laurie isn't deserving of his gruff reputation. He's a tried and true old sea dog, with many years of experience paddling the wild waters of Tasmania and beyond. Neither of us had met him until the day of the departure, but his reputation of being highly opinionated and arrogant was, in my opinion, quite unjust. He reminds me of my father – gruff exterior, yet an old softy underneath, with a heart of gold. Ant agrees.

'Maybe you can send Elli a message, and tell her that I arrived at Maria today and I'll be in Orford tomorrow, and I'll give them a ring . . . I'll call you when I'm on the mainland, so that might be lunchtime or something . . . You've got no need to stress anymore, 'cause we're all fine.'

'Love you, Pookie.'

'Love you too, gorgeous. See ya. Bye.'

He sits there, with the wind whistling through the trees, fingers dancing across the face of the phone, rapidly texting his situation report to Jonathan. Beep. Beep. Beep. Beep.

Back in Glenbrook, a frenzy of highly emotional phone calls begins. I call Andrew's parents, then mine. I burst into tears, telling Mum that I really want to go to Tasmania to pick Ant up. I call Paul when I regain my composure and tell him all I know. I call Juliet, Ben, Teen, Neil. Word gets around.

Back on the beach on Maria Island, Andrew's face is a picture of concentration as he composes his text messages. Then the phone rings. *Hello? Oh Paul, how are ya?* Listens. *Oh, that's good*. Wry smile. *I made a very tough decision.* Listens . . . clears his throat. *Well, I'm actually pretty comfortable that I did make the right one.* He goes on to explain the issues he had, then listens for a long while. Paul can talk!

Yeah. Heavy sigh. *Well, I don't feel great about it, 'cause there's a lot of people put a lot of effort into it . . .* He listens to Paul again for a while and laughs . . . *Fucking oath it was rough! Yeah, it was. Oh, the biggest wave that hit was actually as I was coming back towards the mainland, and I was in the tube, and the whole thing broke on top of me. Yeah, no shit! And I gotta say, I thought that one was gonna throw me over.* Listens. *Well, I think the bubble actually helped, you know, because, I mean it's hard to tell because . . . I probably should have done this but I haven't. I haven't actually tried capsizing in the upright position with the bubble on top, but I think what happened was that I did get thrown, but because it's full of air and it takes time for that air to get expelled, it can't fill up really quick. I tell you what, tying it down properly was a good move, though.*

He laughs loudly as Paul asks whether he's thinking of giving it another go. *Well, it's already crossing my mind, but this is something that needs to be discussed with my wife because she's suffered a bit through this. She's been a nervous wreck.*

Perhaps he was thinking of that time, just a few weeks ago now, although it seems an eternity, when we were lying in bed. Tears rolled down my face and he asked what was wrong. I just want it to be over, I told him. I just want it finished and have you back home, safe and sound.

More vivid still, no doubt, would be his memory of the night the week before that, when we were having our ritual Sunday dinner at Pam and Neil's. The dinner conversation inevitably came around to trip preparation and Neil mentioned a hiccup in the plans. What the... Ant hadn't mentioned anything about it to me.

With good reason, really. The stress of it all was taking its toll. Someone took the lid off the pressure cooker. I exploded. I grabbed the car keys, stormed out, and sped off home rather less than cautiously, fuming. He had chosen not to mention some of the more frustrating issues he was facing – thought it was better that I didn't know because it was upsetting me. Yet it upset me more that he didn't feel that he could tell me about it. In a heat of irrational fury, I pulled into the driveway with a screech, ran inside, slamming every door I could, and bashed both fists as hard as I could against the bathroom door. The bathroom door has large glass panels.

The phone rang. It was Neil. I screamed a tirade of obscenities down the line. Ant arrived home to find me covered in blood, with shattered glass everywhere.

Paul asks if Andrew managed to get any sleep out there. *Oh, I slept a bit. But not really. Actually, as I came back to the mainland, I was hallucinating from lack of sleep. I've had it before, and I've seen some pretty wild things. It's better than any drug you can take.*

He laughs, listens, laughs some more. *I actually... I would like to... well, I shouldn't speak too soon. I'm considering having another crack at it. I'm considering having another crack at it, but I want to talk to Vicki first.*

In the space of a six-minute conversation with Paul, Ant had gone from feeling the hardship of the past few days at sea, to that spark in his eye that indicates his 'considering having another crack' means that nothing short of a global disaster will stop him from a second attempt. The only question is when.

CHAPTER 23

5 December 2006

So there I was in Tassie. Again. I was beginning to feel like a local; this was my third visit in two weeks. I picked up the car and drove east to Dunalley to find Laurie Ford. It had been a logistical challenge to get there, only made possible by the generosity and altruism of my wonderful mother. She had called back about half an hour after I had phoned with the news, to tell me she'd fly back from Queensland to look after Finlay while I went to collect Ant. Oh, no, I told her. She couldn't do that. They'd only just only just arrived up there. It's OK, she had assured me; her friend Jane was on the net as we spoke, booking her an early-morning flight.

I had phoned my friend Penny across the road. I was in tears – again – so she hung up and thirty seconds later was at my front door. It was evening by now, and good ol' pragmatic Penny put Finlay in the bath while I booked flights, ran around the house madly, shoving clothes into bags, and phoned my brother's wife to tell her we'd be coming into Sydney to stay the night. I had an early flight to Hobart, so could she mind Finlay until Grandma arrived on the 10 am flight from Maroochydore? Of course. Nothing's a problem for Jilly.

So, with Elli's instructions, I found Laurie at Dunalley. He led me to a good vantage point, where we walked to the top of the hill and sat down for a long wait. I kept to myself at first, still a little unsure of his grouchy reputation. I soon warmed to him, though, and we sat for hours on the hill, talking about kayaking and relationships and life, and keeping a watchful eye on the water. He remarked that, in his younger days, he had wanted to attempt the Tasman trip, but his wife at the time wouldn't let him. Perhaps that's why they divorced. I made a mental note to mention that to Sharnie Wu.

It was a long day of sitting and watching and waiting. Eventually we drove around to a boat ramp and I sat on the edge of the jetty, with my feet dangling, not quite reaching the seaweedy water below, mesmerised by two gigantic manta rays which appeared to be flirting with me. I could have reached out to pat them if I'd felt so inclined. The graceful fluidity of their movement seemed to wash away all the tension of the past days, weeks, months. They stayed there with me, sharing my sunlight and my sense of peace, knowing that any minute now my husband would be returning safely to land. Well, not that the rays would have even known or cared about that, but it just seemed to me as if they did.

Word of Andrew's tactical retreat spread like wildfire. On Wednesday, 6 December, American Derrick Mayoleth very eloquently summed up the situation on his highly respected and world renowned www.kayakquixotica.com:

At 4 am our time the news that Andrew McAuley was returning to Tasmania had begun to spread around the web. The kink in the plan had been risk of hypothermia. After paddling more than 24 hours and 80 kilometres with a helpful wind and big swells he decided it was time to nap. Although his cockpit canopy worked well and did keep the weather out, he had problems getting warmed up. A standard kayak hull does not retain heat well. This was going to be a problem. And this is one of the things that distinguishes Andrew from so many others. He realised then and there that this could get dangerous. Sure he could paddle on. He could get the testosterone going and 'muscle it out' and let the chips fall. But no. He made the wise and I'd say bravest choice of all, he turned back. Living to fight another day, as they say.

It's hard for anyone to really imagine what energy and emotion go into planning such endeavours. From the day you first decide you will tell one other person of your plans you truly are committed. Sure, you've decided, but telling others makes it real. Then for months on end you imagine and plan, you raise money, you market yourself, you build, you test, you talk, you argue, you sweat, you have nightmares, you ride the rollercoaster, you become single-minded. Other concerns of life must pause. At least for a time. Friends become team members. Family become pillars. You rely on them. Volunteers and wellwishers come out to help in any way they can. Often adding important information and guidance you'd have never imagined. So many faces want you to succeed. For a moment in time, they attach their personal goals to yours. By the time you slip out into the water it must almost seem as if you've lived no other life for as far back as you can remember. In some way you must feel the hopes and expectations of everyone you've known and interacted with in the last few months are now firmly wrapped around you like a second PFD [personal flotation device].

Some 80 kilometres from anywhere, wrapped in a fibreglass tube and at the mercy of a big sea, what do you do when you realise you may have a problem? What goes through your mind when you think going forward may be dangerous? How long is the pause before turning back? Do you see all those faces, do you imagine the press, do you wonder if the sponsors will be miffed? Will the second-guessing start? What about that one idiot who keeps saying it couldn't be done? Boy, will he be all over you!! Do you battle with ego and pride? The mind is a funny place to live all by yourself. It does have strange priorities sometimes . . . This is where wisdom and bravery take over. You realise that everyone that matters to you just wants you home safe. They will be proud of you. They know that just by trying . . . anything . . . you've done more than most. Everyone else can get stuffed.

Andrew will have another go. I know he will. He's a man of substance.

Derrick's post generated some very positive feedback. One chap named Silbs commented:

Congratulations to you, Derrick, on an excellent post of wisdom and to Andrew for his courage to go and to be his own man when the time came to turn back. We can all do well to learn from his lesson on digression [sic] and how it relates to valour.

Ant then posted the following:

Derrick, that's an amazing post that sums up the situation perfectly. Thanks to all the other folk out there for your support. You're right, I will be out there for another crack at it soon. Cheers, Andrew McAuley

The fat lady hadn't sung yet!

CHAPTER 24

Back home, and back to the drawing board – well, the garage at least. Andre Janecki, who had given up his precious time to help Ant finalise things in the days before departure, was back again, slaving away in the garage with Ant and requesting more of my home-made pizza.

Both Andrew and Andre have very analytical minds. Together, they came up with an ingenious system of carving V-shaped channels into the insulating foam on the floor of the cockpit. Then they pierced small holes in the foam for the water to drain through. The underside of the foam had channels running in the opposite direction, leading the water to the electric bilge pump outlet. This method was found to be very successful in keeping the cockpit floor dry. A key problem overcome. Unfortunately it created another. The seemingly insignificant 20-millimetre thickness of the foam reduced Andrew's ability to roll over inside the cockpit, taking the effort from considerable to extreme. Nothing could be done about it now, though.

Another of Ant's brilliant inventions was the hammock system for sleeping. It consisted of three sections of netting, each about 20 centimetres wide, with rigid fibreglass rods sewn into the sides. These hammocks were set to support shoulders, buttocks and legs off the cockpit floor. The reason for three rather than just one long hammock was so that any section could be adjusted to avoid pressure sores. This system had failed on the first attempt, due to overcrowding in the cockpit. We had sewn several models and, after each test, Ant would bring them back for me to resew. I initially sewed a polar fleece lining onto the shadecloth mesh, to make the surface warmer and less abrasive. But the fleece retained water and had the opposite effect.

Upon his unexpected early return to the mainland, Jonathan Bogais called Ant to his 'office' and blasted him for not sticking to the protocol on the day he made that monumental decision to return to Australian shores. Andrew had made what Jonathan considered an unforgivable omission by not giving his position the night of his turnaround. Andrew's reasoning was that the weather was too wild to stop and turn the beacon on and, if we had received the coordinates, there would have been mild panic and confusion. Jonathan didn't accept that excuse and made it perfectly clear that if there were to be a second attempt, the communications plan *must* run to schedule, regardless of any monumental act of God.

And then it was Christmas. A rather different Christmas than we had originally planned. If all had gone well the first time round, we might have been celebrating Christmas in New Zealand with a very weary yet ecstatic Ant. The unexpected delays by the authorities had put paid to that plan. And then, with the aborted attempt behind us, but the second attempt looming, Christmas was a subdued affair in Bathurst. Just Ant,

Finlay, Mum and Dad and me. It was supposed to be a McAuley Christmas and we did think of driving up to Queensland, but it was such a long way, and a singularly focused mind wanted to maximise preparation time for the second assault. Driving to Brisbane and back then rushing around packing to drive south to Tasmania again was simply not viable.

Poppa and Marsie came down to Glenbrook for a brief visit the week before Christmas, though. Dinner that night was awkward. Marsie commented to me later that she was worried. Andrew seemed very tense and stressed – most unlike his usual loving, carefree, enthusiastic self. She wanted so much to go out to the garage, as he worked furiously on last-minute fine-tuning, to tell him she was worried about him, about the trip and to tell him she thought it was too dangerous. Like me, she wanted to tell him not to go. But also like me, she knew she couldn't.

It was an uncomfortable visit. Poppa sensed that Andrew didn't want to discuss the trip. It was indeed the case that Ant was concerned that his parents would grill him too much, and possibly try to talk him out of it, and so both Marsie and Poppa found the visit very stilted, very stressful.

As they sat in the car, Poppa in the driver's seat ready to pull out of the driveway, Andrew leaned in for one final embrace with his dear mother. She told him then, 'I'm so proud of you, my darling, and of everything you have done in your life. So very, very proud.'

'Thanks, Ma,' he said. 'I know all this crazy stuff I do stresses you, so I really appreciate your support. It means so much to me.'

The New Year arrived in a flurry of final preparations, although we did have time to count 2007 in with our closest friends. Well actually, we sort of cheated. I guess it's a sign of age, or maybe just parenthood, that we all crashed well before midnight.

Then, back to business. There was a serious need to declutter, but how, when all items are essential? More netting in the form of small pockets lining the inside of the cockpit would make it a more livable space. These seemingly small adjustments made an enormous difference to Andrew's living quarters. It's all relative, of course.

Less food equated to a little less bulk and a little less weight. So second time round he decided to leave two drybags behind – that's four days' rations. And less water. After all, the Katadyn Survivor-35 manual desalinator was reputedly bombproof. In fact, it was the model favoured by the US army. The only problem with the desalinator is that it is, as stated, manual. Fifteen minutes of hand-pumping yields one litre of fresh drinking water. After paddling all day, it's a task that I'm sure he wouldn't be looking forward to. But, it saved the weight and bulk of carrying more water.

What other necessary items could become unnecessary? Sharnie had investigated breathing apparatus to avoid inhaling the carbon dioxide that might accumulate inside Casper after prolonged periods tucked inside. The yacht ventilators, plus the extra little hatch at the back of the canopy worked well enough. So in the end it was more stuff, taking up more space, and although it wasn't particularly bulky, every small item added up. He also ditched the iPod.

Sea kayakers and sailors spend an inordinate amount of time talking about the weather. The wind, waves and sea state have an enormous influence on progress at sea. By the end of the first week in January, Cyclone Isobel, the first of the Western

Australian tropical cyclone season, had deteriorated into a low pressure system and moved south, making its way across the Great Australian Bight towards Tasmania. This system was forecast to bring some much-needed rain to Victoria and Tasmania. It would also bring some strong winds to the southern Tasman Sea in another day or two. Ant wisely decided to let this one slip through before venturing out there. The summer weather patterns of late deserved a lot of respect. There had been plenty of easterly headwinds recently, so Ant was on weather hold, waiting for the right moment to make the dash towards the Land of the Long White Cloud.

CHAPTER 25

Glenbrook 8 January 2007

It was very early. Finlay's mouth was wide open. His little arms were thrown back over his head, and his Bob the Builder pyjama top had ridden up to expose his tummy. He was fast asleep. My heart broke as Ant leaned in to kiss him ever so gently on the forehead, and whispered, 'I love you, Munchkin. I love you, my little man.'

Tears streamed down my face, but I wiped them surreptitiously on my T-shirt. I don't think he was fooled, though. I was trying to be strong and brave and to have a dry face when the time came to kiss my beautiful Ant goodbye. It's just farewell, after all. Not goodbye.

We'll be in Milford Sound in about a month, waiting for the man and his kayak to tame the Tasman. Any sports psychologist will endorse the benefits of positive visualisation. That's what I was doing. I was visualising that euphoric moment when Ant takes his final strokes towards shore. Finlay is in my arms as I run into the water, up to my waist. I throw my arms around him.

He grabs our little boy and we all burst into tears of pure joy, elation, relief. Our tangled torsos cause the boat to tip, and we all fall into the water and we sit there, all three of us soaking wet and we laugh and cry and hug and kiss and laugh some more . . .

On the eve of heading off, I feel a lot like I'm about to go to war. It feels like the chances of not coming back from the Tasman are similar. It's a scary feeling. I'm scared and frightened, but I cannot turn away from it. Each time I hold my wife close, or kiss my child, I wish I could.

Ant checked the straps on the kayak one last time. I asked if he had his passport. He laughed – a rich, warm laugh, tinged with an ever-so-slight hint of nerves.

The possibility of using the sail this time had been a fierce topic of discussion over the previous weeks. Once more, I urged him to reassess his purist ethics and use the darned sail. It was another risk-reduction factor. The greater the daily mileage, the shorter the trip. Fewer days on the water would significantly decrease the overall risk factor. He didn't give me a definitive answer. I could only hope that once he was on the water good sense would prevail.

I held his hand through the car window as he backed out of the driveway. No mean feat one-handed – it's an awkward driveway, with a couple of seemingly innocuous little kinks. Still holding my hand, he jammed the gearstick into first and drove slowly up the street. I ran after him until our hands slipped apart. Then I ran some more, waving, waving, until he disappeared around the bend in the road. I continued to wave although I knew he could no longer see me. And then I stood, frozen, unable to move, watching the empty road, and the tears flowed unchecked.

Two little surfie dudes. Three-year-old Andrew and his younger brother, Michael, about to hit the gnarly surf at One Mile beach near Nelson Bay, NSW in 1970.

Andrew leading the fifth pitch of his route 'Crash Test Dummies' in the Grose Valley, Blue Mountains, with Vera Wong on belay in 1998. They named the climb after a group of base jumpers who flew past as the climbers were half way up the 200-metre cliff face.

Simon Carter

The first pitch on Marpo Brakk, Nangmah Valley, Pakistan. The 5300-metre peak came within a breath of taking the lives of Andrew's climbing partners, Vera and Ned, on the final pitch. June 1999.

Chris Gleisner

11 December 1999. The day I became Mrs McAuley and the luckiest person on earth.

Finlay's first big adventure; a very proud dad with his 11-week-old son on top of Pigeon House Mountain, Morton National Park, NSW, in August 2003.

Finlay's first kayak lesson with Dad at Dunn's Swamp, Wollemi National Park, NSW in 2004.

The three of us in the National Park down the road from our place in July 2005. Finlay spent much of his first couple of years on Dad or Mum's back exploring 'our backyard'.

Donna Ingram

The McAuley family celebrating the auspicious occasion of Marsie and Poppa's 40th wedding anniversary at Maroochydore in December 2005. *Front from left*: Juliet's husband Shaun with baby Olivia, Juliet, Jilly (Marsie), me, Finlay, Ant. *Back*: Michael, Michael's wife, Nicole, Peter (Poppa).

Ant paddling through brash ice and a pod of humpback whales in the Antarctic Peninsula in March 2006.

Ant in a state of pure contentment in the pristine perfection of the Antarctic Peninsula.

Ant in the shed (where he spent an inordinate amount of time) putting the first coat of paint on Casper in October 2006.

Paul Hewitson and Ant fitting out the kayak in the Mirage workshop in Gosford in October 2006.

Ant going through the motions with Casper on dry land before he hits the water for some real testing. Stainless steel pivot arms allow him to reach back and pull Casper from the rear deck to latch into place over the cockpit coaming, locking him inside with a watertight seal. The small rectangles fibreglassed onto the rear deck are Paul's initiative – stabilising blocks to keep Casper from being buffeted by waves.

Andrew Meares

This classic shot illustrates Ant's characteristic high-bladed paddling technique. It was taken on a training run a couple of weeks prior to the real thing.

Sea anchor – deployed from the bow during non-paddling hours to stop the kayak from broaching by keeping the nose pointed into the weather. He carried two sea anchors, a small one for use in a tailwind to allow drift to the east, and a large one for use in a headwind, to prevent backward drift.

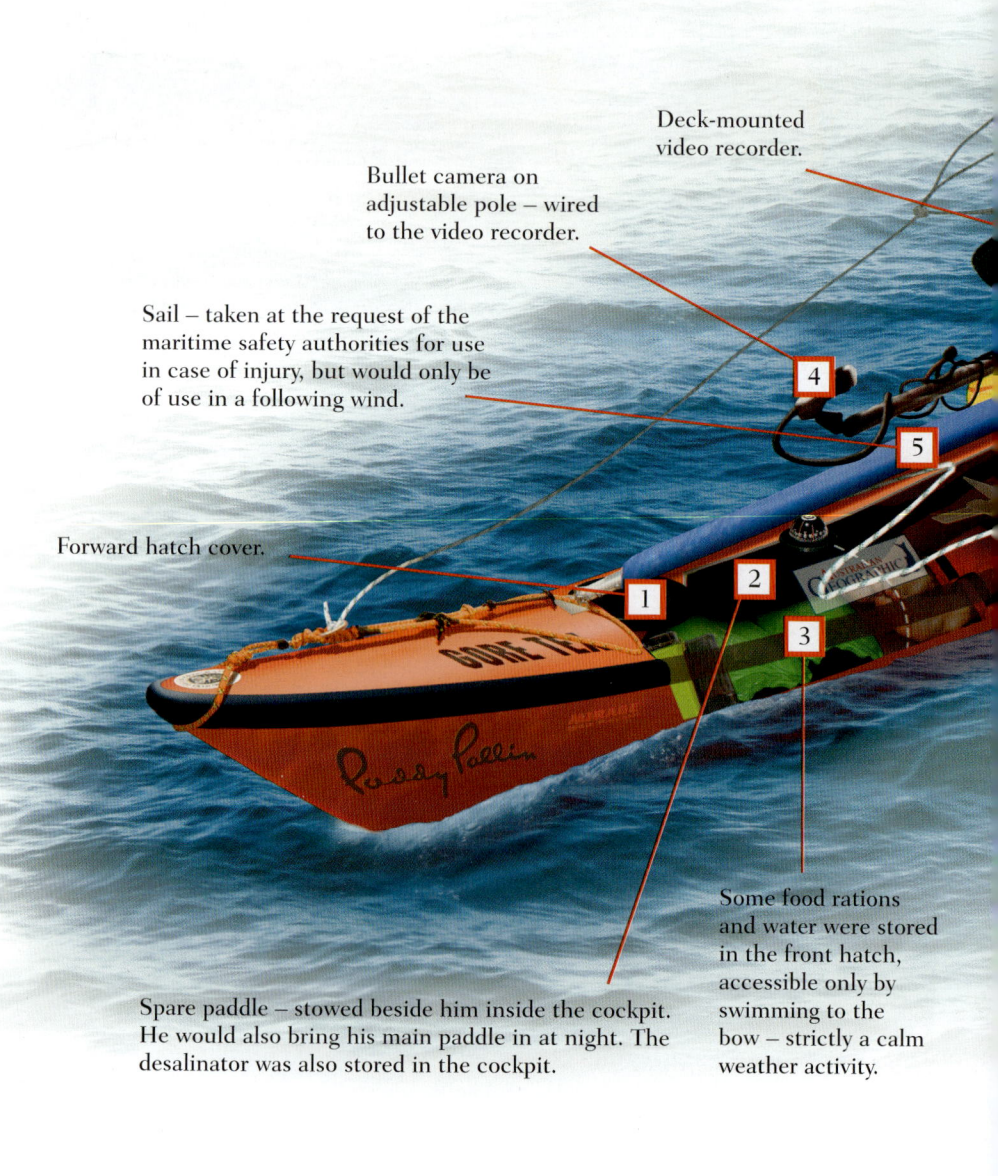

Deck-mounted video recorder.

Bullet camera on adjustable pole – wired to the video recorder.

Sail – taken at the request of the maritime safety authorities for use in case of injury, but would only be of use in a following wind.

Forward hatch cover.

Spare paddle – stowed beside him inside the cockpit. He would also bring his main paddle in at night. The desalinator was also stored in the cockpit.

Some food rations and water were stored in the front hatch, accessible only by swimming to the bow – strictly a calm weather activity.

Andrew left Australia with his EPIRB in a waterproof case, hung around his neck. To my eternal despair, it was found stowed in one of the shadecloth pockets inside the cockpit.

PFD (Personal flotation device) – worn over his Gore-tex cag (paddling jacket with neoprene neck, waist and wrist cuffs to keep water out).

'Air-Only' yacht ventilator – with the aid of another small hatch on Casper's rear wall, it provided adequate ventilation, even when Andrew was locked inside Casper for two full days.

Riding sail – used to point the boat into the wind when the sea anchor was out.

Five-watt solar panel – for recharging all electrical equipment (i.e. sat phones, beacon, GPS, cameras).

Casper the cockpit canopy – sat on the aft deck during paddling hours, and was pulled into place over the cockpit for sleeping and riding out storms. Over-centre latches were clamped down to provide a watertight seal.

Rear hatch – contained the bulk of his food rations, Dromedary bladders full of fresh water, battery recharging bay, medical kit and drysuit. It opened into the cockpit so Andrew could access it when Casper was locked in place over the cockpit.

The arms of the outriggers fitted over ball joints (fishing rod mounts), allowing the outriggers to swivel easily for storage on the fore deck when not in use.

Inflatable outriggers stabilised the kayak when attending to important tasks like messaging, desalinating water and ablutions. The outriggers weren't used in severe weather as they could inhibit the self-righting ability of the vessel in the event of a capsize.

The rudder pedals were hinged to swing out of the way so his feet could slide right down to the bulkhead (indicated here by the white dotted line) for sleeping.

Australian Geographic

Another training run. Ant is taking the kayak offshore for a test sleepover.

Fortescue Bay, Tasmania, on 2 December 2006. I look on with a nervous smile, trying to hold it together, as Ant finishes packing the essentials for a month at sea, filling every available space in and on the kayak.

The customs official (in the background) has just stamped Ant out of the country. It's time for him to depart Australian shores, but I'm most reluctant to let go of him. He had to prise me off him.

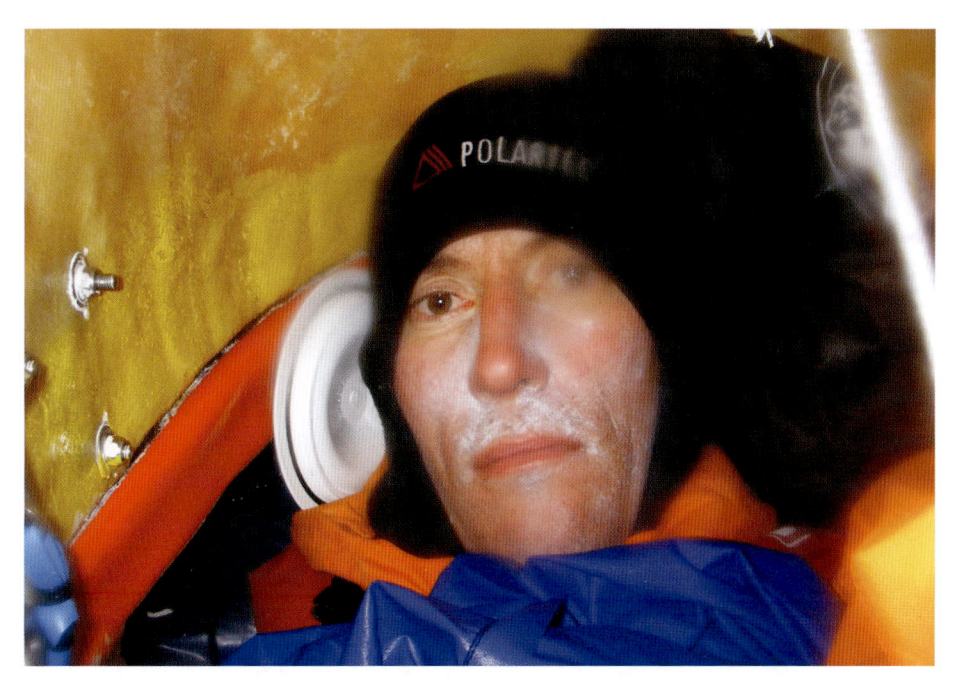

Crunch time. With hypothermia looming inside his ridiculously cramped confines, Ant makes the very difficult but prudent decision to turn the bow back west and live to fight another day. His eyes reflect his disappointment.

A short reprieve. Ant is home for a quiet Christmas with us after aborting the first attempt. This is the very last photo of the three of us together.

January 11 2007. I wasn't there to see Ant paddle out of Fortescue Bay the second time around.

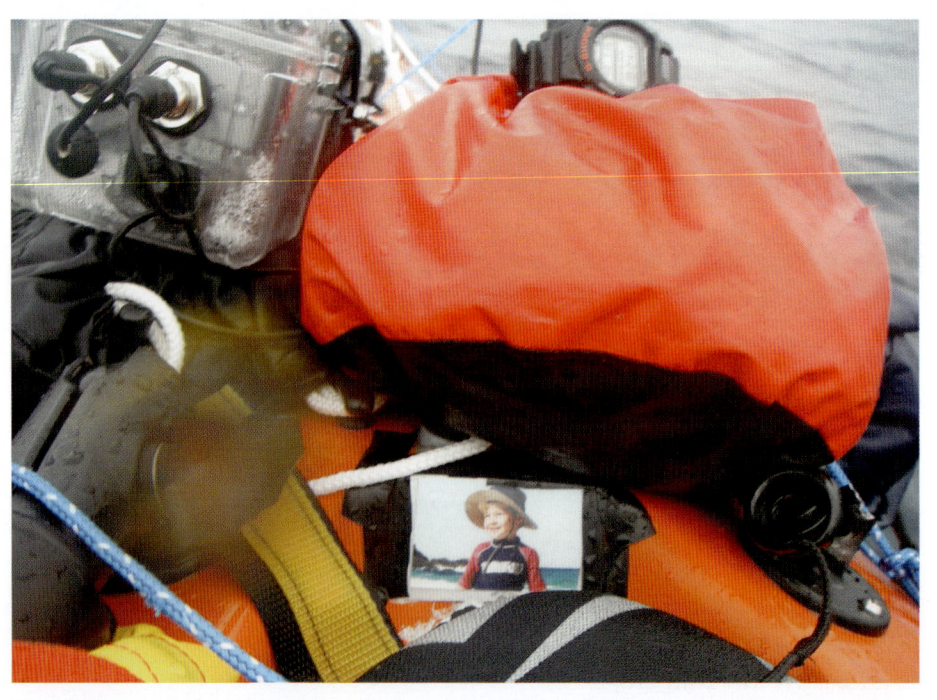

This little picture of his son on the crowded deck is what kept Andrew going for thirty unfathomable days at sea.

'What ya doing there, big guy?' A very welcome visitor in the middle of the Tasman Sea.

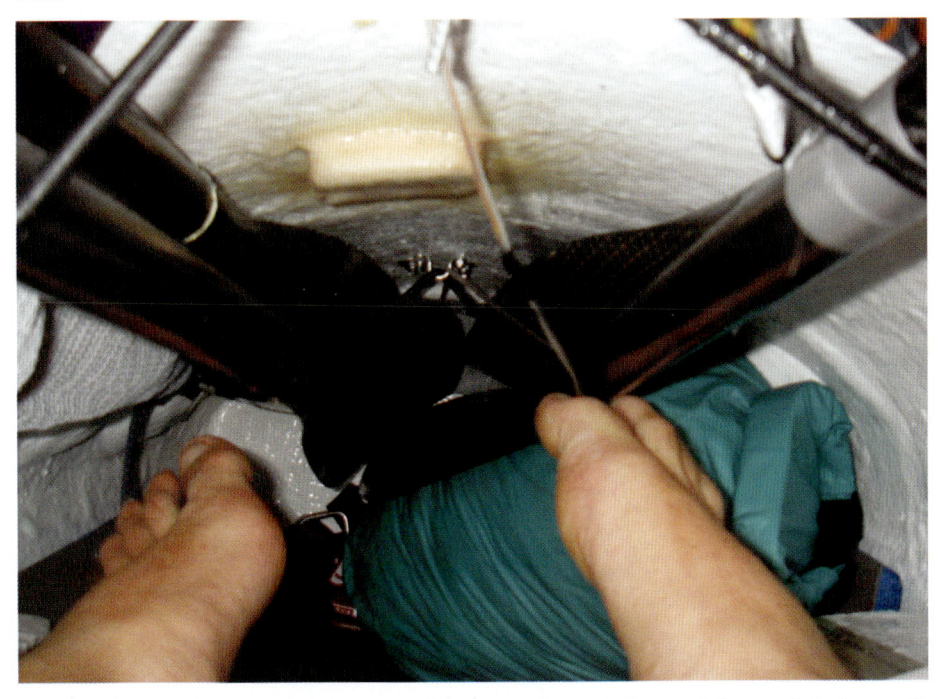

Not an inch to spare. Bunking down for the night with his paddles and drybags of gear, there is barely room for Andrew to wriggle his toes.

One can't begin to imagine what wonders, terrors and delights those soulful eyes had witnessed and were yet to experience. One of Ant's last self-portraits, taken somewhere in the middle of the Tasman Sea below the 40th parallel.

Milford Airfield, February 10 2007. I'm about to take a ride up in the helicopter to look for Ant – at the time believing that he was in no danger. A distraught Finlay didn't want me to leave him. Perhaps he knew more at the time than I did.

Barry Harcourt / The Southland Times

At 1925 NZDT, Saturday February 10 2007, a P3 Orion sighted a semi-submerged kayak. At 2038 NZDT a helicopter arrived at the scene, and the nearby cruise ship *Clipper Odyssey* was tasked to attend. The helicopter crew were unsure yet if Andrew was actually with the kayak.

Rescuers worked tirelessly in search of Andrew. Finn Murphy was winched from the helicopter onto the *Clipper Odyssey* so he could reach the kayak in a Zodiac. The kayak was then winched aboard the *Clipper Odyssey*. Note the inflated yellow outrigger. This suggests that Andrew was not actually paddling at the time of the capsize.

Barnacles on the hull, unintentionally discovered on Day 19 of the voyage, remained firmly attached when the kayak was delivered to dry land after 30 days at sea.

Finlay's fifth birthday present, Aslan, warms his bed and his broken heart.

I guess it was better this way. That's what I needed to tell myself. The raw emotion of that last departure from Fortescue Bay nearly killed me and I know it will be better for Ant. He'll be more focused, less distracted, if I'm not there to see him off. Paul will be there. That's something, I guess. I wanted so much to be in that car with him, driving south to the ferry again. It was a joint decision – a difficult one – that I should stay home this time. I hoped it was the right decision. Everything felt right this time. We'd see him in New Zealand in a month. Give or take.

I turned and walked slowly back home. An overwhelming sense of loneliness suddenly engulfed me. I lay down next to Finlay and cried and cried. He woke up, wrapped his little arms around me and whispered, 'Don't worry. It's OK.'

PART TWO

CHAPTER 26

Fortescue Bay
Day One, 11 January 2007   3.30 pm

The sky was a brilliant, almost cloudless azure. The bay glistened with reflected sunlight and a gentle breeze rustled through the trees lining the water's edge. Silver-lined wavelets licked the shoreline, beckoning to the slender orange craft.

The kayak slithered into the water, with the aid of six burly bystanders, and the first strokes of an incredible journey were drawn. The mood this time was, by all accounts, far more positive than that rain-drenched and windy afternoon just five weeks previously. My absence, I'm sure, had a great deal to do with that. Naturally, I couldn't control the weather – that was a matter of watching the forecast, listening to Jonathan's advice, and then making the move. But my absence allowed Andrew far greater focus on the task at hand, thus a far less emotional exit from Australian shores.

About an hour later, Paul phoned me to report on the successful departure. A wave of nausea swept through me. My legs turned to jelly. It was with some solace that I recalled the intriguing story Ant had told me the previous day. Apparently Paul's wife has a psychic friend. This lady told Paul, back in December, that Andrew shouldn't go. Things weren't right – she could 'see' failure. Naturally Paul thought it imprudent to impart this information back then, regardless of the doubtful accountability of a psychic's predictions. However, since she confidently advised that success was on the horizon for this attempt, he thought this was an appropriate time to share the news. Well, we might scoff at such nonsense, but it's amazing what that little tale did for my confidence. When there's a need, we grab onto the tiniest thread. And I desperately needed to believe in that psychic as my husband paddled off into the unknown. I phoned Juliet and she, too, seemed just that tiny bit more at ease.

At 5.41 pm, Andrew sent a text message from his iridium satellite phone, which was translated somewhere in the ether, through technology that's beyond my understanding, into an email which appeared on my computer screen a few seconds later – the first of the anxiously awaited daily situation reports.

WIND15KTS SOUTH CUM E FEELING GOOD

What a relief it was to get that message, and be assured that all was good on the first day of this epic. What was his position though?

At 5.45 pm, as if he had read my mind, another email appeared.

BEACON ONWHEN I FINISH PADLING 4THEDAY

Well, that answered that question.

Then I logged the first of my daily entries onto www.andrewmcauley.com:

> Well, he's off again! Customs officials stamped Andrew
> out of the country and he departed the shores of Fortescue

Bay, Tasmania, at about 3.30 this afternoon, with light westerlies to push him off shore. The forecast is looking great for the next few days, so he should be able to settle into a good rhythm and get some miles under his belt.

He was all smiles as a small group of friends and wellwishers waved him off and watched him disappear from land. Just think – 30 days (give or take) living in that tiny little kayak all alone at sea! Sounds great doesn't it?!! Wish I was there!

This time he has promised to meet me (his poor old longsuffering wife) in New Zealand!!! Hopefully in a few weeks! Watch this space!!!

Lighthearted, a hint of humour. Everything Ant had asked for. He specifically wanted me to keep the updates upbeat and positive. Taking this approach in some ways helped me to remain positive throughout that incredibly challenging month.

Along with the blog updates, I was entrusted with the task of moving the red dot on the map each day. Of that I was more than capable, but the technical aspects of updating the website daily were beyond my very limited technical abilities. Peter Kappelmann, the webmaster for the New South Wales Sea Kayak Club, saved the day. Each day for a month I wrote a blog, moved the dot a little bit further east, then sent the files to Peter, who made them miraculously appear all around the world via the web.

A 42 degree heatwave hit Glenbrook that afternoon. I lay awake all night, sweltering, and thinking of my beautiful Ant out there. Alone. Cold. Wet. Miserable.

I lay listening to Finlay's broken mumblings. What dreams disturbed his sleep tonight? Was he wondering about Daddy in his tiny kayak on that big ocean? Who knows if three-year-olds are capable of such recondite thoughts? I got up, went to his room and watched him toss and turn, one foot tangled in his sheet. Then I went outside to see if it was any cooler out there. It wasn't. I took a big block of ice out for Noushka. She licked it, then rested her head on it. Maybe I should try that.

I checked my computer in the wee hours, waiting for his coordinates to arrive from the tracking beacon. When they appeared, I logged them into my Google Earth map. He had just dropped off the Continental shelf. On the computer screen, it looked ominous. The sight of it erased any hope of sleep for the rest of that hot, sticky night.

Andrew was asked in an interview, just days before his departure, to put himself in my shoes. 'How do you reckon it all looks from your wife's point of view?'

> Well, I tell you what, it's tough, you know, I really do think it's tough. It's very hard being the one who's left behind, you know. If you're the one who's leaving on a big trip, it's a big adventure, you're excited, you've got things on your mind and you're occupied while you're out there, your mind's very busy on survival, on executing the trip well and safely and so on and you're the one having the big adventure. But if, on the other hand, you're in a position of being left at home, you've got a lot more time on your hands to worry, to let your imagination run riot and really, you know, that's a really difficult position to be in.
>
> So I've got a lot of empathy for that, yeah, and in fact having seen the level of stress in the lead-up to this expedition, and I recognise that it's a high-risk trip, I don't

have a strong desire to ever subject her to that level of concern and stress again.

And I can't deny it. It's hard being the one left behind. For several reasons. Primarily because the stress of worrying about Ant out there, a tiny speck on a huge, wild sea, is so great. I don't expect his quality of sleep to be remotely satisfactory for the next month, but I doubt that I'll sleep well either.

Then part of it's what I might consider purely selfish – being left to do the single parent thing while he's away means that I must be more resourceful in order to swim, get to my yoga classes, get out in the bush on my mountain bike. These things that are very important to me and quite necessary for my well-being take a back seat when Ant's away. And the pressure of trying to maintain some semblance of normality for Finlay's sake . . .

And I miss him. I miss him so much whenever he's away. I feel empty without him around.

The first light of dawn peeped through the gap in the curtains and I wondered if Ant was awake. Did he sleep at all? What was it like out there? I couldn't even begin to imagine.

CHAPTER 27

Tasman Sea, approx. 43.18S, 148.48E
Day Three, 13 January 2007   Early morning

The little hatch at the back of Casper is open, and through it the rise and fall of the big ocean swells are visible. He is lying down on the hull, sleeping bag pulled up to his chin, Polartec thermal beanie on. A tuft of matted fringe protrudes from the beanie at his forehead. Light shines through the fibreglass wall of Casper. He attempts, in the extreme confines of the cockpit, to stretch his right arm over his head. It folds around his head, elbow jammed into one wall of Casper, fingers touching the rear wall.

Well, it's the morning of day three and I've had a, well a pretty crappy night really. His voice sounds tired, his eyes echo that. *I wasn't too cold but I was wet and I didn't take enough care to keep the cockpit dry before I went down for bed.* He reaches down to pull the sleeping bag higher around his neck and pulls the beanie further down over his forehead. He rests his long fingers on the crown of his head.

And it's quite rough. It's quite rough at the moment. I'm not really sure what it's doing outside but I had waves breaking right over the top of the cockpit a number of times and breaking into the hatch here behind me a few times. It seems to have backed off a little bit now but I had a front through the night that was quite a strong one, and a taste of what the Tasman can dish up. And it was manageable but I hope I don't get anything too much worse than that . . .

So it's day three. I've been wondering lots of things. Wondering what the hell I'm doing here. He folds his arm back and tucks it behind his head, to make a headrest. *Wondering how quickly I can get this done because my progress hasn't been as fast as I had hoped so I gotta get out there and get some good miles in. I've only done 70 ks. In two days. That's 35 ks a day.* He closes his eyes and grimaces as if the mere thought of it is abhorrent. *It's not enough. It won't even get me there in forty days.* He rolls his eyes heavenward. *So, I'm gonna put in a big one today. There's a bit of wind there. Hopefully it'll help. So I'll get out there and get into it.* He lets out a heavy sigh. *It's interesting the things you think of here. I've been thinking of little jobs that I needed to do for Vicki, like register her website. I'm tempted to send her a message to do that . . . Lots of little things pop into my head. There's another wave over the canopy.* A shadow of the wave is visible through the thin fibreglass walls of Casper. Water covers the open mouth of the hatch. Miraculously, none enters.

Anyway, at least it's sunny outside. Joy. Joy . . . You really wonder why you do these things sometimes. Bloody hell. I'll be honest – right now I really don't want to be here. I want to be on dry land, not suffering. Right now I'm suffering. It's so tight inside this cockpit. It's just so tight. I can hardly do anything. And it's hard. It's really, really hard. But . . . when it's all over I'll be glad of it . . . I think . . . I hope. He shuts his eyes tight. Another big wave breaks over the kayak, buffeting the tiny craft.

CHAPTER 28

13 January 2007

Seals swim with incredible grace through glistening clear water. A large pod frolic in the surf, catching waves with majestic ease. Several of the seals peel off from the other surfers and glide through whitewash to calm blue waters.

Suddenly, a monstrous set of jaws erupts out of the calm. Row upon deadly row of razor-sharp teeth fill the cavernous mouth. The creature propels its entire massive body several metres out of the water. The vice-like jaws snap shut on the tail of a seal. The monster rolls in mid-air then crashes down with a thunderous splash. The seal is flung high into the air on impact, escaping the jaws of death. Momentarily. The beast thrashes its tail with overbearing violence, then cuts sharply through the now churning water after its prey.

'If surprise fails,' David Attenborough's sonorous voice penetrated the loungeroom, 'there will be a chase. The shark is faster on a straight course, but it can't turn as sharply as a seal. It's agility versus power.'

The gigantic fins of the great white thrash and churn. The seal turns sharply in a desperate attempt to flee its prey. The monster propels its body up again from the water, rising even higher into the air. Now the seal is clenched firmly between the deadly jaws. No escape this time.

'Once the seals have finished breeding, then the giant sharks will move on,' David Attenborough continued in a very clinical, matter-of-fact tone. 'It's now becoming clear that great whites migrate thousands of miles across the oceans to harvest seasonal abundances in different seas.'

I rarely watch TV. I have no idea what prompted me to watch it this night, and I cursed my inappropriate channel selection. I pressed the off button, tossed the remote onto the coffee table, and went to bed. Perfect viewing to ensure another sleepless night.

CHAPTER 29

Tasman Sea, approx. 43.27S, 149.42E
13 January 2007   Late evening

He sits upright, in the paddling position, his mood positive.

So it's day 3 and today I've seen two sharks. One followed right behind the boat. He was, like, THAT far from the rear of the boat. He shoves his hand into the camera lens and indicates with his thumb and forefinger a distance of mere centimetres. *He looked like a great white. Don't know how big he was. Very glad he didn't have a chunk. And the other one was HUGE.* The enormousness of the shark is emphasised by his exaggerated facial expression. *He was like five metres – four and a half – five metres. Jumped about five metres into the air and landed all of about 50 metres away from me. That was incredible. Never seen anything like that in my life.* His features are animated with the thrill of his experiences. His voice is light and brimming with enthusiasm.

Also saw a bluebottle. Well, I saw heaps of bluebottles. One of them got wrapped around my paddle, which was no fun.

Umm. Had a rough night last night. It was pretty gnarly. Strong south-westerly winds. Thirty knots — something like that. I was just being bounced around like you wouldn't believe and the outriggers were sort of right up high and not really doing anything at all.

Didn't get much sleep at all. And I broke an outrigger some time today. Well, I've got it here but I'll probably chuck it. So, it's been a pretty eventful day.

Good progress under sail for a fair bit of today, then it glassed off to nothing. Right now I've got a little bit of a tail wind again, and it's 9 o'clock. I'm gonna make the most of it and probably go through till, I don't know, 10 or 11. See how I feel.

Beautiful sunset there behind me. Pretty happy to be here. Got a bit of a rash starting on my stomach. A bit worried about that, so I've gotta take care. And well, actually, I just want to be there. The sooner the better. He looks off into the distance. *Ah, but it's gonna be a long trip. It could be anything up to about 30 days.*

Then, with a sudden burst of zeal, he shoves his face right into the camera, and shouts, ALL RIGHT THEN, with a sparkle in his eyes.

CHAPTER 30

Tasman Sea, approx. 43.30S, 150.15E
Day Four, 14 January 2007

The dead of night. An ink-black ocean beneath a coal-black sky. It's calm. Just a gentle rhythmic sloshing of waves against the hull. The inside of the cockpit is blacker than black.

Well, last night I had the boat parked rear to the wind for a change to try to promote progress and I lost the rear hatch cover of the bubble here. And so I had a bag full of clothes stuffed in the hole but it still let heaps of waves and water in. I was having a miserable time – very cold and stuff, and I thought, I've learnt the meaning of suffering. I know what suffering is all about.

Well today, I capsized in 30 knots [55 km/h] of wind. Huge swells. Lost a bit of gear . . . had to empty my huge cockpit which is about . . . I don't know . . . 90 or 100 litres or something. And it was all pretty full on. And I thought, here I've learnt the meaning of the word extreme. This really IS extreme. It's full on man, it's fuckin' full on. I really could die. I mean, it's an excellent, excellent, EXCELLENT adventure . . . provided I make it. It's something that's really out there . . . it's more full on than anything I ever imagined. So, it's just wild . . . It's a true, true stunning adventure.

I just hope I haven't bitten off more than I can chew, 'cause there's a few little things going wrong but, I mean, I still feel pretty good. I just need a good run with the wind and the weather and hopefully I'll get there really soon because right now I just want it to be over . . .

And when it is over, I'll look back and I'll be stoked. I'll be stoked . . . that I did it. But I'm looking forward to it finishing right now. It's hard. It's hard going. But . . . a smile that can't be seen but can be heard in his next words spreads across his face. A cheeky grin . . . *it's kinda fun at the same time.*

I have been wondering . . . there was something in the paper – I was quoted in an article the other day – an extreme kayaker. And I was just wondering, am I extreme? I dunno? But I guess, if liking this stuff makes me extreme, then maybe I am . . . I don't think of it that way. I just like it. It's better than . . . watching soap operas or something. He gives a high-pitched little chuckle, amused by his own train of thought.

Ah yes, just to record for posterity, in case I didn't get it on the camera the other day. First night I had a couple of – either whales or dolphins – not sure which – blowing just outside the kayak. I couldn't see them. It was at night when I was sleeping. He inhales noisily and exhales with a sharp whistling breath to imitate the creatures. *Yeah, it was amazing. Many times. Um yeah, didn't see what it was – either whales or dolphins. Not really sure which. And that was amazing. Really nice. Really nice.* His voice is full of warmth at the thought.

So the first day was southerly out of Fortescue Bay and I didn't really make that much ground. About 30 k or something.

The second day was a bit of a slog. Not much wind. I could see land for most of it and I made 70 or 80 altogether.

The third day got a little bit windier to start with I think, and it was raining . . . So I lost sight of the mainland and was able to motor on . . . It was the third day yesterday and I saw two sharks. One leapt out of the water and did, like, a backflip and landed and that was amazing, and the other one was following the kayak which was both amazing and scary. And I saw something else land, but I only saw the splash. I didn't see what it was, but I reckon it must have been a shark given the guy I saw jumping in the air. He was huge. He was about four and a half metres long probably. Really huge animal, and jumped out, maybe five metres up in the air and did like this backflip. Yeah, it was wild. But it wasn't towards me. It was as if he was worried about something else . . .

I had a crappy night last night. In fact, every night's been pretty crappy really. But today's been exciting. Lots of albatross. It was a slog to start with, and then the wind built up to about 30 knots [55 km/h] and huge seas. Really big seas. And I came out of the boat. Capsized after the position report to Jonathan . . . totally unplanned. And a bit scary to be honest. It reminded me how vulnerable I am. Really, really vulnerable. Vulnerable. Vulnerable. So, I've gotta be very very careful. Very careful if I'm gonna make it. I'm gonna turn on the GPS in a sec to find out how far I've come. Think I've had a pretty good day. Hopefully about 80 ks or something . . . Hope for more good weather tomorrow.

CHAPTER 31

Tasman Sea, approx. 43.43S, 150.43E
Day Five, 15 January 2007

Daytime. He sits upright, in the paddling position, with sunglasses on and his face smeared with zinc. The hood of his bright yellow cag is pulled up over his head and fastened around the neck.

Well, it's day five, and the war of attrition continues. I've done about 200 ks, which is only 50 ks a day average. The first day was a bit short, only half a day really, but nonetheless, I was hoping to have done a bit more.

Had a capsize yesterday. That was pretty gnarly . . . Big, big, big seas. Very scary, and it left me feeling very vulnerable. Makes you realise what a speck on the sea you are out here in the middle of the Tasman. Just how vulnerable you are, you know. I'm right on the bloody edge here, and I guess I'd blinded myself to that a little bit. So I'll be very careful not to let anything like that happen again . . .

Day five. The weather's pretty calm today. It was big yesterday and it was a rough night.

Miserable inside the cockpit. Bloody miserable. Oh, it's hard to rest and I took a sleeping tablet last night for the first time 'cause I just wasn't sleeping properly and it's just . . . the conditions are abominable. No matter how hard I try and dry out the water inside, I think the water's being stashed under the foam. The foam's acting like a reservoir because it's not glued down completely and so this water just keeps seeping up through it and it can't get to the pump at the rear because my head and shoulders are holding the seat down so . . . living in the cockpit is just hard going. And it's very difficult to recover properly from hard days of paddling, too.

Yeah, so it's just a tough trip. A very, very tough trip. Anyway, I'm kinda enjoying it, I guess. His facial expression, however, starkly contradicts these words. His bright hood is juxtaposed against his grimace and the thick blanket of steel-grey cloud covering the sky. *I'll keep plugging on today.*

All sorts of things going on. In the capsize I lost a bit of gear. I lost a cup and spoon. Earlier that morning I lost my bailer, which is also my poo bottle. I'm gonna have to find something else to poo into, although I haven't done too many of them. I've only done one in five days. Think it might be time to do another one today. And I've gotta start trying to look after my skin because my bottom's starting to hurt a bit and I can feel a rash around my tummy. These are the sorts of things that happen from paddling so far so long, sleeping in a wet cockpit where it's very hard to maintain personal hygiene.

This is a tough trip. It's a real adventure. It really is. I just hope I get there in one piece. I have to get there in one piece. I'm optimistic but I'm scared about approaching the New Zealand coast. Anyway, there's a lot of water to cross before I have to worry about that. I've only done about 200. There's another 1400 to go . . . His face distorts as he spits out that ludicrous distance. *It's a long way, 1400. I don't want to think about it. Let's focus on doing 80 today, I think. Much easier, yeaahh.*

So, who knows when I'm gonna get there. It's gonna be a good 30-day trip, I think. I'd like to do it quicker. People have suggested I'll do it in under 20 but I don't know where they got that number from. They've got misplaced faith in my abilities. I think it's gonna take me a bit longer.

Anyway, back into it . . . Here we go.

All sorts of songs running through my head. He breaks into a very enthusiastic, if somewhat off-key, rendition of 'I can see clearly now, the rain has gone'. You can almost see the cogs turning as he racks his brain to find another suitable tune. He hums a few bars of 'Comfortably Numb'. *Yeah, OK! I know I can't sing, but anyway, I enjoy it.*

Lots of albatross out here . . . I'm not sorry that I didn't bring the iPod. Who needs a bloody iPod. Just one more piece of shit.

Umm . . . YEAH . . . he shouts to the albatross and any other creature that he hasn't yet managed to scare off. *Don't think I'll be doing this one again in a hurry. I think I'll have had enough of paddling for a little while after this trip. Anyway, back into it!*

CHAPTER 32

15 January 2007

Very early this morning I woke from an inadequate night's sleep to check my email. Ant will have turned the tracking beacon on as soon as he woke from his far, far less adequate sleep, so his position should be logged. He switched the beacon on at the end of each paddling day, and then first thing in the morning. That way, we could track his overnight drift. When the satellites pick up the beacon, it sends an automatic transmission to all the email addresses of the support team – me, Paul, Mike, Jonathan, Ant's dad and Fastwave Communications, a Perth-based company which kindly supplied Ant with the beacon and the tracking support.

TRACKING BEACON NOTWORKING MAYBEBATTERY WILTRY+CHARGE TONIT.POS43,30 155,15.

Not the message I was hoping for. It's very early days to be experiencing equipment failure. We hoped it was, as Ant suggested, a battery problem. He had a five-watt solar panel on the rear deck, wired up to a charging base inside the rear hatch.

He had 6000 milliamps of battery power (2 × 3000 milliamp batteries). The solar panel was capable of charging both batteries, from completely flat, in 15 hours of sunlight. Not that he'd run both batteries right down. He'd use one while the other was charging, so he always had one fully charged battery at any given time. Charging batteries shouldn't be a difficult task, although *everything* is difficult when you're in a tiny, cramped kayak in the middle of a relentless sea.

I sent an email to Nick Daws at Fastwave, hoping he might be able to do a bit of remote troubleshooting. A couple of hours later I received his reply:

The battery was fully charged when sent to Andrew, so given that he has only sent a few messages, it should be OK. However, if it was inadvertently left on when not outside, it could have been running but not sent signals, resulting in battery discharge. There is a little LED on the unit that indicates if the battery is operating . . . can you ask Andrew if he can see if this is on. If not, the battery is flat. The only possible solution is for Andrew then to plug the unit into his solar panel with the charger we provided. It may take a while to get sufficient charge to send a signal.

I sent a text message to Ant's satphone, knowing he would pick it up when he checked for Jonathan's weather forecast.

The hours dragged on. I tried to speed the day up by taking Finlay for a walk down into the gorge in the National Park at the end of our street. We searched for tadpoles in the creek, played in the rock pools, hunted for trolls under the little bridge, almost trod on a snake, but none of that took my mind off Ant, the Tasman Sea and the beacon.

When we returned home, I sat anxiously by the computer waiting for the 5.30 pm report. He was punctual, but the brevity of the message provided poor relief from my anxiety.

WIND15KT+NTH.POS43,43 150,43.

Is that all? No other comments? It worried me. I could read a lot between the lines. Rather, the lack of lines to read between made me aware of how acutely demanding every single action must be.

I plotted his position on Google Earth then phoned Paul to compare notes and to discuss the beacon issue, which Paul assured me was not an issue at all. It would charge, there would be no problem. I was grateful to have his positive support. We discussed Ant's progress – only 43 kilometres today, and a similar distance yesterday. He'd need to increase his daily average to make landfall in a month. He did pack rations for 36 days, but I fervently hoped he wouldn't need them.

That night I logged a flippant blog on www.andrewmcauley.com in an attempt to lift my spirits, if nothing else:

> *While we're lounging around, sipping our warm tea and maybe having a bowl of icecream and reading a novel before bedtime, Andrew is still clocking up the miles out there.*
>
> *He'll bunk down around midnight – not much else to do really, other than paddle. He has no books, no mini DVD player, he didn't even take the iPod this time. So I guess he'll be singing to himself (it's a good thing he's so far from civilisation!) He's cruising along, averaging around 50 kilometres a day, and feeling good.*

I stretched the truth somewhat in assuming that he was feeling good.

CHAPTER 33

16 January 2007

I lay in bed after another sleepless night, wondering what it might have been like to marry a mere mortal. No doubt far less satisfying, but probably far less stressful. I wouldn't change my Ant for anyone – not even Viggo Mortensen. And with that thought, I dragged myself out of bed early and trudged into the study, pausing to listen to Finlay's soft little snores on the way.

At 8.18 am, after what seemed an eternity of staring at the computer screen, the email I was waiting for appeared.

BEACON NOT WKG.CHARGERFLASHES RED ORANGE GREENWEN ATACHED. BACKUP SATFONE ALSO CARKED IT.ALL OK.CAPSIZED BYA BIGWAVE2 DAYS AGO,NOFILM THO!

Actually, *not* the message I was waiting for. I was after the tracking beacon coordinates. This was not at all good. Capsized *two* days ago. Oh, God! I phoned Fastwave, then hung up when I realised that it wasn't even 4.30 in the morning over the other side of the country. So I phoned Paul and we spent the next hour considering the impact on the expedition of the loss of two vital pieces of equipment. Paul pointed out that Andrew was obviously fine; he still had the good humour to comment on the misfortune of not filming the capsize, as if that were the greatest of his worries.

Paul's attempts at reassurance fell short, though. This was a most unsatisfactory situation, having serious equipment failures so early in the expedition, with such a long way yet to go. With the secondary satphone out of action, there was no further room for error, or mishap, or ill luck, or whatever you want to call it. The next call was to Sharon Trueman, asking if she could mind Finlay for a few hours. I needed time to think.

Kieran Lawton, a long-time climbing buddy, had been at Fortescue Bay on the 11th to wave Andrew off. Actually his send-off was even more enthusiastic than the other well-wishers on shore that day – he swam out from the rocks a bit further out in the bay to give him one final wet good luck hug. Kieran happened to phone me this morning, to see how I was coping at home. I told him of the beacon and satphone drama, and we ran through a host of possible outcomes. In the end, he suggested I contact AMSA (Australian Maritime Safety Authority). I did so reluctantly, knowing that they'd recommend he abort the expedition.

Unfortunately for me, the woman I spoke to more than recommended that he return to Tasmania, she insisted on it. When I tried to reason with her that the tracking beacon wasn't necessarily a problem, because he had three – not one, not two, but *three* GPSs with which to send coordinates from – she argued that having only one functioning satphone was unacceptable. This woman's demeanour was overbearing. My head felt like it was about to explode. I told her that I'd get Paul to call her and discuss the issue, knowing that he would remain more composed than me.

Paul Hewitson argued at length that the reason Andrew took back-ups was precisely in case something like this happened. He had not lost his ability to communicate with us because the primary satellite phone was still working. He had not lost the ability to notify us of his position because he had three functioning GPSs. He would, as he had done the past two mornings, send his coordinates manually via satphone. Paul used what I thought was an excellent analogy – nobody carries four spare tyres in their car, do they? The woman remained steadfast. We should notify him that he had to return to shore. Paul argued that with winds and current, it was probably quicker for him to continue his easterly course.

Later that day I had a call from the manager at the Australian Rescue Coordination Centre (Australian Search and Rescue – AusSAR). Whereas he was far more reasonable to talk to, he still recommended that Andrew return to Tasmania. Alternatively, he said, you should arrange – at your expense, of course – an equipment drop. He was still just within range of the long-range aircraft. They could drop him an aviation band radio (a tracking device worn on the wrist). He should have had one anyway, the man said. Why then, I argued, was this not suggested before, back at our meetings with MAST and the Tasmanian Water Police? Andrew had specifically stated that if there were any other safety device they felt he should have, he would get it. There was never any mention of this aviation band radio, although it certainly sounded like an indispensable piece of equipment.

The upshot was that Andrew had turned around once before, back in December. He would be more than reluctant to do so this time, not after the effort to get this far. Not when all else was going well. And he would not accept an equipment drop. The ethos of this trip was for a *solo, unassisted* journey.

More lengthy discussions with Paul ensued. I phoned and emailed Fastwave. No response.

Andre Janecki ('Grasshopper') emailed his opinion on the matter at hand:

> *Even the best electronics can fail, but this is often related to two issues (unlike my English!)*
> 1. *the solar/batteries regulator/charger is 'unstable'*
> 2. *the condensation affects one brand/model at higher rate*
>
> *The good news however is that the problem may be only intermittent . . . Cleaning and drying the exposed battery terminals as well as the antenna contacts (and last – do a reset of the unit if possible – but talk to the supplier tech support first)*
>
> *One alternative would be to organise a 'drop down' at least of the tracking beacon. Remember, pilots would love to do such a delivery, after all they are always ready to fly somewhere!*
>
> *Fingers crossed all the time, Vicki*

Believe me, I had every appendage crossed. It was good to have Andre's optimistic perspective. With Andre's help and the man from AusSAR, we researched the options for an equipment drop. Twenty thousand dollars, we were told. At the end of that long and stressful day, Paul and I made the executive decision to leave Ant to do the hard work out there, without knowledge of the AusSAR upheaval back on dry land.

CHAPTER 34

Tasman Sea, approx. 43.54S, 151.10E
Day Six, 16 January 2007

Water sloshes, with more force tonight, on the hull. A speck on the sea, in the dark, dark night. The dull light of an LED beam shines into a tired balaclava-clad face. Soulful eyes stare into the camera. The hatch at the back of Casper is open, allowing the ominous dark to steal into the scant shelter of the cockpit.

Well, it's day six today, and outside it's blowing about . . . oh, it'd be approaching 30 knots. Yeah, definitely around 30 knots. The sea state's building up quite a lot and it's pretty rough. And just while I was packing the gear up today, putting the sea anchor out and so on, it made me realise just how close to the edge I really am.

This is a trip that has taken me closer to the edge, nearer to my limit than any other trip has ever done. And in fact I wonder if I'm exceeding my limit at times. I'm a bit worried to be honest because it's just such a difficult, dangerous trip. I've never done anything as hard as this and I hope I, well I never will do anything as hard as this again in the future. That's a promise, Vic. Because, I'm scared . . . that I might not make it and the ocean is just such a powerful place that it can just snuff you out.

I capsized a couple of days ago and . . . that made me feel how vulnerable I really am. And this cockpit area that I'm sleeping in is just ridiculous, you know. It's wet all the time. I can't dry off. I've got pressure sores on my backside already. It's only day six. I'm looking at 30 days for this trip. God, I hope I can do it a lot quicker than that, but I'm not sure because my average is just slightly under 50 ks a day, and that's a 30-day trip.

Drops of icy ocean splash in through the open hatch, showering his face. *So, there goes another wave right through the hatch there. So it's howling. It's windy. There's big waves. I'm in a kayak. I'm in the middle of nowhere. I'd rather be at home. I can't wait for this to finish. I can't wait for this trip to finish.*

You know, I live for adventure. I love it and I savour it. But on this particular occasion, it's just . . . that . . . far . . . out there. I'm so extended and it's so dangerous, that I'm looking forward to it being over. I really am. But I've got a long way to go. I've only done 350 ks, and I've gotta do 1600, so . . . He gives a false and almost disgusted sort of laugh as if to confirm what most of the population would regard as an absurd situation. *I'm only just scraping the surface. I'm right at the beginning.*

There's an awful lot of paddling in front of me and I've gotta keep it together. I don't know how I'm gonna do that but I've gotta keep it together and really focus and make sure that I pull this off successfully because I've just got too many things to go back to. I've got a beautiful wife. I've got a beautiful son, little Finlay. He's just the most gorgeous kid in the world. I really love him. I love you, Googie Egg. Can't wait to see you again. Daddy'll be home soon, OK?

In the very faint head torch lighting, his zinc-smeared face distorts into a grimace. *I've got weddings to go to: I've got a wedding in February with Ben and Urs; I've got John and Jed's in March. I've got heaps of friends. I've got a lot of people who want me back. I've got a great family. My sister, brother, Mum and Dad. Everyone. I just . . . I gotta get back in one piece.*

But I'm scared because this trip makes me realise that I might not get back, you know. I've never been able to say that about a trip before but on this one I can say it with all sincerity because it's just such a hard trip. It really is such a hard trip and I'll never, ever, ever do anything as hard and as dangerous as this again.

Crossing Antarctica is nothing compared to this, man. Fair dinkum, this is just so out there. So extending. It's funny 'cause I kinda love it and I'm . . . I fear it as well. I guess everything that I've ever learnt in two decades of outdoor adventure is coming together in this trip. And still, I think I can pull it off. I think I can. I think I can pull it off. I just need a little bit of luck with the weather. But it's tough man, it's tough.

And if you get just that little bit unlucky then you might not pull it off, you know. It's that close to the edge, so . . . I gotta do it . . . I gotta stay positive.

CHAPTER 35

Glenbrook 17 January 2007 5.30 pm

I'd just finished bathing Finlay, had a shower and was drying myself when the phone rang.

'Hi, gorgeous,' said the slightly muffled voice on the other end.

'Pookie!' I screamed. 'Oh Pookie, it's so good to hear your voice.'

'Yours too, beautiful. How are you?'

'Good,' I lied. 'More importantly, how are you?'

'Yeah, good. Great,' he lied back. 'How's Googie?'

'He's pretty good – he's missing you. Keeps talking about you, asking when you're gonna get to New Zeelum. What's it like out there?'

'Well, you know, it's a barrel of fun! Don't think I'll be doing anything like this again!'

'Yeah, I've heard that one before!' We both laughed. Words cannot express my delight in hearing his beautiful laugh. A tired and muffled laugh, but his laugh, all the same.

Back in August 2004, Ant phoned me from his kayak in the middle of the Gulf of Carpentaria. He'd been three days at sea, living and sleeping in his kayak, and he estimated it would be another three or four days before he set foot on land. He told me then, with no uncertainty, 'I will never, *ever* do anything like this *ever* again!'

I did laugh at the time, because I knew him too well. I said I'd give him a week to forget the immediacy of the suffering, then he'd be keen for bigger and better challenges. It was only a matter of days. When I picked him up from the airport, looking rather gaunt, just two days after he made landfall in Nhulunbuy, he told me that he reckoned the Tasman was possible. He reckoned he could do it. How short his memory is.

In fact he confided to me later that the thought occurred to him even as he was lying in Gove District Hospital, under the watchful eye of his Aunt Suzie, who fortuitously happened to be director of nursing there, with a saline drip and intravenous antibiotic tubes hanging from his arm. He had arrived in Nhulunbuy in high fever, with massive salt sores covering most of his body. Aunt Suzie admitted him straight to hospital. Perhaps the combination of antibiotics, painkillers and his general euphoria at having made landfall after seven days at sea led to the almost instantaneous eradication of the pain and suffering, and his thoughts very soon drifted to the Tasman Sea. By the time he arrived home from the Gulf, his grand plan was well and truly in the making.

'No!' he said emphatically. 'This time *I really do* mean it! I won't be setting foot in a kayak for a l-o-n-ggg time after this one!' And this time, I believed him.

I asked him about the capsize. He sort of glossed over it, not wanting to cause me panic with the details. Likewise, I neglected to tell him of the stress back home with AMSA.

He did tell me, though, that amongst the casualties of the capsize were his bailing bucket/poo bottle and his spoon. It didn't immediately occur to me what a huge loss the spoon was.

We spoke of his food intake. He had too much food, he told me. He wasn't getting through his daily rations. I told him he must. It was critical that he maintained his energy. His diet had been scientifically calculated. He must eat it all.

'How's your mum's cake?' I asked.

'Awesome!'

'No injuries, sore bits, rashes, or anything?'

'My bum's a bit sore. It's a bit of an effort to put cream on it.'

We talked about the weather. He had finished paddling early today — about 3.30 pm — due to the particularly unpleasant 40-knot [75 km/h] northerlies. Thankfully a westerly change was due overnight, but in the meantime he'd battened down the hatches and would have been twiddling his thumbs, if he'd had enough room. He was paddling conservatively, for which I was grateful. All in all, he told me the experience was amazing. 'The total immersion of mind, body and soul in the raw elements is just incredible. Something I'll never forget,' he said. 'Mind you, I can't wait for it to be finished!'

'Well, you're closer than you were before!'

Back in 2002, we had paddled across Backstairs Passage to Kangaroo Island. We had planned a circumnavigation. After our first night on the island, we left our beautiful campsite in Pink Bay, accompanied by a convoy of seals, shot through a tidal race rounding Cape Willoughby, and then settled in for the long paddle across D'Estrees Bay.

After five or more hours of paddling, I asked how far to go. He replied, with a cheeky grin, 'We're closer than we were before!' From that day, whenever I was foolish enough to ask how much further, his reply was always the same.

CHAPTER 36

Tasman Sea, approx. 44.13S, 151.44E
Day Seven, 17 January 2007

All's dark inside the cockpit, with Casper clamped down tight. He is again attempting to rest. He wears his balaclava, pulled right down so that his eyes barely peek out beneath. What's to see anyway? With the light off, there is nothing but darkness. A chill, depressing darkness. The sound of waves battering the kayak is constant and frequent.

Well, this storm outside has gotten a lot worse. This is my first really big storm. I've had a couple of little ones up to this point, but I'm getting waves over the boat every few seconds now and it's really rough out there. And it came up as a bit of a surprise because it was largely unforecast. I thought this was the blow that was due sometime on Thursday. Maybe there is still something due Thursday and this is something else. I dunno. I'll have to hear a little bit later on but anyway it's very rough. And if it stays like this I won't be paddling tomorrow. I'll be staying in this little chicken coop, which will be a barrel of fun. And . . . hoping that everything holds up.

I can't believe that I'm doing this. It really is . . . dangerous . . . I've been knocked down already. A couple of times. I've not actually capsized yet [whilst locked inside the cockpit canopy. He *has* capsized while paddling]. *Haven't gone right upside down. I hope that doesn't happen. I'll be quite happy if I do the whole trip and not go upside down once.*

It's scary. The ocean is so powerful out there. So powerful. It's a lot more powerful than me. And I hope it lets me live through this . . . and get to New Zealand. All I wanna do is get to New Zealand and get off the water. I can't wait to get off the water.

CHAPTER 37

Tasman Sea, approx. 44.07S, 152.11E
Day Eight, 18 January 2007

Daytime. Light filters through the layers of fibreglass that make up the shell of Casper. He rolls his body, with difficulty, onto his right side, to alleviate pressure sores. His arms are squeezed back to tuck in behind his head.

I feel like I'm in a padded prison cell. His voice is almost slurred – a combination perhaps of fatigue, seasickness and the effects of carbon dioxide build-up inside the cockpit canopy. His breathing is laboured.

I've got waves washing over the cockpit. It's pretty windy outside. He takes a long, laboured inhalation. *Not as bad as last night. I was capsized a couple of times during the night* – he pauses for another deep breath – *and thankfully the capsule worked as advertised and the boat* – deep breath – *didn't stay upside down, which is a relief.* Deep breath.

So right now – slow, deep breath – *it's still pretty windy so I'm gonna . . . it sounds like . . . it feels like it's gonna be OK for paddling . . . I've just gotta be super, super careful . . . I'm gonna have some breakfast before I venture out into the big, bad world, and when I do . . . I'm just gonna be really careful. The last thing I want is another capsize. I really don't want to –* he pauses yet again to catch his breath, and to allow the noise of a huge wave crashing over the cockpit to pass – *capsize again. There's another wave.*

It's pretty dangerous out there, really. I just want to paddle conservatively and stay upright . . . But I've gotta make progress as well. I'm not gonna make progress if I sit in here all day . . . I'll get out there and give it a go, I think.

CHAPTER 38

18 January 2007

From the moment the phone rang, I knew it was going to be another one of those days. It was the gentleman from AMSA, whose name escapes me. He advised that Andrew was now more than 193 nautical miles [358 kilometres] from land and approaching the utmost limit of the long-range choppers. I must ask him to turn around, otherwise organise the equipment drop. I told the man that I would allow no-one but Andrew to make that decision and I would speak to him this evening.

A major headache was brewing as I called Paul. The phone bill was going to be horrendous this month. I then sent a text message to Ant's satphone, asking him to call me this evening.

At 5 pm I was sitting by the phone, waiting for my second call in two days – a most unusual treat. And sure enough, it was only minutes later that I was advising Ant of AMSA's request, to which I knew exactly how he'd respond. Turn back? Out of the question! Equipment drop? Out of the question! The conversation was brief. We were both very aware of conserving battery power on this, his only remaining satphone.

And that was that. All I could do was pray that there would be no further mishaps with equipment or craft, and least of all with the paddler.

That evening, Jonathan sent Andrew the following forecast:

HOPE YOU ARE OK. YOU ARE IN NTH PART OF COMPRESS ZONE. FAST MOVING TROUGH JUST FOLLOWED BY NTH PART OF FRONT CLOSING ON YOUR POS BUT MOVING SE. YOU ARE IN NTH QUADRANT OF GALE WARNING. YOUR POS: N/NE QUADRANT OF LOW = WIND: FOR THU W TO NW EASING TO F5 THEN 4/5 LATER. BEWARE SEAS. THEN RIDGE = SE/SW FOR DAY

It didn't sound too promising, although Ant's reply appeared positive. I hoped our phone conversation about the AMSA business hadn't worried him, but then again, knowing of his tremendous and enviable ability to overcome adversity, he wouldn't give it a second thought. Water off a duck's back.

WIND 10KTS SE (YUK!)SKY LOW CLOUD.POS 44 07S, 152 11E. FOOD4THEDAY:CHOCOLATE.YUM!

Good thing I'd slipped a few extra bars in the shopping trolley. Now seemed as good a time as any to indulge. With sticky chocolate fingers, I typed that evening's blog:

*One whole week's gone by and Andrew is almost
one-quarter of the way across. So he's right on target for the
estimated 30-day crossing.*
  *Those nasty northerlies were replaced by a gentle
10 knot sou-easter, so he had a bit of a headwind, but it
was a far better day than yesterday.*

Casper (the cockpit canopy) is certainly earning his keep! Andrew was very excited to report that he capsized several times during the night, but Casper simply popped him upright every time, and he was all smiles! Good on ya, Casper!

All sounded fine for the following night's report too.

WIND 10,15KTS NW (YAY!)SKY LOW CLOUD,RAIN. POS 44 17S,152 46E. BUM A BIT BETTA NOW V. LUV YA'S ALL!

I took it as a sign that he was in good spirits. And then the evening of the 20th . . .

WIND 10KTS NNE SKY LOW CLOUD,RAIN.POS 44 19S,153 10E. ALL OK.ARE WE THERE YET?!

CHAPTER 39

Tasman Sea, approx. 44.30S, 153.80E
Day 11, 21 January 2007

Heavy fog obscures the view of the elusive horizon. A lone albatross glides effortlessly overhead, circles back and comes in to land as light as a feather on the steel-grey water, less than a metre from the kayak's bow. He floats down the starboard side, closer and closer. He inspects, with great interest, the strange orange creature floating on the sea, in the middle of nowhere. His head turns this way and that. Long pink legs propel his body closer, closer, until his beady black eyes stare up into the eyes of the big creature. He stops, stares and then cruises down past the stern, has a close inspection of the rudder, then comes back to the man. A drop of water glistens on his beak as a ray of sunshine pierces the fog.

What're ya doing there, big guy? The bird pauses, nods, the drop falls and he turns his head and paddles away to the south. The man in the orange kayak stares after the bird for a long while, then he too paddles off, pointing the bow resolutely to the east.

CHAPTER 40

21 January 2007

Tonight's web entry reported:

I could sense the excitement in Andrew's text message this evening. He'll pass the one-third way mark tonight. A momentous occasion – wonder if there'll be a flashing neon sign out there. He'll be celebrating with a Back Country Cuisine of some exotic flavour, heated using one of those flameless heating kits. He'll probably even have dessert tonight. Back Country Cuisine Apricot Crumble or something like that! (His ration packs have a dessert for every second day.)

As I prepared dinner that night, I truly wondered how he was faring with his Mountain Oven flameless heating kit. He needed to desalinate water first. This act alone expended more energy than he'd feel up to after paddling all day. Fifteen minutes of pumping the Katadyn Survivor-35 desalinator yields one litre of drinkable water. And that's the physical energy. Imagine the mental energy required to focus on stabilising the kayak – deploying the drogue line to keep the bow pointed into the waves and setting up the inflatable outriggers. A huge effort to keep the boat steady enough to balance the collection vessel between his legs while he hand pumps the seawater through the filter, and avoids letting it spill over into the cockpit.

After completing that exhausting task, he would then pour some of his desalinated ration into the foil Mountain Oven satchel then, ironically, add a sodium tablet, which creates a chemical reaction with the heat pad. Then he would put a packet of Back Country Cuisine into the satchel, wait a minute, and, voila! A hot meal, ready to eat straight out of the packet. All this balanced in his lap while trying to avoid getting burnt from the heat of it. We experimented with this method of cooking at home. I was amazed by the heat it generated – certainly hot enough to scald if care wasn't taken.

As if that weren't challenge enough, eating his hot meal had suddenly become that much more difficult seven days ago when he lost his spoon to the sea.

I thought back on my day, chatting with other mums in the park as we pushed swings for excited little children. They spoke of mundane things, but my mind was so removed from the everyday. What are you doing next week? What are you cooking for dinner? Have you seen the latest . . . ? Did you read about . . . ? Don't know. Don't know. Don't care. No.

I was aware of the need to remain focused on the normality of life at home with a three-year-old, but often I felt that I was there in body only. My spirit was out in the Tasman with the other most important thing in my life. I was longing for that day, only a couple of weeks from now, when I'd run into the water and wrap my arms around him and cry for joy and sheer relief.

CHAPTER 41

Tasman Sea, approx. 44.32S, 154.03E
Day 12, 22 January 2007

Daytime. Light filters in through Casper. He sits up slightly, as much as that is possible in the claustrophobic confines. His balaclava covers his face as usual, and his sleeping bag is pulled right up over his ears, neck and cheeks. A dark stubble of a moustache is growing. His face is set into a permanent scowl. His voice, though, is strong.

Well, I've got a little bit of catching up to do on my video diary, so I'm gonna pretend – it's day 12 today. But um, well, if we go back a few days to day . . . nine. Let me think . . . day 11 . . . ah shit. OK, we'll just go backwards from yesterday. Or today. OK, I tell you how it's going today.

I spoke to Jonathan the weatherman last night. He sent his forecast through. There's gonna be a gale hit me today. Sou-west to sou-east gale from a low pressure system and that makes me scared. I'm scared. In fact my hand's shaking holding the camera. I'm worried about that and I'm worried about what's gonna happen. I hope that it's not too dangerous. I had hoped to put my drysuit on last night in advance of the gale hitting but it was too rough, so I couldn't do that. So, I haven't got my drysuit on. His voice is laced with more than a hint of annoyance. *Hopefully it's no worse than the last one, which blew over very quickly. Ah, but you don't know until these things hit you and pass, so, fingers crossed. It's an inevitable part of this crossing of the Tasman, and I chose to do it knowing that these things would happen, but it doesn't make me any less scared about them.*

Yesterday, day 11, I passed the one-third waypoint. One-third of the way across the Tasman, which is really good. I had a great day, with good north-westers all day. Fifteen to 20 knots – maybe 25 [28–46 km/h] actually, and yeah, it was really good. Best day's travel so far. I was feeling great.

But day nine – I was gonna record a piece to the camera on the night of day nine. And if I did, this is what I would have said. I would have said, today was a real slog. It was calm all day. It was brutally hard work and I barely made 50 ks. I'm losing confidence that this trip is actually achievable, if every day's like this. It's gonna be so hard, it's gonna take a long time and I'm sure some part of my body's going to break down trying to get to New Zealand.

I need some tailwinds. Jonathan's forecast south-east headwinds tomorrow, which means it's another brutally hard day of slogging with no wind assistance.

But I saw some whales – I think they might be baleen whales. Short stumpy head, white belly and many of them, splashing playfully around the kayak, which was really nice. And I had an albatross visit me as well. So the calmness was nice. It was beautiful out there. Something very different. That was the morning of day nine, or day 10 or something.

Anyway I woke up the next morning expecting south-easterly headwinds, and happy, happy. Joy, joy. I had the very best day that

I've had, with good nor-westers all day, so that was fantastic. Quite a contrast to the forecast that I had, but nonetheless the forecasts are a comforting thing, because I know when the nasty stuff's gonna hit, like today, or some time tonight apparently.

So. His voice is strong, loud and full of enthusiasm. *It's time to get into it!*

CHAPTER 42

Tasman Sea, approx. 44.25S, 154.27E
22 January 2007

Howling winds scream through the cold, dark afternoon. The sea state is horrendous. Mountainous iron grey swells swallow up the sky. Whitecapped waves crash over the deck, engulfing the tiny craft, making it seem ever so vulnerable. The drogue line is taut off the bow.

The camera swings around to focus in on the stubbly, weatherbeaten face. The days at sea have etched deep lines into those beautifully carved features. Strands of long hair have escaped the beanie and are plastered across his face, wringing wet. He squints into the harsh gale-force winds and shouts at the camera. *This is what a gale looks like from near the centre of a low and . . .* Ice-cold spray slaps him in the face. He shakes his head to flick off the water, braces for another face full of ocean spray . . . *I was gonna start paddling today, but –* A wall of water looms up behind him – *it's getting up a bit too feisty, so I've decided not to. I'm gonna tuck back under and go back to sleep for a while.*

SOLO

It's a bit frustrating 'cause I could make some good ground, but it looks a bit dangerous to me. I don't want to go over. It's pretty wild. The kayak is tossed side to side, swallowed up by the ferocious seas.

CHAPTER 43

Tasman Sea, approx. 44.40S, 155.31E
Day 13, 23 January 2007

Pitch black. An eerie ghost of a face appears in the very corner of the otherwise pitch-black screen. Just nose, mouth, and barely a glimmer of eyes. The sound of water beating against the hull is tedious, never ending.

I'm feeling a little bit dejected at the moment. He clears his throat. *I'm finding that this trip is really taking me right to my limit . . . I'm right at my limit. I'm not sure whether I can . . . pull it off.* His voice is drained, exhausted.

It's just so hard. Not so much the paddling each day, but living in this fucking little cabin-cockpit thing. Each night. And you just can't move. You can't do anything. Can't even put cream on my arse to get rid of these pressure sores and salt sores because it's so tight . . . I'm just finding it very, very difficult. He clears his throat again. *Much more so than I imagined I would. I really feel that I'm right at my limit and this is about . . . as much as I can handle. So I've gotta really focus on . . . hanging in there. I'm a third of the way through the trip. I've got two-thirds to go. And I've just gotta . . . make sure I don't lose it . . . and keep mental strength . . . and hang in there . . . to the end . . . because . . . surely I can just repeat what I've already done.*

CHAPTER 44

23 *January 2007*

> *Suffering produces endurance, and endurance produces character, and character produces hope.*
> *— St Paul (Romans 5:3–4)*

Suffering is all relative, he would often tell me. It helps to deal with adversity in our day-to-day lives, adds a bit of perspective.

WIND 25,30KTS NW SKY CIR,CUM.POS 44 40S, 155 31E. ALL OK.BOAT LITER NOW GOING WEL. 970 KM TO GO!

His messages remain positive. That is a very good thing. How does he even contemplate the 970 kilometres to go? After Andrew's Gulf trip, Ian Dewey of Australian Canoeing told him he couldn't fathom how anyone can even consider such a distance in a kayak. How, Ian asked, did he manage to keep going?

While I can't deny that the physical challenge involved in this paddle was enormous, I think the mental challenge was by far the most important aspect. It is very difficult to stay focused sometimes, and in particular to cut down the rest breaks and meal breaks and get back into paddling. I tackled this by breaking the trip down into daily targets, and then breaking each day into smaller hourly targets. My watch was very important as there are no landmarks to judge your progress.

He further elaborated on this incredible ability to persevere one evening, not long before leaving for the Tasman. He told me that sometimes even an hour can be too long, so he would simply focus on five minutes. When that five minutes was up, all he needed do was repeat that, then another five, and again, and again, and again. But the trick was, he told me, not to focus on the again and again. Think only of the now. Remain in the now. And of course, the key to it all, remain calm and level-headed. Many times in the past couple of weeks, well months really, I have needed to remind myself of that singular fact. Remain calm.

Jonathan's analysis of the weather, however, in no way induced a sense of calm. 'We have a situation developing at the moment, because there is a storm building. Now we also have a depression in Western Australia. This is the type of system that concerns me because we could get a convergence between two systems. Convergence means that both systems are going to merge, then intensify, and steam straight through. So he's going to be rolled over, literally, by the system.'

CHAPTER 45

Glenbrook
Day 14, 24 January 2007

WIND 15,20KTS SW SKY CIR,CUM.POS 44 37S, 156 22E. ALL OK.COMPLETE ROL 4CASPER+ME LAST NITE WAS RUF 35KTS.LUVU2GGS!

Tonight's web entry read:

Imagine being inside a washing machine on full spin cycle. That's what it must have been like for Andrew last night when he and Casper did a complete roll in very rough seas. It didn't dampen his spirits though. He clocked up close to 70 kilometres today in 15–20 knot [28–37 km/h] sou-westerlies and all's well.

The washing machine analogy was pertinent today. I had a load of washing on this morning and when it came to the spin cycle, the machine bounced across the laundry floor with such force that it ripped the hose from the connection, resulting in a minor flood. When I finally cleaned up the mess and took the clothes out to the line, a snake slithered off into the lomandras. I stalked back inside, dragging Finlay and Noushka with me. An eventful day at home, yet one I'm sure Ant would gladly have swapped for.

The snake encounter brought to mind another incident a few months back. Finlay and I went out to open the gates for Daddy to drive the car in when he came home from his training paddle. It was just on dusk and I stepped over a curled-up fern frond on the ground. Just as Finlay was about to tread on it, the fern uncurled and slithered from under his foot. I screamed, scooped him into my arms and ran inside. I had to run back out to coax Noushka inside as the 'fern' slithered towards the back door.

At that moment the car came up the driveway and I yelled out to Ant that a tiger snake was loitering at the door. 'Yeah, right,' he yelled back. A few seconds later he stopped in his tracks and said, 'Yeah, actually, you *are* right!'

Armed with his paddle, he flicked it out of the way, but it slithered straight back to the door. So he picked it up on the paddle blade with the idea of carrying him to the bush down the road. The snake hissed in annoyance. He was only a youngster, but I'm sure a bite would still be enough to put paid to Ant's Tasman exploits. I voiced my concern but Ant flicked the poor snake all the way out the driveway and down the road. By the time they made it to the National Park fence, the snake must have felt that he, too, had been caught in the spin cycle. He stopped struggling and just sat there on the paddle blade for the last hundred metres.

All ended well, and I prayed that it would do so across the Tasman.

CHAPTER 46

Day 15, 25 January 2007

After all the years of planning and preparation, he's finally out there – literally in the middle of the Tasman now! He'll paddle past that flashing neon halfway banner early tomorrow morning, so I reckon he's feeling pretty happy with himself. It's been two weeks since Andrew had his last glimpse of land, and another two before he'll set eyes on it again. And what a glorious sight that will be!

Andrew made close to 70 kilometres again today, with a 25 knot [46 km/h] following breeze. He had some fast downwind runs in squally conditions this afternoon.

To think what is possible if you just keep plugging on, five minutes at a time. Then five minutes more, and another five. And there you are – halfway from Australia, halfway to New Zealand. It would be difficult for anyone to imagine how he must be feeling out there. What a strange mix of emotions. Exhaustion, trepidation, elation. Having made it this far must be such a boost to his flagging morale. I'd like to think the physical pain from two weeks at sea cramped up in that tiny bath toy would be alleviated somewhat by the magnitude of this milestone.

His log the following day, Australia Day, read: WIND 15,20KTS NW SKYCIR.POS 44 49S,158 13E.WAS 20,25KTS 4MUCH OF2DAY.WHALE NEXT2METHIS MORN+FUR SEAL 2NITES AGO.THKS4 NEWS P.OVER HALF,GO GO

What an amazing treat that would have been for him, to be escorted across the halfway mark by a whale. The absolute joy of his intimate interaction with the creatures of the sea is almost palpable. After all, that is the essence of his journey, the total immersion of body and mind in this unpredictable environment. The joy, the fear, the excitement, the love, the loathing of his experience is what drives him to places where others dare not go.

Robin Knox-Johnston, while in the Southern Ocean during his first ever non-stop solo round the world voyage, commented on the regularity of interactions with wildlife:

People talk about the empty sea and sky, but in my experience, more often than not, some form of life is in view. There are many varieties of seabirds which spend their whole lives, apart from the breeding season, living miles away from land. Most common during my voyage were petrels and albatross. The stormy petrels seem far too fluffy and delicate to live in such a merciless environment, yet even in the roughest weathers they are to be seen skitting low across the water, reacting instantly to the changing airflow caused by the waves inches below and extending one tiny, fragile leg beneath them to gauge their height above the waves.

As with Robin Knox-Johnston, each wildlife sighting would no doubt have provided extraordinary and welcome relief from Andrew's self-imposed solitary confinement.

CHAPTER 47

Day 17, 27 January 2007

WIND 25KTS WNW SKYLOWCLD,RAIN.POS 45 00S, 158 49E. NOPICNIC2DAY35KTNTH 4MOST.WIL STARTMOVINGNTH.PRESUREAPROX987URWATCH-OUTOF BATRYTHIS MOR

Morale was very high in the supporters' camp by now. He was actually doing it! Not that there was ever any doubt from my perspective. The trickle of supportive emails that made their way across my desktop from the onset of this history-making voyage had by now increased to a steady flow. It was taking me longer and longer as the days passed to reply to each and every message. I hoped the positive vibes were reaching Ant in the middle of the Tasman Sea, and I liked to believe that they buoyed him up, and gave him that extra drive to continue for hour after hour, day after day.

The news about his watch disturbed me. He relied on it and not only to stay punctual with his evening situation reports.

It also had a barometer, which he would be sorry to be without. Even though Jonathan's forecasts were for the best part reliable, the barometer was a useful tool for confirming the conditions. And of course there was that psychological aspect – with no landmarks, the watch became almost a guide. A century ago, of course, he would have used celestial navigation. No GPSs or watches or such sophisticated equipment back then, yet no problems with batteries running out, either. In many ways, the seamen of old were more self-sufficient. Actually, Ant was adept at navigating without the mod cons, but without the watch to mark off those hours, I can only imagine how much more mentally gruelling the trip would become.

Even more disturbing was the conversation I had with Finlay over breakfast this morning. He boldly announced, 'When I'm as big as Dad, I'll borrow his kayak and paddle across the Tasman Sea to New Zeelum!' Excellent.

CHAPTER 48

Day 19, 29 January 2007

WIND 20,30KTS SW SKYCUM.POS 44 26S,160 45E. THUNDERHEADS+SQALS TO40KTS BRIEFLY. BARNACLS ON HUL!DONT ASKHOWINO!

He has only so many characters with which to construct his message. That and the fact that spelling and punctuation would be low on his priority list when he was battling huge seas to text his messages home meant that sometimes it was like deciphering code.

Barnacles on the hull? Don't ask how I know? Doesn't leave much to the imagination, really. Yet obviously he recovered from the situation and the unintended dunking hadn't dampened his wit. This, again, I took as a very good sign. He was obviously still strong, both mentally and physically, and I was now in little doubt indeed that he would make it.

The emails were flooding in, offering encouragement and support, not only for Ant, but for the support crew back home, which was gratifying.

Vic, you are doing a brilliant job on the blog. I'm hooked into keeping up with Andrew's day. He is amazing! God bless, Love Gail & Shane

I replied to my long-time friends from Melbourne,

Thanks guys. I'm doing my best – I think I'll hit the boss up for a pay rise! This business of web updates and replying to all his fan mail has turned into a full-time job!

Huw Kingston wrote:

What he is attempting is utterly incredible and beyond the pale for us mere mortals. To achieve this crossing really does mark a stamp in adventuring in a time when there is so much esoteric claptrap going on!!

Margot Todhunter: *Go the dot!*

Laurie Ford:

G'day long-suffering wife, I'm glad to see he survived the current low pressure OK. They don't get any lower than that – 960 mbar is fairly extreme. If he can handle that then he can handle anything out there. What a rip-roaring ride eh?

I replied to Laurie:

Apparently there's another potentially nasty low coming through tomorrow, but after that he's home and hosed! Only about 560 kilometres to go!!!

The previous night's report had stated that it was a very rough night, with many capsizes, and he was LOKING FWD 2 GETTING THER! No kidding!

CHAPTER 49

Day 20, 30 January 2007

Until tonight, he had been fairly punctual with his situation reports, even with the loss of his watch. The GPS tells the time, although he wasn't about to waste batteries by turning it on regularly to check the passing hours. This, of all nights, was one when I anxiously awaited his message. The forecast was not good and I sat by the computer all afternoon in a state of anxiety. Email messages flew back and forth between Paul and me for about an hour from 5.30 pm. Heard anything yet? No, you? No.

Jonathan's text to Ant today was:

TROUGH NEAR YOUR POS TUE LATE AFT. WINDS W TO NW INCREASING TO F5/6. FRONT MOVING FAST WILL FOLLOW EARLY WED. WINDS W/SW F6/7, COULD REACH F8. BEWARE.

6.30 pm. Nothing.

7.00 pm. The phone rang. It was Ant's dad calling from Boat Harbour. They were holidaying in New South Wales and there was no internet access or phone reception at the house where they were staying. He had to drive up to the top of a hill a few streets away to call me for the update. I hadn't told him about the AMSA affair back in the first week. The trip was nerve-racking enough for Andrew's parents without them stressing about issues that were out of their control.

Tonight I had no option but to tell Poppa that the report hadn't yet come through. He was aware that only one satellite phone was working and he knew the forecast wasn't favourable, but I tried to sound convincing when I told him that it wasn't as bad as expected (a little white lie) and that Andrew had probably just lost track of time, what with his watch being broken and all. I'm not sure that he bought it, but what else could he do? Just as I was trying to protect him, he also remained positive for my sake.

7.30 pm. He was two hours late. My anxiety was increasing to a point not far short of a nervous breakdown. Finlay had me in tears because he wouldn't go to bed. He wouldn't eat his dinner, wouldn't brush his teeth, wouldn't do anything I asked of him. He seemed to have an uncanny ability, which I guess all kids do, of feeding off my stress, and totally misbehaving, as if that might somehow help.

8.00 pm. The phone rang again. It was Paul. He theorised that yesterday's capsize might have affected his primary satphone. I chose to disagree. Although what could we do but wait? And the tears flowed all over the keyboard.

8.38 pm. Yet again the phone rang. It was his brother Mike, saying the message had just come through. And sure enough, in that second, the report appeared on my screen. Never in my life have I breathed a heavier sigh of relief.

WIND25KTSNWSKYRAIN.POSWILSEND2MOROW. WILD DAY WITH 35KT NTHLY B4 CHANG.GGS PLS BRINGPENTAX CAM+ CHARGER+ BENSCAM +GPSMSTIKR

True to his word, at 5.38 the following morning he sent his coordinates – 44.36S, 167.44E, plus a few more abbreviated instructions for me to decipher. Again, his attention to all these reminders to bring cameras, chargers, another GPSM sticker for his boat, indicated that his focus remained strong. I wasn't sure why he needed the sticker. I could only assume that the other one had begun to peel off, which would cause drag as it was near to the waterline, in which case he would have ripped it off, and he wouldn't want to disappoint his generous sponsor by having no GPSM sticker on the kayak on arrival in New Zealand.

Some light humour from one of our many faithful supporters boosted my spirits a little:

Along with all the stuff Andrew wants don't forget a spare can of deodorant for when he first gets out of the boat. :~)

I replied in jest:

Yeah! That was the first thing I packed!!! I hope the quarantine people don't bring sniffer dogs!

Another wellwisher wrote:

Words aren't enough. Your controlled and courageous wisdom in returning on your first attempt to come back so soon after fine tuning is just amazing.

Seeing your updates has become a daily 'hold my breath' ritual – and what a wife you have to be so sparkling in her reports.

Best wishes for your last 500 kilometres. Your wife and son greeting you in NZ will be a perfect finish!!

David Gibbins – Newcastle – who thinks it's a bit of an effort just getting his kayak down from the garage roof!!

CHAPTER 50

Day 21, 31 January 2007

Winds howled with such ferocity to make the bravest of men cower. The sea roared in supreme fury. Wave after wave, of inconceivable power, smashed down on that minute orange speck, slamming, rolling, pitching, hurling, propelling the insignificant vessel.

The wrath swept far and wide. Two hundred nautical miles [370 kilometres] west-north-west of the tiny kayak, a yacht lost its mast in the storm. Tasmanian police reported the 11-metre sloop *Trident Three* ran into trouble in heavy seas on its return voyage to Australia from New Zealand and was in need of assistance.

Imagine the courage needed to maintain even the slightest note of composure amidst the raging maelstrom – the visual deprivation, the unbearable overstimulus of auditory faculties, the physical thrashing of the body against the walls of his confines, no control over the situation, nothing he can do but lie there, in a state of who knows what terror. How does the mind cope with such torment? The lone paddler would lie in those claustrophobic confines in surrender. I would like to think, though, that he was capable – and I know he was – of removing his mind from the physical presence to a calmer place that would sustain him through the nightmare.

Jonathan's text that evening would have appeared as a gross understatement:

HI A. DEEP LOW 975 @ 50.0S FRM YOU POS MOVING SE. FRCST: GALE NW TO SW F7/8 TO 9. WINDS F10 STH @W OF YOU WILL BRING HIGH SEAS. WILL EASE BY THU. DANGEROUS CONDITIONS. TAKE GOOD CARE. J

Ant's response:

WIND 35,40KTS WNW SKYCLEAR.POS44,39S161, 50E.WIND TO 40KTS+ALL DAY,NO PADL SEAS HUGE+CONFUSED.HOPING IT ABATES SOON!J CAN U GIVE 4DAY4C NOW?

The request for a four-day forecast could only be seen as a need to mentally brace himself for what lay ahead, to harness an even greater level of mental fortitude. I know he was capable of that. Paul commented that Andrew had the best safety equipment that money can't buy – experience and wit.

CHAPTER 51

Queenstown, New Zealand
Day 22, 1 February 2007

From a cruising altitude of 40,000 feet, the Tasman looked benign. Finlay and I took the easy passage across the ditch, in Air New Zealand economy class luxury. Little did I know at the time that the sea below was churning up 30-foot [9 metre] swells.

It was with mixed emotions that we stepped off the plane. We were now closer to Ant than we were back at home, and justifiably thrilled with the anticipation of our reunion, which promised to be only a week away. Our excitement was heavily laced with trepidation, though. I knew he'd had difficulty accessing recent tidal charts for the approach to the coast, so he was to some extent paddling into the unknown. The ocean topography off the coast of Milford Sound consists of deep troughs and ridges, which tend to cause unpredictable currents. Jonathan had warned him of this. He had expressed his concern about approaching the coast on more than one occasion. But he was so close now. He had come so far. It was nearly over.

My brother's very close friends, Greg and Jane Turner, generously offered to accommodate us for the duration of our New Zealand visit. I had never actually met the Turners, but they welcomed us like family and were the epitome of true New Zealand hospitality. We couldn't have asked for better hosts. The plan was to stay in Queenstown for a few days until Ant neared the coast. Due to the uncertainty of the currents, there was a slight possibility of him missing Milford Sound, so we needed to keep in mind other potential landing sites up or down the coast, preferably with road access, or a helicopter landing area at the very least.

The forecast, I realised when I checked that afternoon, was grim and our first day in Queenstown progressed from exacting to totally nerve-racking. Finlay refused to eat what Jane had cooked for him. I burst into tears – the strain of the past month was taking its toll, made infinitely worse by the lack of a situation report. Jane took me in her arms and let me cry out those pent-up tears.

I checked and rechecked my email every 10 minutes. Nothing. It was, to me, the longest and most painful night in history. Phoned Paul late that night, although it was two hours earlier back home. He emailed a satellite image of a vicious low pressure system in the Tasman Sea, looming over the exact location of that tiny orange kayak. I phoned Jonathan for some reassurance.

'Um.' There was a long pause. I sensed his hesitation.

Jonathan later added an interesting perspective to this moment:

When I first met Andrew it was at their house in Glenbrook and I sat down between them. I had Andrew on my left and Vicki on my right and I was amazed by the magnetism there, there was so much energy between the two and that had a strong impact on my decision to get involved.

Vicki was very strong, very determined, very passionate about it. There was a communication between the two. In fact it was amusing because, during the course of the conversation someone asked me what it's like to experience big seas, very big seas, and I could see Andrew trying to tell me 'Jonathan, don't say anything, Vicki's there' and I could see Vicki looking at me, begging for an answer and I decided to explain it to her so that both knew straight away that it was extremely dangerous. And that's something that I wanted them to know all along.

But despite this, I could feel that intensity between the two. I never really saw them together later on. I avoided it. I looked at this project from a technical perspective. I knew that it was an extremely complex project, and I wanted to detach myself from any emotional issue. It was a one-on-one with Andrew and I did not want any interference from anyone.

One of the rare contacts I had with Vicki was towards the end of the big storm when finally she called me. She managed not to interfere. But she could not handle this. She called me and her words were, 'Jonathan, can you tell me that it's going to get better?' And I did not answer. I did not answer because I knew it was not going to get better yet. Yes, the wind would ease but anyone who has been in big storms, and I'm very experienced at that, knows that this is the most dangerous part of the storm because the wind will ease but the seas will get even more dangerous. And there's a gap of about 12 to 14 hours there which can be very, very extreme and that's exactly what Andrew was going to experience. So I was very, very shy answering and . . . tried to be very nice but I certainly didn't give her any . . . I did not lie to her.

Jonathan had sailed in that fateful 1998 Sydney to Hobart yacht race. Back then, tumultuous winds of up to 80 knots [150 km/h] whipped the sea into a state of sheer chaos, causing waves of 20 metres and more to pummel the fleet. Tragically, six lives were lost. Miraculously no others were. Conditions this day, Jonathan told me frankly, were of similar force and intensity.

Jane sensed my growing terror as she bade me a late goodnight. The rest of the household had long since gone to bed. I sat by the computer, waiting, praying. After midnight New Zealand time (20:33 Aus EDST) a message appeared and I cried with relief.

WIND DROPTO25KTS SW SKYCUM.POS WILSEND IN MORN.A GOOD DAY ABOUT80 KILOMETRES ITHINK.TERIFYING START THEN SETLED ABIT. BROKE APIVOT ARM ONCANOPY BE OK

CHAPTER 52

Day 23, 2 February 2007

Dawn broke with renewed promise. Incredible, isn't it, how a hint of sunshine can lighten one's outlook? The weather here in Queenstown was warm and calm. It seemed to bode well for the Tasman Sea, a few hundred kilometres west of Milford Sound, about 400 kilometres as the crow flies from where I was standing.

A good part of the day was spent on the phone. As luck would have it, the Turners' two children, Jack and Charlie, hit it off with Finlay and they kept him entertained while I attended to business. Paul and I discussed last night's stress, and in particular the disturbing fact of Casper's broken pivot arm. 'BE OK' he had said.

We could only assume that the problem wasn't too severe. The stainless steel pivot arms attached the cockpit canopy to the rear deck and allowed Ant to reach over his head and pull the canopy onto the cockpit coaming where over-centre latches clamped it in its watertight place. These arms were welded to steel plates which were bolted onto Casper and onto the rear deck. The deck and Casper were reinforced where the bolts held. It was the most workable of many designs we had considered. Paul assured me that Casper had survived this far and would continue to do so until the journey's end.

I phoned Brett Mackay at New Zealand Customs and Kevin Kennett at Quarantine to let them know I was in the country and to update them on Andrew's progress. They were to be at Milford Sound to administer and legalise his arrival.

Anticipation was high. Calls were coming from many New Zealand media sources, wanting to know more of this incredible man. Meanwhile, Mike was fielding an ever-increasing chorus of media calls back home. More and more followers were emailing and phoning. The support was heartening. This epic journey was nearing a close, and that day could not come soon enough.

POS 44 07S 163 07E SKY STRATOS WIND 15KTS SW,ABATED FROM BLDY WINDY THISMORN. DESALINATING ALL WATER NOW.LOOKGFWD TO ABEERAT MILFORD!THKSALL

After posting on the web blog that Ant was looking forward to a beer at Milford, Sydney paddler Lee Killingsworth emailed his recommendation:

The local Speights beer and big Bluff green-lipped clams as entree before a big lamb roast for Andrew's first big meal. After all, you are in NZ.

Hope the low coming Monday pm is user-friendly with the pre-frontal nor-westers helping his progress. I've been tracking the weather progs twice a day and wishing the lows buzz off south and the nor-easters go away. Hope his final runway has all the lights on for the landing.

> As is often said, we are all rooting for him to get it done and dusted.

In a following email, Lee added:

> Vicki, if he doesn't enjoy a cold Speights on landing then he should paddle back – via Cape Horn!!!

Nothing like a bit of email banter to lighten the mood.

> Righto, Lee, I'll tell him you said to do that! Maybe I'll get him to phone you to personally deliver his reply!!!

CHAPTER 53

Day 24, 3 February 2007

POS 44 19S 163 58E SKY LOW CLDWIND 30KTS NW WAS LITE THIS MORN.LOOKS LIKE ANUTHA BUMPY NITE.SLEEP WELL YA'LL!

With only 300 kilometres (162 nautical miles) to go, spirits are high and anticipation is soaring. Ant will be visualising the mouth of Milford Sound. He knows it's only a few days' paddle away. Physically and psychologically it's a far more appealing position to be in than what he faced a few weeks ago.

Day 25, 4 February 2007

POS 44 12S 164 23E SKY CLEARWIND CALM WAS 30KT STH THEN 15KT E 4MUCH OF2DAY.SATF BAT IS LOW WIL CHARGE 2NITE.HOPE NO CURENT NEAR COAST.

Easterlies blowing at 15 knots [28 km/h] don't look that bad on paper, though with the finish so enticingly close but still not quite within reach it would be torture. Now that we were in New Zealand, his progress seemed unbearably slow.

That afternoon, I received an astute email from Australian adventurer and leader of the first Australian expedition to the Arctic in 1986, Earl de Blonville.

I have just been alerted to Andrew's progress. It's almost unbelievable.

Please convey to him if possible my most sincere encouragement at this difficult point. From experience I know that being almost there can be worse that being in the middle. As overall fatigue catches up, near (which is relative) can be a very difficult place when you want it all to end. I wish him every strength, all courage and a kind breeze to help his cruise to the beach.

And congratulations for an astonishing feat. I mean, just to have the balls to try is fantastic.

In my view, this feat counts alongside Messner and Habeler's ground-breaking Everest without oxygen. The doctors and scientists could prove such a climb was physiologically impossible. But then, they just went and did it!

Doing what apparently can't be done (according to 'experts') opens up new understandings for all human possibility.

The repercussions of this achievement will be felt around the world by all mariners and sea kayakers.

My reply:

Hi Earl, Your insight is quite uncanny. Andrew is indeed at that very difficult point of being almost there, but has battled with strong currents to make very little progress the last two days. I'd almost say soul-destroying, but I know it will take more than that to break Andrew's soul!

    Vicki (Andrew's very patient wife)

Day 26, 5 February 2007

POS 44 18S 164 39E SKY CUMWIND CALM. ADVERSECURENT RUNING SW,SLOW PROGRES. HOPE I GET OUT OF IT SOON.WAS HOPING 4 MUCH BIGER DAY!GOT MSG PAUL

Winds and currents were conspiring against us. Headwinds yesterday and a strong south-easterly current all day. From his coordinates, it appears that he drifted to the west overnight. The net result was a mere, heartbreaking 25 kilometres progress for the day.

I received another insightful message from Earl de Blonville.

At this time the rocket fuel will be almost drained.

    He can only carry thoughts of family and self for so long. When a person's unconscious self comes more to the fore, he is more vulnerable to old fears and uncertainties. Could I recommend that you provide him with a new motivation, something greater than himself. Something that might be unaccustomed and therefore will take him a while to explore as he paddles. Well, certainly long enough to get him to the beach.

    And that something would also prepare him for the new world he will inevitably face. For he will no longer be just Andrew who pushes himself, but a miracle man who has alerted us to something greater that dwells within each of us.

Think how Ed Hillary came to surpass being just a climber and came to represent mankind finally reaching an ultimate summit.

So try and focus Andrew, if you can, on how he will explain that superhuman power that he has discovered within himself and how he will help others to discover it within themselves also.

Let him see the bigger picture so that he gets out of that dark space a man can fall into when the shore appears teasingly close yet seems to never get any closer.

Shortly afterwards, another email from Earl appeared, offering sage advice:

For your part, imagine that he already is there, safe and well. Create the reality of him being on the beach, standing and looking back out to sea, being really present to how you're feeling and what happens next (The Big Meal of course).

Then try and see him travelling up the NZ hinterland. What car is he in? Which airport does he fly from? Where is the kayak? Which press is present?

Imagine how he travels back to OZ. Imagine what the press will be saying when he gets to Sydney. Think hard about how Andrew will be feeling, after the initial emotion washes over.

The more real you imagine the homecoming, the more you'll transmit those thoughts to him, as I imagine you're quite close. He'll get it.

Whatever you do, don't think at all about your worry. It tends to transmit too easily.

All the best. And give him a cold one from me!

CHAPTER 54

Day 27, Tuesday, 6 February 2007

Jen Peedom flew into Queenstown this morning, with her camera, to film Ant's history-making arrival. She had been brought onto the documentary project when Ben Deacon realised that he didn't have the resources to do it on his own. Jen worked for a prominent Australian filmmaking company, Essential Media and Entertainment, and it was the company which secured the funding to produce the documentary. Ant and I met her for the first time when she came to our place just before the second departure, to film more interviews. You know how sometimes, when you meet a person, you develop an instant rapport? Well, it was like that with Jen. It felt as if I'd found a long-lost sister.

Poppa and Juliet arrived on the afternoon flight. Juliet's six-month-old baby Caitlin was breastfeeding, so she accompanied her mum and Poppa. Her beautiful little smiling face was a beacon of light amidst our collective anxiety. And then that evening we all met up with Paul Hewitson and his mate Phil, who had just arrived in town. We were accumulating quite a cheer squad.

I was expecting a phone call from Ant that night – I had sent a message asking him to call. I needed to discuss logistics. We had chosen a quaint little pub to dine in and, unfortunately for us, it proved to be very popular with the locals, making it difficult to have a conversation for the noise. When I heard the phone, I ran outside to the relative quiet, Jen and her camera hot on my heels.

His voice was muffled (the phone was double-drybagged, so as not to risk water damage) but he sounded strong and focused. I didn't tell him his dad and Juliet were here. It would be a wonderful surprise for him in a few days time. The conversation was brief. The phone was running very low on battery power and he wasn't certain it would recharge, so we hurriedly discussed all we needed to. Ben wanted me to make sure Ant filmed his final day at sea and his momentous paddle down the fiord. I needed to ascertain his estimate of arrival, so I could have the relevant authorities in place. And, I just needed to hear his voice.

He wanted us to relocate to Milford Sound since he was obviously on course for landfall at Milford. I told him there was no mobile or internet access at Milford, so we would go to Te Anau and, when we received his message, we'd go on to Milford. Paul and I planned to hire kayaks and paddle out to meet him coming up the fiord.

If the satphone batteries died, we would hear no more from him. If that was the case, he said, we should be in Milford by Saturday.

He was feeling good, and relieved that the elusive Land of the Long White Cloud was almost within reach.

Jonathan's text that night, however, warned that he should be off the water by Friday – three days away.

ANDREW. FRONT ENTERING TASMAN IS ACTIVE AND WILL COME TO MILFORD SOUND BY FRIDAY AT THE LATEST. YOU WILL GET VRBL WITH E TO NE WINDS FOR TUESDAY. NOT GOOD BUT MAKE THE BEST. FINAL APPROACH WILL BE WITH S F4. DONT WORRY ABOUT CURRENTS. I'D LIKE YOU TO BE ON LAND BEFORE THE FRONT, SPECIALLY CLOSE TO LAND. FRONT MOVING SLOWLY FOR NOW SO SHOULD BE OK. WILL BE SAFE TILL THURSDAY LATE AFTERNOON. J

Andrew, as we know, had expressed his concerns about the approach to the coast. Jonathan agreed that this was probably the crux of the expedition:

From the beginning my biggest concern was the approach to New Zealand. My concern actually was the last 50 to 100 miles from New Zealand. That's due to the topography of the land. You move from very deep water to slightly shallower water very, very quickly. There you have currents and of course you have local conditions, so you may have south-westerly currents, which is the case there, with additional currents from the north, which is what you experience in those specific waters. And on top of that you have surface currents created by local winds. You get those sea conditions that can be very treacherous and this part of New Zealand is notoriously dangerous. On a good day you can get rogue waves, not big waves but a two or three metre set as we call them that can come out of nowhere. Not big, but powerful and very dangerous. And that was my biggest concern.

Ant's position report arrived just minutes after our phone conversation.

> POS 44 31S 165 11E SKY CLEARWIND CALM,LITE NEHEADWINEARLIER. SORY4QIKCAL GGSCANT WAIT2CU,MAYBE SAT.BULET CAM LENSE CRAKED. HARD SLOG2DAY

He seemed to have escaped the main force of that damned current. He clocked up 50 kilometres today, leaving only 200 to go – the longest 200 kilometres (108 nautical miles) in the history of paddling. Last week we had expected him in on Wednesday or Thursday. Jonathan says it needs to be Friday. Ant was thinking Saturday, maybe Sunday.

CHAPTER 55

Day 28, Wednesday, 7 February 2007

I took the scenic drive to Te Anau the following day, with Jen beside me and Finlay secured in the back seat; Poppa, Juliet and baby Caitlin travelled separately. Before we left, we had a media circus to contend with. Television news crews intruded on our gracious hosts' home, and the phone was running hot with calls from local and international press. Back home, Mike was swamped with calls.

One more little task I did before leaving Queenstown was to book a series of massages and physiotherapy sessions for Ant upon our return. Both Jen and Jane, in their wisdom, insisted I make massage appointments for myself too. They noticed the stress was taking its toll and, as Jen pointed out on our drive south, the reunion and the end of the epic would have a profound effect on me, as well as on Ant. There would be a time of rediscovery, re-energising, soul-searching, not unlike a soldier returning from the front. We would both be in need of nurturing.

Due to the battery problem, we weren't sure if we'd hear from him that night. It was with great relief that his report came through at 8.17 pm New Zealand time.

POS 44 24S 165 41E SKY LITECIR,WIND LITE+VAR. SATF BAT VERY LOW CANT CHARGE.ASUME ARIVAL SUN MORN 9AM SHARP?! IF U DONTHEAR OTHERWISE.ALL OK!

Sunday, 9 am sharp! Those who know him well know that he's not renowned for his punctuality, but I've learnt, over the years with Ant, to expect the unexpected. I wrote on the blog:

> *He's right on target. You have to hand it to him – that's some pretty impressive navigation – not to mention paddling – to be right in line for the mouth of Milford Sound. Conditions are looking OK for the last couple of days. Fingers crossed they stay that way.*

Day 29, Thursday, 8 February 2007

Again, we were pleasantly surprised to receive this evening's situation report. We expected it might be the last.

POS 44 38S 166 13E SKYLOWCLOUD, WIND LITE+N.CLOSER THAN I WAS B4!J'S FCAST OF SW SHOULD MEAN LANDFAL SUN MORN AS PLAND.M PLSTEL A.MEARES SMH

I laughed. 'Closer than I was B4!' I could imagine his cheeky grin as he ran his fingers over the keypad.

CHAPTER 56

Day 30, Friday, 9 February 2007

It was Friday. Media attention was intensifying, and it was something that I had never, until this trip, experienced. Radio interviews followed interviews with the press and television. I was a tightly wound spring. A recoil was inevitable, but at the forefront of my mind were the words of Earl de Blonville: 'Whatever you do, don't think at all about your worry. It tends to transmit too easily.'

Sure enough, that afternoon following yet another radio interview, with Alan Jones back in Australia, the explosion occurred. Juliet asked me to recount the interview. I told her simply that I couldn't really remember what I had said, or what he had said, even though it was just minutes ago. My head was reeling. She was clearly upset with me. She told me that she was more informed when she was back home. I stormed off in a cloud of expletives, venting weeks and months of pent-up anxiety and frustration on poor old Jen, who listened, consoled and rationalised. Being an accomplished mountaineer herself, she understood the minefield of emotions that accompany any challenging expedition, and she was well aware that heightened emotions are not exclusive to the adventurers. In fact, they are very often more intense among the supporting parties.

Juliet and I are as close as real sisters, and it was not long before we both hugged and chorused, 'Sorry ... No, I'm sorry ... No, no I'm sorry', and told each other we couldn't wait until this was over.

I needed to escape from everyone for a while, so I took Finlay on an excursion across Lake Te Anau, to the magnificent Glow Worm caves. We have glow worms near home, but none to compare with this. It was a worthwhile distraction.

Word came through that Paul Caffyn was coming from his home on the west coast to meet Andrew at the mouth of Milford Sound. A New Zealand couple from Christchurch, Martin and Fiona Fraser, upon hearing of Andrew's adventure and his imminent arrival, had changed their holiday plans to drive to Te Anau instead. They had intentions of paddling out with Paul Caffyn. It appeared that Ant would have a flotilla to escort him down the fiord for those final, painful yet blissful miles.

We dined that night at another noisy restaurant. What is it with New Zealand and noisy eating establishments? In the middle of our steaks, Paul's phone rang, then Poppa's. Poppa, being a bit hard of hearing, went outside to answer his call. Paul leant over to me and asked for Andrew's call sign.

'Huh?'

'RCCNZ [the New Zealand Rescue Co-ordination Centre] on the line. Wants to know Andrew's call sign.'

'Huh? What for?' I asked in confusion.

'They got a VHF call on Channel 16. Someone identifying themselves as "Kayak 1".'

'Wha-what? When?'

'They received a muffled call from Kayak 1 about an hour ago. Everything's OK. Do you think it's Andrew?'

'Hmm . . . Kayak 1,' I nodded. 'Yeah, that's definitely him.'

Jen pulled the camera out and started filming. Poppa came back in, saying Mike was on the phone, asking the same question as Paul. Caitlin started to cry. We left our half-eaten steaks and exited. I assume someone paid the bill.

It was almost 9 pm. The man from RCCNZ told Paul the transmission came through at 1913 New Zealand Daylight Time. That would make it around the time the situation report was due, Paul rationalised.

'We've been expecting the battery to go flat. This is good news, actually. He must be closer than expected if he is within VHF range. He's obviously within sight of land. His last message said he'd be in Sunday. He might be trying to tell us he'll be in tomorrow instead.'

Paul's logic was sound. Channel 16 on the VHF band is for hailing and for distress messaging. The Maritime Operations Centre (MOC) operates and monitors the New Zealand distress and safety radio network. This is a network of radio stations tuned to maritime frequencies and linked to the MOC. When the MOC operator receives a maritime transmission on Channel 16, he will establish the nature of the call, then switch it over to the appropriate channel.

John Seward from RCCNZ wanted to speak to me. He would call back in half an hour, so we adjourned to the motel, Leanne Malcolm and Damon Forde from TV3 in tow, cameras at the ready.

I answered on the first ring. John Seward introduced himself as the operations manager of New Zealand Search and Rescue Region, and asked if I would listen to a brief snippet of the transmission they had received. He hoped I could identify, or otherwise, Andrew's voice. MOC receives a substantial number of hoax radio calls on the distress and safety network in any given year of operation. 'We haven't discounted the possibility of a hoax,' John told me.

'This is Kayak 1. Do you copy?'

'Er, would you mind replaying that?' I asked.

'I'll repeat it as many times as necessary. Take your time.'

I listened a few more times, then told John that I would put the phone on loudspeaker, so the others could hear.

'Mmm. Sounds like the person is drunk,' Poppa said, as we all huddled over the phone, as if that would allow us to hear more clearly.

'Yeah,' said Paul. 'That's not him.'

'There were some other words in there,' John told me. 'There's more to the transmission than that. We're having great difficulty in deciphering it.'

'Right,' I replied. My feeble brain couldn't, at the time, come up with a more intelligent question or comment.

'That's part of the reason that we're, you know, taking this precaution. We'll get the helicopter out. We'll do it tonight because, you know, in the worst circumstance, if Andrew *is* in need of assistance, well, we don't want to leave him out there overnight.'

'No,' I agreed. A huge drain on resources, I thought.

Again I asked John to replay the snippet. Again Paul and Poppa insisted it wasn't Andrew. The voice, as Poppa said, was slurred, as if drunk.

'Yes,' I told John Seward. 'I'm not entirely certain, but I think it's him.'

At 2135 NZDT, Richard Hayes at Southern Lakes Helicopters was notified that a solo kayaker might need rescuing. At the same time, a fishing vessel *Te Wai* advised that they were three hours steaming from the dead reckoning position and were standing by on Channel 16.

At 2329 NZDT, Richard Hayes was flying through heavy fog on a dead reckoning of 44.37S, 166.50E.

And then, around midnight, across the Tasman Sea at our house in Glenbrook, my neighbour Penny reported that the otherwise placid Noushka turned her muzzle to the sky and howled – a piteous, languid howl that echoed long into the night.

CHAPTER 57

Saturday, 10 February 2007

The road to Milford Sound would have to be one of the most beautiful drives in the world. As I drove along that spectacular winding road, flanked by snow-crowned mountains, Jen asked how I was coping.

'I must say, I'm feeling very nervous. I really don't think it's him, but the whole situation is . . . not a pleasant one.'

Early this morning, before we hit the road for Milford Sound, I'd had another call from John Seward. He told me they'd spent all night trying to decipher more of the message. 'Help. I need a rescue' were the words of the caller, John told me.

'No! Andrew wouldn't say *Help*,' I told him. 'He'd follow the correct protocol – he would issue a Mayday. It's not him!' So, no, it must not be him.

'I just hope that Andrew is oblivious to all this and he's merrily paddling away out there, doing what he's doing,' I said to Jen. 'And we'll expect to see him on Sunday morning, as planned.'

We discussed Ant's attitude towards responsible adventuring, his prime precept being to eliminate risk as far as possible, but then, if a situation arose, to have the self-sufficiency to get yourself out of the problem, or accept the consequences. He had always considered it a tough call to risk the lives of others in a rescue scenario. 'Ant will be totally pissed off when he hears about this drama.' Then we speculated about the source of the hoax call.

Driving towards that amazing tunnel chiselled through the mountain, Finlay called from the back seat, as he sucked on a lollipop, 'I can't wait to see Dad!'

'Neither can I, my little pea.'

And his little fist thrust the orange lollipop to the sky, as if he were brandishing a sword.

Then I broke into song to lift an ever-increasing sense of foreboding. 'We're off to see the Wizard, the wonderful wizard of Aus . . .' Shortly afterwards we made a hasty stop on the verge. I wasn't quite quick enough in getting the door open. Finlay vomited all over the back seat. I don't believe my singing had anything to do with it. Could have been my driving, though.

Upon our arrival in Milford, we were swarmed by news cameras. I had barely opened my car door when I was bombarded. I said to the television cameras that Andrew was happily paddling away out there, oblivious to all this upheaval. A man from the Christchurch Press wanted to photograph Finlay and me. Everywhere I looked, people were staring. I was nonplussed and more than a little uncomfortable.

Leanne Malcolm was trying to organise to send me up in a TV3 chopper, with the aim of flying out to find Ant and having an air-to-sea chat on film. Leaning against the fence at the airfield was a tall man in police rescue overalls. I walked up to him and shook hands. He introduced himself as Constable

Finn Murphy. Finlay thought he must be related, because he shared the same name, although Finn then explained that his full name was Fintan. I apologised for all the fuss of the search and he listened to me babbling on about Andrew paddling away, heading for the mouth of Milford Sound, and what a spectacular sight that would be. I saw genuine concern in his piercing blue eyes and knew him at once to be a trusting and comforting soul.

The chopper was now ready. Poppa, Damon Forde and Jen, with their respective cameras, and I donned orange safety suits. Finlay was distraught as I prised his little arms from my neck. Juliet and Leanne made promises of icecream back at the café. He reluctantly let go.

I had high hopes of spotting him, but 'Oh, well, you know, it was a little disappointing not seeing him out there but it's an awfully big ocean and we only covered a very small area, so it's certainly understandable that we didn't spot him,' I calmly reported to the horde of journalists when we touched down an hour or so later. 'It's pretty difficult to see a tiny little kayak.' In truth, the ocean was calm and clear. We easily spotted large clumps of seaweed, seals, and a fish leaping from the water.

Richard Hayes, the helicopter pilot initially deployed for the search, was asked about the conditions overnight. 'It was a brilliant night. No cloud cover at all, and a million stars and a half moon, so there was a good chance of seeing him.' He then elaborated, 'Well, we're sort of working on where RCC *think* he may be. It's not to say that he's not a few miles to the north.'

At dinner that evening at the Blue Duck café, the atmosphere was positive. We were all there – Poppa, Juliet and baby Caitlin, Paul, Phil, Finlay and I. Leanne and Damon were dining with other journalists in a different booth. Finn Murphy came into the café, looked around, spotted me, then slid into the booth to brief me on the search. And at that moment another search and rescue officer came in to tell Finn of a possible sighting. He left immediately and a buzz of excitement rippled throughout the café.

'Looking good,' I said to Jen's video camera. 'They've had a possible sighting, so they're just going up to confirm. We'll hear back in half an hour or so.'

Finlay passed a potato chip to Poppa and together they crunched through the conversation.

'Sounds good,' said Jen.

'Yes, well, we won't get our hopes up too high yet. But yes, I'm feeling confident that's him.' I let out a deep sigh. 'We may all be able to sleep tonight!' Nervous laughter spread across the table.

We walked back to Milford Lodge in the twilight. Getting Finlay showered and ready for bed was a task, due to his increasing excitement. 'Only one more sleep, then we'll see Daddy.' They turn the generators off at the Lodge at 10 pm, so I needed him settled in bed by then. I lost track of the time, but I was expecting news of the sighting any minute.

It was now after 10 o'clock and the lights hadn't yet gone out. The generators were still humming. I was trying, with little success, to settle a very exhilarated little boy and get him to sleep. There was a knock on the door. I answered it and in stepped a policeman who introduced himself as Constable James Ure of Te Anau police, and with him, a woman he introduced as Margaret from Victim Support. Before he had time to say another word, Margaret took a step towards me, arms outstretched, wearing a sombre expression, full of empathy. I pushed her away.

'*What* is she doing here?' I demanded.

'The kayak has been found. Your husband isn't with it.'

PART THREE

CHAPTER 58

10 February 2007

The room was spinning and the cold, stark walls were closing in on me, suffocating me. I was shrinking as the room spun more violently and a bestial shriek came rushing from my lungs and up to my throat and lodged there. Stuck. No noise escaped. It was a nightmare, surely. I opened my eyes and Margaret was still there, as was the young police constable James.

'No. No! It's not his boat. It's not him.'

The look of pity from them both was terrifying.

My voice raised several octaves, 'It must be someone else's kayak! It's not him! I tell you, it's not him! It's not his kayak! What colour is it?'

Margaret took another step towards me. I stepped back, hands pushed resolutely in front of me as a blockade. 'It's not him! YOU GO OUT THERE AND FIND HIM!' And I scooped the now wailing Finlay into my arms and sank to the floor, descending deeper into the nightmare.

A thick, dark, impenetrable fog engulfed my senses. I vaguely recall Juliet coming in from the room next door to ask what was going on. I remember her hysterical tone. I remember Jen's comforting voice. Someone tried to take Finlay from me, but I locked my arms around him, my lifeline. I think Poppa came in sometime later as I lay comatose with my precious boy tight in my grasp.

The night dragged on. And on. The soft murmur of indistinguishable voices penetrated the room like the maddening buzz of mosquitoes. Doors banged. Footsteps echoed. The hum of the generators became an incessant roar.

I lay taut in the bunk, sightless eyes staring at nothing, cradling my sleeping boy. Merciless waves washed through my mind. I could not dispel the image of my beautiful Ant, lost in that cold, unrelenting sea. Don't lose hope, I thought to myself, and to him. Don't lose hope.

As the last vestiges of that seemingly never-ending night were replaced by the dim light of dawn, I prayed the nightmare would end. Jen's gentle arms lifted me from the bunk and supported my weight down the corridors to the bathroom, to wash away the horrors of the night. There was no strength in my legs. There was nothing.

I don't recall seeing Poppa or Juliet that morning, or Paul. I do remember the intrusive horde of journalists staring through the car windows as Jen drove us out the gates. I do remember James the police officer driving ahead of us. I remember a van coming around a sharp bend on the wrong side of the road. James screeched to a halt. So did Jen. Through glazed eyes I watched James gesticulating wildly to the foreigners in the van.

I remember stopping for Finlay to vomit. I did the same. And then his little socks were full of burrs from walking through the undergrowth to a trickling stream to wash our faces. And then James was there, to see if we were alright. No.

CHAPTER 59

11 February 2007

Then we were back at the Te Anau Great Lakes Holiday Park. No point staying in Milford Sound. Communication is so limited there. The owners, Silvia and Brett, did all they could to make our stay easier. Silvia offered me food. No, thank you. She found some toys for Finlay. Jen took him out to the playground. Bruce Fraser and his wife brought a bucket of berries from their berry farm. Other locals rallied to offer support. More toys were brought in to keep Finlay occupied as the news of the tragedy spread.

I lay on the bed, staring at the ceiling. Poppa rushed in, asking whether Andrew had a drysuit. Yes, I told him. A police officer came, asking if he had a drysuit. YES I told him. John Seward phoned, asking if he had a drysuit. YES!! I told him.

Silvia came in. Finn Murphy was on the phone. He wanted to update me on the search. I leapt from the bed and ran to the office to take the call. He had been out all night and was clearly drained. The kayak was found some miles north of the directed search area, upturned on an angle, with its stern submerged. No sign of Andrew yet. The air force Orion was still in the area and they were expanding the search. Conditions were good for the search today, he promised, and the water temperature was about 16 degrees, warmer than usual for this time of year. I went back to the room and collapsed on the bed. What more could I do?

Poppa and Juliet came in. The kayak had arrived at Doubtful Sound. A helicopter was going to take them to see it. I'm coming too, I said. Oh no, we thought you should stay and rest, Poppa said. Oh no, I'm coming, I said.

And Finn called back to say that the chopper couldn't go until he arrived back in Te Anau. He would accompany us. James Ure took Finlay to his house. Finlay, who thankfully understood little of what was going on at the time, was thrilled to ride in a police car. James had a boy of similar age, and a young baby. James' lovely wife Melanie was so welcoming and kindhearted. I knew I was leaving my little boy in good hands.

As we walked out along the jetty to the helipad – me, Poppa, Juliet with baby Caitlin, Paul, Jen, the exhausted Finn Murphy and a fat journalist from Christchurch Press who had apparently paid for the charter – I heard Juliet ask with a note of hysteria, 'What if they don't find him? He's my brother. He's . . .'

Her voice faded. My mind went numb and my legs failed me. Finn lunged out to catch me.

My brain, with the fall, had tuned out from the dark reality. Caitlin was screaming in the back seat of the helicopter and Juliet was distraught. Finn told her to put the baby on the breast, that might settle her. I blocked it all out and stared in detached wonder at the majestic scenery as we flew over the rugged mountain ranges.

And there she was. That tiny orange kayak that had come so far, through so much. If the kayak could make it, surely my husband would. I recall scrutinising the craft with an analytical aloofness. I pointed out the bent steel pivot arm to Paul and Finn. The other arm, along with Casper the canopy, was gone. I noted the barnacles Ant had spoken of. There were scratches on the hull. These, Finn advised, were made as they dragged her up onto the *Clipper Odyssey* – the ship that brought her in. The rear hatch cover was missing and strands of seaweed clung to the empty hatch rim. The little laminated picture of Finlay was in perfect condition, stuck firmly to the deck just in front of the cockpit coaming so that Ant would have his eyes on his goal for the entire journey – to get back to his little boy.

Poppa and Juliet had never before even seen the kayak. The immensity of the challenge their son and brother had set himself was realised at the sight of it, and it was desperately heart-wrenching.

I went over to the detective's four-wheel-drive, where the contents of the kayak were spread across the back. I picked up each drybag and opened them one by one to note the water-logged contents. His medical kit seemed intact, apart from a couple of Nurofens and sleeping pills removed from their blister packs. I opened another bag. Food. Another. Food again. Then more food. So much food remaining. Another. All the video footage of his journey was swimming inside. I beckoned to Jen, handed her the sopping drybag, and walked back again to be with the kayak.

There, still tucked firmly in the netting on the port side of the cockpit, I saw the EPIRB. In an instant, my resolve failed. An animal-like howl escaped my lips. I slumped in utter despair.

SOLO

Jen wrapped her arms around me and led my shaking body back to the helicopter. Again my legs faltered, this time pulling Jen down with me. Again, Finn was there to soften the landing, and we sat in the dirt, the three of us, Finn's strong and comforting arms encircling us.

CHAPTER 60

Mum and Dad were there, waiting, as soon as we arrived back from Doubtful Sound. How was it that they were here? Only yesterday, I had spoken to them from the Milford airfield. Someone had mentioned that the Australian media was reporting news of the distress call and the subsequent search. I had phoned Mum to let them know that Ant was OK. We thought it was a hoax call, I told her. Everything was fine. Ant was just happily paddling away, oblivious to all this upheaval. Mum had agreed that all was fine, although she must have known otherwise.

As it happened, the Australian media and thus the Australian public knew more than we did. My parents were at my brother's place in Sydney when I called them. Peter drove Dad the three hours back to Bathurst to collect their passports and they had caught the first flight to New Zealand this morning. Greg and Jane had picked them up at the airport and driven them down here, to Te Anau.

I had never seen my father cry, but he held me tight and together we wept a river.

Then there were more questions. Does he have a drysuit? How many times did I have to answer, YES! Is it a drysuit or an immersion suit? Is there a difference? It's a Kokotat Gore-Tex Expedition Dry Suit. How tall is he? 1.9 metres. What does he weigh? 72 kilos. At least he was when he started. The search continued.

By Monday, I hadn't slept or eaten since James Ure walked into that room on Saturday night. Marsie and Michael arrived around midday in a state of distress. Gavin Brown, Consul-General of the Australian High Commission, arrived. The search was into its 60th hour. The sea temperature was 16 degrees. Models were studied to determine the likelihood of survival. The Australian government had intervened the night before when New Zealand authorities had spoken of calling off the search. One more day, they insisted. This was it, the last day.

I remember nothing of it, except 7.30 pm. Sergeant Tod Hollebon of Te Anau police called the family together on Monday, 12 February. At 7.30 pm he approached me, laid a tender hand on my shoulder and said, 'The search is over. Andrew has not been found.'

My world dissolved.

CHAPTER 61

More than a month later, a package arrived in the mail. I knew from the postmark what it was and left it on my desk unopened. Later, I called Paul. I didn't use that customary greeting, 'How are you?' We don't ask that of one another anymore.

'The tape has arrived. Will you come and listen to it with me? I can't do it on my own.'

He drove down from the central coast the following day.

[Sounds of water] Ky (muffled) . . . kayak 1 . . .
Fiordland maritime radio. Fiordland maritime radio. Any station calling. Over.
Can you copy? This is kayak 1. Do you copy? Over.
Kayak 1. This is Fiordland maritime radio. Roger you loud and clear. Go ahead.
I have an emergency situation. I'm in a kayak about 30 kilometres from Milford Sound.

SOLO

I need a . . . I need a rescue.

Kayak 1. Kayak 1. This is Fiordland maritime radio. Roger. Understand you have an emergency situation. Now please repeat your message. Over.

Situation (muffled extra syllable) . . .

Kayak 1. Kayak 1. Your signal is muffled. Please repeat your message. Please repeat your message. Over.

I'm in (five muffled syllables) . . . My kayak's sinking.

Kayak 1. This is Fiordland maritime radio. Just confirm your kayak is sinking. Over.

[nine-second pause]

I've lost (muffled) . . .

Kayak 1. This is Fiordland maritime radio. What kind of assistance do you require? Over.

[nine-second pause]

Kayak 1. Kayak 1. This is Fiordland maritime radio. What kind of assistance do you require? Over.

[five-second pause]

Kayak 1. Kayak 1. This is Fiordland maritime radio. Do you copy? Over.

I fell off (three more muffled syllables) . . . I've lost . . . Oh, no.

[five-second pause]

Kayak 1. Kayak 1. What kind of assistance do you require? Over.

Kayak 1. Kayak 1. This is Fiordland maritime radio. Can I have your position? Your position. Over.

Kayak 1. Kayak 1. This is Fiordland maritime radio. Do you copy? Over.

Kayak 1. Kayak 1. This is Fiordland maritime radio. Fiordland maritime radio. Do you copy? Over.

All stations. All stations. All stations. This is Fiordland maritime radio. Fiordland maritime radio. Fiordland maritime radio.

It's one nine one three New Zealand daylight time on Fiordland channel one six. A call for help was heard. No other information was received. Any stations with further information, please advise. This is Fiordland maritime radio listening channel one six.

I froze. I was speechless. Then angry tears became a torrent.

'*Roger you loud and clear,*' the MOC operator had said. Devastated was a grossly inadequate description of my state. To veer down that dangerous path of 'if onlys' was not only foolish, but pointless. Too late now for 'if only'. But, if only John Seward had played more of the tape that Friday night. He had said to me the rest of the message was indecipherable. Both Paul and I were shocked, stunned, mortified to hear the clarity of Andrew's voice. 'I have an emergency situation. I'm in a kayak about 30 kilometres from Milford Sound. I need a . . . I need a rescue.'

Craig Smith, skipper of the fishing vessel *Te Wai*, had copied the initial distress call of Kayak 1 shortly after 7 pm on Friday the 9th. He heard only maritime radio's response, not both sides of the conversation. He had contacted maritime radio at that time advising that he was two hours steaming from that position. He had asked if they wanted him to respond.

This, the skipper advised, would have given him the highest probability of locating the kayak, since at that time they had a good few hours daylight remaining. 'A southerly had blown up in the afternoon,' he later reported. 'It was 20 knots on the coast and would have been up to 25 knots where the kayaker was. The sea conditions were trying, with a short, sharp chop. The current drift was to the north, of 0.5 to 0.75 knots.'

It was approaching dark three hours later when RCCNZ tasked *Te Wai* to assist in the search. By then, the fishing vessel had steamed one hour further away from the area. The daylight was lost.

That fateful Saturday in February, the day after the distress call, when we were gathered at the Milford airfield (still believing that it was not actually a distress call), Paul had questioned the pilot, Richard Hayes, who flew out on the initial search the previous night about the dead reckoning position. He showed the pilot, Lloyd Matheson – Southern Lakes Helicopters operations manager and search adviser – and Finn Murphy his computer model of Andrew's progress, his calculations of wind and current drift, and his estimated coordinates of the kayak at the time of the call. Paul explained that, for the previous three days, Andrew had been drifting north of his travel line. The search area was south of that line.

Finn advised RCCNZ of Paul's theory that they were searching too far to the south, and requested that Richard Hayes fly on a course further to the north. Richard then spoke to RCCNZ to reiterate Finn's evidence and that of Craig Smith, skipper of *Te Wai*, and was told that RCCNZ were assessing the new information. Shortly afterwards, RCCNZ phoned back and advised that the P3 Orion would soon be in the area and the Southern Lakes chopper must remain on standby. Richard Hayes protested this decision, advising that 'conditions were optimum for searching now as it was about to go south-west and in another hour the sea state would hamper search conditions'.

Data later downloaded by the Electronic Crime Lab in Dunedin from the two GPS units found onboard the kayak showed Andrew's last recorded position to be 44°29.680'S, 166°38.074'E on 9 February at 2:38:43 pm. Paul's estimate was on a direct line from the 2.38 pm GPS coordinates to the mouth of Milford Sound. RCCNZ's dead reckoning, the position to which Richard Hayes had flown late on the night of Friday 9th, was approximately 11 nautical miles [20.4 kilometres] further south. The unmanned kayak was found, 24 hours after the distress call, 20 nautical miles [37 kilometres] due north of RCCNZ's dead reckoning.

And then, 'if only' opens a Pandora's box. If only the tracking beacon hadn't failed – a faulty piece of equipment that was not up to the task. I discovered afterwards that Andrew was testing a prototype. The model never made it to production. If only he had paid that extra $7000 for the 'Argos' tracking beacon. If only I had forked out $20 000 for an aviation band to be flown out to him after the beacon failure. If only the pivot arm on Casper hadn't failed. If only he had activated the EPIRB. If only he had decided to abort the second attempt.

If only, if only, if only . . .

CHAPTER 62

Grief is a grossly misunderstood entity. Some might consider it a circumstance. I now know it to be a living creature inside one's body. A parasite. One with the ability to plunder your very soul, to gouge the deepest hole in your heart until nothing remains.

If you let it. And it's so easy, so very easy to let it. But, you can't reject it either. And it takes almighty strength to remould the parasite and allow it to become a symbiosis.

If you delve deep enough, something good and kind and genuine can come from it. My friend Donna did, and Lara, and Kate. I didn't know them before my world was lost, but then, at preschool one day, as I fought to expunge the parasite, these women came to me and offered their support. And Donna gave me a little book, *Grief Therapy* by Karen Katafiasz. In the opening pages I read, 'There is no way out of grief, only through grief.' Yes. It's a long, dark road, a seemingly never-ending tunnel, but through it we must travel. And, in my experience, it can't be done alone. But such is the paradox, there is no other way, ultimately, than alone.

The next sentence in Donna's little book read:

> Only by letting ourselves experience grief can we move beyond it. Beyond – not to the old way of being what was once 'normal'; not to denial of our hurt; not to resentment and bitterness. But beyond to fully integrating loss into life, to richer understanding, renewed purpose, deeper spirituality, rebirth.

Beyond is good in theory, but there is no getting *through*, no passing *beyond*, without hurdles. Sometimes gargantuan, sometimes soul-destroying, life-threatening hurdles. But necessary, I guess, and ultimately worth the effort of conquering.

Two days after the search was called off, we flew out over the Tasman Sea, to 44°24.0'S, 166°56.0'E – the estimated coordinates of Andrew's last position and about 7 nautical miles [13 kilometres] south of where the kayak was found. We were there – me holding Finlay in my lap, Dad next to me holding my hand, Marsie, Poppa, Juliet and Mike – all together, yet all very much alone in our dark tunnel that was not yet grief, for there was not, as yet, acceptance, and grief can't exist without acceptance. The lack of seats relieved Mum of being exposed to her fear of helicopters. She found her own dark tunnel of shock and disbelief on solid ground.

Finlay had painted a picture to present to Daddy upon his arrival. He presented it now to the sea. We threw flowers as the chopper hovered low over the water, the mountain peaks of the Milford region clearly visible in the distance. I read aloud a message, then dropped it after the painting and the flowers. Juliet unstrapped her watch and dropped it out the window. His had stopped, after all. Andrew's Tasman Solo expedition had now become a solo journey for each of us, far more terrifying than any of us, least of all Ant, could have envisaged.

Mark Deaker, the Southern Lakes helicopter pilot, then set his course for the mouth of Milford Sound, where Ant should have come. I can't begin to imagine how it would have felt for him to enter the calm water of the sound, surrounded by such rugged beauty. A perfect ending that was not to be.

The pilot then flew us over the highest mountain in the fiordlands, dropped the chopper to land on a saddle and we, each one of us, threw a snowball or two for Ant. Dad collected a bag of snow for Finlay to throw at Grandma. On Mount Tukoko, looking out over the Tasman Sea, I felt a certain peace. There we were, in two of Andrew's favourite playgrounds. Precious memories came flooding back of all our magnificent adventures together on the water and in the mountains. But what now? There's no coming back, is there? There will be no more adventures with you, my beautiful Ant. The slightest glimpse of peace, and in a moment gone on the stiffening breeze.

That terrible day when we flew back west across the Tasman, my heart was wrenched forever apart. Coming home without my husband was the hardest thing I have done in my life. Robyn was there to meet us — Mum and Dad, Finlay and I. And Peter and Jilly and the kids, and Jen, and a room full of others, and there was a dreadful awkwardness. What to do? What to say? I felt sick to the core. There were tears, though none from me. My eyes had shed enough to fill an ocean and now they were vacant and a deep, dark, lonely emptiness filled the space behind my rib cage. For his part, Finlay handled it all incredibly well. 'Kids are remarkably resilient,' Finn Murphy wisely told me when I had asked him what on earth Finlay would do without his father.

CHAPTER 63

Life around me continued, as it must. Mine was in stasis. I became an empty shell – numb, non-functional. But my little boy needed me. I needed him. And for Ant's sake, each morning I dragged myself from a sleepless night to face the reality of living. Grandma and Donnie came to stay with us for a while. They were, I think, too afraid to leave us alone. They cooked, they cleaned, they did everything that my non-functioning mind and body could not.

The consequences of grief are widespread. And much stems from misunderstanding – an inability to accept the wretched thing. People don't know how to react, what to do, if grief has never visited them. Some turn away, or cross to the other side of the road, or bury their heads in the sand. If I say something, will it upset her? If I don't, will that upset her? Best to turn a blind eye. I experienced a lot of that blatant avoidance. It cut deep each time. I saw and heard nothing of a couple of very close friends for six months after Ant died. But then

I was suffocating in my grief and in the constant overwhelming presence of those wellwishers who didn't turn their backs. To each and every one of the kind-hearted and compassionate souls who came bearing kind words, hugs, flowers, food, gifts, I thank you now. I couldn't at the time. I could do nothing but sit and stare vacantly and mumble incoherent platitudes. Or sometimes, in irrational frustration, just walk away, leaving my parents to serve tea and make inane conversation.

Richard, in his medical capacity, encouraged me to get back in the pool and swim. That had always been my one great release, ploughing out the kilometres. But I couldn't. I was asphyxiating on land, but the pain was tenfold in the water. I panicked. I couldn't breathe, couldn't relax, couldn't find my rhythm. Could think of nothing but my husband, and his final hours. So I walked. Grandma and Donnie kept Finlay entertained while I walked and walked through the bush. And in their concern for my welfare, they asked my friends to accompany me. But I always said no. I needed space. I needed solitude.

'Think of Finlay,' Mum called out one day as I headed out the door in a fit of inconsolable tears. 'He needs you. Don't do anything . . .' she left the sentence hanging. Steep cliffs plunge into the gorge down the road. I can't say that I didn't think about it. Many times. But each time, a bird would swoop down or a snake or lizard would slither by, as if they were watching out for me, and I would think of Finlay, and I would think how terribly disappointed Ant would be in me.

And in the solitude of the bush, our backyard as Finlay calls it, my mind would clutch at feeble straws. Could he have somehow, miraculously, swum to shore? After he had proved the impossible was, in fact, possible, surely this too was possible. I would think of the miracle of Lincoln Hall on Everest. He survived. But then, Sue Fear. She didn't. Then a lyrebird would appear on the path in front of me and sing and the stupidity of those hopeless thoughts was brushed aside. Sometimes I'd walk in the rain and not even notice I was wet. Once a little azure kingfisher followed me, or rather I followed him, for almost three hours. He fluttered ahead, hovered, and when I caught up, he'd buzz around my head and fly off again.

Kathy Riley from Australian Geographic sent me a version of the beautiful Mary Frye poem:

Do not stand at my grave and weep
I am not there; I do not sleep.
I am a thousand winds that blow,
I am the diamond glints on snow,
I am the sunlight on ripened grain,
I am the gentle autumn rain.
When you awaken in the morning's hush
I am the swift uplifting rush
Of quiet birds in circling flight.
I am the soft stars that shine at night.
Do not stand at my grave and cry,
I am not there; I did not die.

In those words, I found a small glimmer of something akin to hope. Each time the wind whistled through the trees, with each encounter with the creatures of the bush, I thought of Ant, just being.

When finally the friends that had kept their distance saw me again, they told me that they simply didn't know what to say at the time. Anything, anything at all, I told them. Tell me what your kids are doing at school. Tell me you don't know what to say, but at least tell me that. Often there is simply nothing that can be said, but a hug can say more than any words. The smallest rift can become a chasm if you let it. Good friends are too precious for that. And when my world ended, I needed, always will need, my very good friends. And Finlay needs them. Although, as I've said, grief is a solo journey. So who's to know, really, the right or wrong path to tread?

March 2007

There were the hurdles, ceaseless. The bank provided one and I had no energy to jump it. I just knocked it down and ploughed clumsily through. My credit card was cancelled because it was Andrew's card. I was the secondary card holder. We had joint accounts, we shared everything. Then a window envelope from Medibank Private arrived in the mail, addressed to Mr Andrew P McAuley. Our health insurance premiums were going up. The next automatic deduction from the credit card would have the newly deducted charges. Bloody hell!

I phoned Medibank and told them what no woman should ever have to, that my husband had passed away. The bank cancelled my credit card, I told the woman, so I could no longer have deductions taken from the credit card, and could they please cancel my husband's membership altogether. The operator politely explained that, due to the Privacy Act, my husband would have to cancel it himself. I then somewhat less than politely asked if she was deaf. Didn't she hear me say my husband was dead? I'm sorry, she insisted, due to the Privacy Act, he must cancel it himself. After a stream of expletives down the line, interspersed with angry tears, my sister-in-law Jilly gently prised the phone from my grip and eventually, although not without difficulty, sorted through the issue.

I phoned the bank when I had regained what little composure was left in me and explained that Medibank wouldn't cancel Andrew's membership, and so what would happen with the payments? Well, even though the card had been cancelled, they'd still debit it. And by the way, the banker said, I notice you have been accessing Andrew's internet banking, so I've just cancelled that too – you know, Privacy Act and all! So, then I couldn't see what my mortgage or investment accounts were doing, and I had no way of paying off the mortgage. Oh yes, you can just ring me and I'll transfer money onto the mortgage for you, she said. Gee, thanks!

Shortly after the bank/Medibank drama, John Seward called from New Zealand to warn me that some news crews had requested the tape of Andrew's distress call. In contrast to the Privacy Act, the Freedom of Information Act meant that he had to hand the tape over, thus it was all over the evening news. The irony was pointed.

> *Vicki will live with the memories of the great man she married. Finlay will know his father as one of the greatest adventurers of modern times. I feel saddened for all his family and close friends, and those who were his closest paddling partners.*
>
> *I never had the fortune of paddling with Andrew but did speak with him prior to his departure. I put him in the same category as many of the early explorers.*
>
> *Andrew – a man with courage such as his is extremely rare. His spirit, courage and determination will remain with us forever.*

This was an email Paul forwarded to me from his friend Henry. Yes, it's comforting to know that others hold Ant's achievements in such high regard, but it doesn't ease the pain.

March 2007

Resilient he may be, but Finlay over the past month has been exhibiting tremendous anger and frustration. A friend who has done some work with child bereavement assured me that this is all very normal, and a good thing. Apparently he needs to vent his frustrations. Claire suggested a large cushion for him to vent his anger on. I'm at a loss, though. How can I manage his outbursts when I can't cope with mine? I'll need a room full of cushions myself. Fortunately we're blessed with a wonderful support network of family and friends, who are all doing their best to ease our burden and our pain.

Friday, 23 March

A nightmare. Sick with the flu, I needed to go to the doctor. Finlay wanted to come, but he wouldn't get in the car when I was running late, so I lost all patience and screamed at him. Mum and Dad came running out and I screamed at them too, and they took Finlay. I slammed the car door, which now doesn't close properly, and screeched off to the doctor, almost wiping out the gate as I reversed out the drive. I arrived in a blubbering mess and the doctor made me stay there for several hours to settle down before I could go home.

A couple of days later, Mum and Dad took Finlay to Sydney with them, so I could have some 'time out', which I desperately needed. I felt like such a failure – as if I'd been sent to the naughty corner and they were taking him away as punishment. Obviously they thought I wasn't coping – which was very true. Nonetheless, I was devastated about coping poorly enough that they felt they needed to take him away for a few days.

And here, another paradox. All I had wanted was to be alone, yet now that I was, I was totally overwhelmed by the deepest, darkest loneliness. Being sick, of course, didn't help matters at all. I stayed up very late watching movies, eating chocolate. I thought of those many times that I'd be working into the wee hours and Ant would always come into the study and tell me to finish up and come to bed. He couldn't sleep if I wasn't in bed. How it used to annoy me. How I so desperately wished he were here to annoy me now.

I took a sleeping tablet the doctor had given me. It caused me to wake up with such nausea and lethargy that I found it difficult to function properly. I guess I could liken the sensation to a hangover, although, since I never drink, I wouldn't know. It was a horrible, out of control feeling, so I vowed never to take another.

Thursday, 29 March

What was happening to me? My life was taking on a surreal quality. I was trapped in a Salvador Dali painting – well, maybe a cross between Dali and Escher. Try as I might, I couldn't find the exit.

I rushed home from preschool drop-off because it had started to rain and I had a line full of washing. I stopped, startled, to see a huge dark blob in the pool. The filter was on, so the little sprinklers were confusing the scene more. Then I looked to the back door – it was wide open. Inside, on the tile floor that Ant and I had laid when I was nine months pregnant, the drawers of the cupboard were strewn, with contents sprawled across the floor. My heart went through my mouth.

Then I remembered that I'd started to clean the drawers out because they were annoying me – just one of many, many frustrating things in my life at the moment. Typical of my very distracted actions of the past however long – seems like an eternity – I start things and move on to something else, and never manage to finish anything. But that didn't explain the door, or did it? I remember leaving, going back to get something and leaving again. I guess I forgot to close the door.

First thing I checked was my computer. Phew! Still there. No other sign of anything out of place. I went back to check the mysterious blob in the pool. The doona cover had blown over the fence into the pool.

CHAPTER 64

'Closure.' What's that supposed to mean? It's a word bandied about by experts and the like as if it is some God-given tool to erase the pain. To me, it seems unattainable. Andrew's body was never found, there was nothing but the kayak and the memories – and the unrelenting nightmares.

But in an effort to make at least some slight sense of the word, I made the journey back across the Tasman on 5 April, the day before Good Friday. Jen Peedom, my pillar of support, accompanied me to RCCNZ headquarters in Wellington. It was a trip that was simultaneously excruciating and rewarding, and very necessary for me to find some answers . . . or something.

John Seward collected us from the airport and drove us out of town to RCCNZ's base at Avalon, where we were warmly welcomed by the general manager, Chris Raley. Paul Hewitson had intended coming, but work commitments got in the way. Mike also had considered accompanying me but family commitments, in particular his seven-month-old baby, impeded his plans.

The visit was as good as could be expected. Actually, I went over with no expectations – less risk of disappointment that way. The entire MOC and RCCNZ staff were considerate and mindful of how difficult it was for me to be there. Our meeting was very thorough, and I think we even managed to put a few more pieces of the puzzle together. I came away with a much clearer picture of what had most likely happened that day. More importantly, I satisfied myself that they had conducted a meticulous and extensive search.

New Zealand's Search and Rescue Region (NZSRR) covers 30 million square kilometres of the Pacific Ocean, ranging from 300 nautical miles [550 kilometres] south of the Equator to the South Pole, halfway to Australia to the west to halfway to Chile to the east – one of the largest search and rescue catchments in the world. RCCNZ had received 103 distress calls and 133 hoax calls in the past twelve months. Of all those received, the untraceable calls were categorised as unresolved incidents. In each instance, every effort was made to identify the caller. Generally speaking, the profile of a hoax caller is a young male under 16 years of age, with the frequency of hoax calls increasing over the school holiday period. In this case, there was nothing to identify the caller as Andrew. There was, in fact, dispute among the MOC operators as to the nationality, and even the age, of the caller.

The 'Debrief for "KAYAK 1" – Andrew McAuley SAR Incident Report' noted:

Richard Hayes [the helicopter pilot] considered that an earlier call-out would have enabled the first search to be conducted in daylight, however it was noted that while a

Distress Phase had been declared, evaluation of the situation was under way and it was not possible to task immediately as there was no known drift start position. This had not been assisted by the broken, incomprehensible radio message. It was noted that the land-based VHF receiver had a theoretical range of 75 nautical miles [140 kilometres], however the swell (reported as 2–3+ metres) may have accounted for the breaks in transmission.

We know certain facts, and from the facts we can make assumptions. It's the closest we'll come to understanding the events of those tragic hours of 9 February 2007. We know that Andrew reported Casper breaking a pivot arm after that huge storm of 30–31 January. That welding job was most likely his undoing. We know he had capsized several times earlier in the trip and had on each occasion managed to right himself. I think it's likely that, in this instance, he was either preparing to or packing up from desalinating water. A full five-litre bladder was found, fixed beneath the shock cords, on the front deck. Andrew wouldn't paddle with the water sitting there because it would destabilise the kayak.

We also know of his and Jonathan's concern regarding the approach to the coast. 'On a good day you can get rogue waves, not big waves but a two or three metre set as we call them that can come out of nowhere. Not big, but powerful and very dangerous,' Jonathan had said.

We can hazard a guess that one of these rogue waves caught him off guard. Due to Casper's broken pivot arm, Andrew was unable to right the kayak because Casper would have filled with water – the weight of it being close to 100 kilograms, therefore making it impossible to right the boat. Andrew would most likely have tried for ages, possibly hours, to sort things out, or try to pull Casper off, or anything to be able to get the kayak upright. By the time he finally grabbed the VHF radio, he was most probably already hypothermic, as is evidenced by his slurred speech in the recording of the distress call to RCCNZ.

Why he didn't grab the EPIRB straight away is anyone's guess, and his most calamitous error, but the boat was obviously swept away from his grip by another huge wave while he was making the call. His message, 'Oh no! I've lost . . .' indicates that he had lost his hold. The EPIRB was still in the kayak when it was recovered. Perhaps he couldn't find it, upside down in the cold, dark churning sea. It was tucked into one of the side pockets inside the cockpit – within easy reach if the kayak were upright, but perhaps very difficult to access from underneath.

I was under the impression that he was going to have his EPIRB tied around his neck at all times – at least that's what he led me to believe. I also thought he'd have his PFD on at all times, but photos from a camera SD card retrieved from the kayak show several self-portraits. In none of them is he wearing a PFD, except those taken on day one. As Paul later said, the bulk of it and the chafing would have driven him crazy. Paddling is far less encumbered without it.

Rescue authorities believe he was not still above water by the time the kayak was located, even though they estimated he could have been up to several nautical miles away from his boat, taking into account the different rate of drift of a person and a kayak. Search conditions were so clear that every tiny speck of seaweed was visible during the search that day.

As for the rest, we'll never know, and it haunts me.

John Seward, for his part, reasoned that although the RCC staff were fully cognisant of the severity of the situation that Friday night of 9 February, it was a judgement call on his behalf not to alarm me by playing more of that garbled distress call over the phone. Whether that was a right or wrong judgement, I accept his sincerity in trying to protect me from distress when he's absolutely correct in stating that they really had no way of confirming the authenticity or severity of the situation at the time. In retrospect, it might have given Ant extra precious and possibly life-saving hours, but then retrospect is a ridiculously dangerous tool.

The following day, Good Friday, Jen and I met with Martijn Kleinjes, the director of the electronic crime lab. He had been working for weeks on the video tapes that were retrieved from the kayak. We were hoping that the forensic scientists might have been able to salvage something from the tapes. Unfortunately, the corrosion from the prolonged exposure to salt water was too great. Of the two video cameras mounted on the kayak, one was completely ruined, but inside it was the only undamaged tape. It was blank. The only surviving video footage was found on an undamaged SD card from the Pentax Optio camera, along with a total of 66 photos. Apparently SD cards are more stable than tapes. The video footage shows nothing later than day 12 of the journey.

We had all hoped – me, Jen, the police, RCCNZ – to discover a glimpse of his last days at sea, but luck was not with us. Still, I couldn't fault the consideration and dedication of Martijn at the crime lab in spending the time to show Jen and me the processes involved in the attempted salvage operation.

While I was in Wellington, Finlay flew to Queenstown with Aunty Jilly and his cousins, Tom and Jess. I met them there the following day. We spent Easter Sunday hunting eggs and bunnies with the Turners and friends. Then we drove back down to Te Anau, where the kayak was still in police custody. Tod, Finn and James welcomed us back like old friends, making a difficult trip far less so. We talked about what had happened, we sorted through the gear and I brought some of it home with me. The kayak needed to remain, in case the coroner wanted to look at it. An inquest into the incident had been opened. There was dispute initially over who should take on the responsibility of the inquest – Australia or New Zealand. Andrew is an Australian citizen. The kayak was found in international waters. New Zealand's territory extends only 12 nautical miles (22 kilometres) from shore. Who knows how long it will take? I had been hoping to organise freighting the kayak home, but I guess there's no great rush.

Coming home from New Zealand that second time in a matter of months was only slightly less traumatic than the first. The depth of loss and loneliness and despair seems insurmountable and so much more real this time. Even though I have my beautiful little boy as a constant reminder of his dad, that unshakable emptiness remains.

An incident with the flight put life into perspective. Apparently a problem with the loading bay meant luggage couldn't be unloaded from the incoming flight to Queenstown, which was the plane we were to board. We departed Queenstown with the luggage belonging to the incoming passengers. The luggage belonging to all passengers travelling to Sydney remained at Queenstown airport. People complained and vented frustrations, but it made me realise that, in the scheme of things, the luggage inconvenience was nothing. Nothing at all. When we arrived in Sydney, one man was in a rage. He was heading up the coast immediately, to be best man at a mate's wedding. The suit was in his luggage. This was a (several expletives) disaster.

No, I felt like telling him, I've come home without my husband. That, kind sir, is a disaster.

It got me thinking about so many of life's little annoyances, and I made a mental note to be more tolerant of stuff like that, because 'stuff' simply isn't important. Life is what's important, and we should just get out there and do what Ant was doing – live it to the fullest!

Wednesday, 9 May

I woke up this morning, after a total of two and a half hours sleep, with a plan to achieve something, and by lunchtime I managed to order Finlay's birthday present, phone Terry Davis (CEO of Coca Cola Amatil), organise Ant's group certificate, wrap Mother's Day presents for Marsie and my mum, construct my Ikea office drawers for the study, and go for a walk, which ended up being a run. I ran the Euroka – Nepean River – Bennett's Ridge – kangaroos circuit, which usually takes me over two hours, in just over an hour. I walked out of the gorge, but the endorphin release was amazing.

Tuesday, 15 May

After a really, really lousy week of hitting an all-time low, I was feeling a little bit better this afternoon, possibly a result of the aggressive acupuncture I had yesterday, and my yoga practice today. My acupuncturist, Rick, has identified a definite need for me to make time for peaceful deep breathing and being in the bush, concentrating on the 'bigness' of everything. And I need to make time for yoga practice as often as possible!

I'm thinking of Ant *all* the time – every thought is occupied with him, and I'm missing him more than you could ever imagine. Spoke to Paul yesterday, who said that would happen – that things get much worse for a while when it really sinks in that he's not coming back, and I truly realise his absence.

Saturday, 19 May

Letters of condolence are still arriving daily in the mail, as are the emails. Today, an inspiring email arrived from Chris Smith in the UK . . .

I'm so sorry to hear about Andrew's death. I only know of Andrew through his video of his Antarctic trip and whilst I didn't know him, I do know what it takes to achieve the things he has done. I'm saddened by the news but he made his life count for something, which is more than most ever do.

I will be leaving for a solo kayak expedition to northern Greenland next year and I will sit on a lonely piece of ice somewhere and smile as I remember him (and you). I'll remember him as I think he would want to be remembered. My Great Uncle was Ernest Shackleton, who I know was one of Andrew's kindred spirits. Maybe they'll sit with me for a while in Greenland and watch the midnight sun. I'm sure they will.

Here's to Andrew, you and your son

I replied, thanking him sincerely for 'thinking of Andrew, and me and my precious little boy, Finlay. He turns four this weekend, and it will no doubt be a very sad day for me at least – hopefully not for Finn, as he'll be too excited with presents and birthday cake.'

From my limited knowledge of Andrew I would certainly say he was cast from a similar mould as Great Uncle Shackers (as he's fondly known in the house). There's no doubt that Andrew possessed something special. His achievements speak for themselves on that front. And as for Finn growing up to possess the same strength and attributes, we have a saying over here (and maybe you do there) which is 'Behind every good man is a strong woman'. I'm lucky enough to have a strong woman (Liz) behind me and it would seem it's one thing that Andrew and I have in common. Finn will be OK, as will you. Our family motto is: 'Through adversity we conquer'. It's not a bad motto and I've never been able to argue with it.

I hope Finn eats far too much cake on Sunday and is every bit as badly behaved as any self-respecting four-year-old should be.

Remember the motto!
Chris

Sunday, 27 May

Finlay's fourth birthday. We flew to Brisbane to celebrate it with Marsie and Poppa. It was the first we'd seen of them since the Memorial Service at Watson's Bay in February. As they left my brother's house that February evening, I held tight onto Marsie's hand, tears pouring down my face, and begged, 'Don't forget about us,' as if their departure symbolised all that remained of Andrew was walking out that door, away from me, away from Finlay.

'Oh little Vic,' she cried. 'How could you say that? We will always love you. We'll always be there for you.' And we parted in a stream of tears. I wept a river down

Father Stuart's shirt as he tried, in vain, to ease my sorrow.

And then here, at Brisbane airport, more shirts were stained with tears.

Marsie and Poppa took us, along with Juliet, her husband Sean and their two girls, to Australia Zoo for Finn's birthday. Marsie had gone to great trouble to make the event special for her little grandson. She baked a cake in the shape of a train. He was thrilled. He devoured all the wheels (soft jube ring thingos) and the lights (jumbo Smarties) and windows (Smarties) and all the bright green icing, but not the cake. Kids always seem to prefer the icing to the actual cake.

And then, after a day with crocodiles, tigers and elephants, we went to the beach at Maroochydore. Daddy would have been so proud to see his little man on the boogie board Marsie and Poppa gave him. I was overcome with profound sadness to think of Ant missing out on all these very beautiful and special occasions.

Monday, 11 June

Can't sleep. Can't do anything. Last week I thought I had hit rock bottom. This week I've slipped through a fissure in the rock. I truly know that my precious little angel Finlay is really that, because without him, I wouldn't be here. Life is not worth living without my beautiful Ant, and the pain of missing him so much is becoming unbearable. I hope I can hang in there for Finlay's sake – I have to. I must. And I'll do it not only for Finlay, but for my Ant, and for Mum and Dad. I think after all we've been through, it would kill them. Please help me, Ant. Please be there to guide me.

I'm devastated about the effect my constant tears are having on Finlay. I'm perpetually sick in the stomach from missing Ant so much. It's all too much for me to cope with and I've been wondering if sometimes Ant might have thought that I love Finlay more than him, but I will always love Ant more than anything in the world, and I will always love Finlay more than anything in the world too, because I can love them both that much, because the love for my husband and my love for my child is a different sort of love, but each love is so intense that it breaks my heart. My heart is half dead now without Ant, but I must keep the other half beating strong for our beautiful little boy.

Saturday, 16 June

My sister threw me a lifeline. I wasn't coping. Robyn knew it. Her husband Mark came all the way down from Coffs Harbour to pick us up and drove us all the way back up there. But not before Ben Deacon threw another lifeline. He drove to our place from the Eastern Suburbs in the pouring rain to take me to see this man he thought I needed to see in Castle Hill. Thus I had the first of what was to become many appointments with an amazing man, Bernie Brown. Bernie has plentiful and broad-ranging experience as a counsellor and it was almost with relief that I poured out my soul to him. Jen described him as a big teddy bear. A fitting analogy. It was nearly 3 pm by the time Ben dropped me home, so Mark, Finlay and I didn't head off for our long drive north in the torrential rain until after 4. Mark's up with technology. He has a DVD in the car, so Googie watched three movies on the eight-hour trip and managed to ask 'Are we there yet?' only once! Incredible.

Our time in Coffs was good for both Finlay and me. He had his big cousins to play with, although Sam, being seven years older, probably thought it annoying to have a four-year-old following his every footstep. I had Robyn to test her culinary expertise on me, and force me to eat her plentiful supplies of chocolate. I regained the kilos I'd lost over the past months. I had wasted away. I slept a bit, yet the sleep remained haunted by nightmares. I practised yoga every morning, to help clear my head, and it was with a tinge of regret that we came home after a couple of weeks to face reality again.

Wednesday, 11 July

This morning Finlay called me as he lay in bed and was very excited to announce that he'd had a dream, and Daddy was in it. 'I had a dream. I went into it through my eyes and I was in Antarctica and Daddy was climbing past and he said hello. Daddy came into my dream!' I told him that is very, very precious, and he must hold on to his dreams! He was overjoyed to have Daddy in his dream – it made his day, and mine too. I took him ice skating. He told me that Daddy was much better than me. Yeah, well, even Finn is better than me, although I managed not to fall over at all, and he fell over heaps, but that's because he wanted to go fast, like the big guys. You know the saying, the older you are the harder you fall. And it hurts.

Tuesday 17 July

Whenever we see the evening star, Finlay shouts with such excitement, 'Daddy! There's Daddy, the brightest star!'

Tonight he was shining brightly near the quarter moon. We stood outside in the freezing night and together we made a wish.

'Star light, star bright, first star we see tonight. I wish I may, I wish I might, have the wish I wish tonight,' we chanted together in a soft whisper.

Finlay asked, 'What did you wish for?'

'I wish that Daddy will watch over us, and guide us and protect us forever, and that he always knows how very, very much we love him.'

He whispered, 'I wish Daddy will come back to life and come back to us.'

I cried.

CHAPTER 65

7 August 2007

I wrote in my journal when I woke on Tuesday morning: *Happy Birthday Pookie.*

It would break my heart except it's already damaged beyond repair, to have to wake up to your 40th birthday today, without you! Why is life so cruel? You, of all people deserve to be celebrating a wonderful 40 years of life. You, the one person I know who has the ability to reach out and grab life, and live it to the fullest, and squeeze every last bit of excitement out of it. Perhaps that was the problem – perhaps you squeezed too hard – but who can deny that you gave hope and encouragement and strength and inspiration to others, and taught the rest of us the meaning of life. The really difficult part now is trying to live the lessons you taught me, without you. But I try, Pookie! I'm trying really hard because it's so very important to me that our beautiful little angel grows up with every opportunity to develop the life skills that you gave me, and that he grows up with your strength of character and your enduring passion for life and for adventure.

And in that vein, I decided that we'd celebrate your birthday as we most likely would if you were still here amongst us mortals – we had a birthday weekend for you out in the Wolgan Valley. It was a bit chilly – well, freezing actually. But we rugged up in fleece and down jackets, and our warmest sleeping bags, and Finlay had a ball, playing with the other kids – Em, Kasey, Nic & Bec, Mela. You should have seen him, Pookie – it was beautiful to watch his excitement as he explored in the creek, found wombats and possums, and climbed boulders and ran and played till the icy chill of winter called the children to the campfire.

On Sunday morning we all ventured for a walk along the Pipeline track to the lookout up top. Remember that we actually had vague ideas of getting married up there! Imagine how impressed all the oldies would have been about that!! The Crabbs turned back before we got to the river, the actual start of the track, but everyone else (Artie with baby Justine in the front pouch) and Lurene, Mark and Teen, Vera, the Crankies and of course Googie and me) made it to the lookout after a considerably longer time than I told them it would take!! They all thought that was a very Andy McAuley thing to do – to say it was only a short walk with one tiny steep bit, when in actual fact it took three times longer and was much steeper! But everyone thought it was very beautiful to be up there. You would have been so proud of Googie – he walked almost all the way – I just had to carry him up a couple of really hard bits. He was a real champion. I told him how proud you'd be, and that made him so happy!

Googie and I put a birthday card in a slit in the rock up the top, and covered it with more stones (after we quietly read what I wrote in it for you, with tears flowing so much that it obscured my vision and smudged the card). Then he said that you would come down in the night to get it, because you're

a shooting star, so you can do that – zoom down to get it, then zoom back up into the night sky. Did you get it? I hope you did.

The sky was so bright and clear out there. You sort of forget that, when you're used to looking at the night sky back home, with the city glow dulling the visibility. It was almost hard to distinguish you, the brightest star in the sky, from the others, because all the stars were bright out there. I haven't been out there for a while, and I almost forgot how very beautiful it is. It's always been a very special place for us – it holds precious and beautiful memories. Do you remember the fireflies? Well, you couldn't forget really, could you?!

On Ant's actual birthday, we went out on Sydney Harbour in Jonathan's yacht. Richard and Sharnie and baby Darsen came with us because they couldn't make it on the weekend. I needed to celebrate his actual birthday with friends. The thought of being alone was too much to contemplate. Finlay was seasick, but when Richard told him how his dad was really seasick on the way to Antarctica, he thought this yachting business wasn't so bad after all. Like father, like son.

On sunset, we dropped anchor in the bay below the zoo and lit candles on his birthday cake and sang happy birthday with a chorus of animal noises. Jen was there, and Ben and Urs, and Pat Spiers, whom Finlay loves because he brings fart bombs whenever he visits. Finlay said 'I'll blow out the candles for Daddy' and my eyes leaked, and so did his, and that broke my already shattered heart. I looked up into the night sky, and there, shining down on us with an almost discernible wink, was our brightest star.

CHAPTER 66

On Thursday, 20 September 2007, Finlay and I had the tremendous honour of accepting the *Australian Geographic* Lifetime of Adventure Award on Andrew's behalf. Marsie, Poppa, Juliet and Mike all came to Sydney for the occasion. I applauded *Australian Geographic* in my acceptance speech 'for being so bold as to issue this award posthumously, the first time in the history of the awards. It truly proves your commitment in supporting and encouraging the spirit of adventure. May there always be someone out there, like Andrew, who is willing to push boundaries, and give it all they've got.'

An email from Don and Margie McIntyre arrived in my inbox the following morning.

We never really got to say hello . . . but we spent a bit of time with Andrew over the years. We had hoped to be at the awards last night, but were beaten by circumstances so did not make it. Congratulations to you and Andrew on the award. Adventure is such a pure thing and I have to tell you Andrew's last journey has been a real inspiration to us. He succeeded and I thought of him often when recently flying a gyro copter solo around Australia. I was not really a close friend of Andrew's but strangely now . . . I feel I am? . . . I will think of him on all future adventures for sure. In Andrew's lifetime he has done even more than he would imagine.

Three days later it was my birthday. Ant used to laugh at my enthusiasm for birthdays. I'd count down the weeks, the days, with the excitement of a child. Not this year. Marsie, Poppa and Juliet were still with us, though – that was almost like having some small part of him there – and they did a wonderful job of making it a special one for me, and that I appreciated more than I can say. Marsie and Poppa later brought their very good friends Pammy and Gal over to our place for a visit, and Finlay was excited to show them Daddy's award. Pammy picked it up, donned her glasses to make out the tiny inscription, and read, 'Andrew McAuley. For your extraordinary lifetime spent pushing the boundaries of discovery and promoting the spirit of adventure.'

Then Finlay took the medal from Pammy and said, 'No, that's not what it says. Here, I'll read it. It says (and his little finger traced the words around the medal), "This is a special award for my daddy because he deserves it because he was brave and paddled his kayak and went all the way from Australia to New Zealand and he died. But he didn't die because he loves us and he's up in the sky and he watches over us forever and he is the brightest star in the sky. Dadda is a shooting star! Zoom!"'

* * *

Back at the beginning of January, when life was filled with promise and thoughts of bold new horizons, I booked a yoga retreat at Byron Bay in October. When my world ended, friends and family and Lulu Bull, the yoga teacher who was running the retreat, encouraged me to go. It would be good for me. With Finlay, I flew to Coffs Harbour, then Robyn drove me the further two hours north to Byron Bay, and then she drove home to Coffs with Finlay. She took the week off work to look after him.

Two days into the retreat I seriously doubted the wisdom in going. Yoga has a peculiar way of drawing emotions to the fore. I found many of the poses, in particular the 'corpse pose', *svanasana*, confronting. Not a session passed without me weeping uncontrollably, and by the end of day two I was ready to throw in the towel. Not only that, since the day my Ant died, I had become claustrophobic. I couldn't bear pulling the blankets up over my head, which Finlay always liked to do. I couldn't stand rolling my legs back over my head in the plough pose, or *halasana*. Many of the poses seemed to constrict my breathing. I was suffocating.

I guess being at the retreat, in that environment of peace and tranquillity and calm, made me realise that in truth I needed the diversions of everyday life with Finlay to keep me going, to distract me from myself. At the retreat, I was very much in the present and that was a lonely and frightening place to be. The emotional drain of being there was overwhelming. Perhaps it was the shock of realising that what I assumed would be a positive and life-affirming experience was actually quite the opposite. All I wanted was to be home with my little boy, in our own space, our own house with the birthday tree in the front yard that Daddy and Finlay planted together on his first birthday.

* * *

Thursday, 1 November, was Noushka's 14th birthday. I bought her a special bone. Googie and I took her for a birthday walk, but we didn't quite make it to the park gates. Her back legs were faltering, and I didn't know what I was to do if she collapsed and couldn't get back up again. I had a very strong reminiscence of when Ant and I used to walk her down there every evening after dark, and we'd always sneakily keep each other distracted and then make a dash for the gate to be the first one to touch it. Even when we were too wrapped up in conversation, one of us would still make a burst for the gate. Funny what little games we played that are now such precious memories for me. Noushka's getting old – the life expectancy for a Malamute is, after all, 10 to 12. I think there won't be too many more walks to the park gates anymore, and I'll miss those chances to reminisce.

Then, just a few days later, I had to call the vet. Blake is an old friend from Bathurst and he came over and bribed Noushka out from under the kitchen table with a dog biscuit. She came reluctantly, then almost bit Blake's hand off as he gave her an injection. She wouldn't get up and after Blake left she was crying, which was most uncharacteristic – Malamutes are a stoic breed. She tried to get up but couldn't. I let here lie there to calm down so she could gather her strength for another attempt.

I phoned Blake again later and he gave her a cortisone injection. He then put a towel under her tummy, pulled her up to standing and walked her, with the support of the towel, around the back yard to the grevillea near the pool, where she lay down. It broke my already shattered heart to see her like this.

CHAPTER 67

In early December, as I prepared to journey across the Tasman for the that time that year, news broke of the fraudulent Englishman who had faked his own death for the insurance claims. It was revealed that his wife was complicit in the scheme of his alleged drowning off the English coast when his boat sank. I wondered what the coroner, whom I was about to meet, would make of this.

On Monday 10 December, the inquest into the death of Andrew McAuley was held in the coroner's court at Invercargill, New Zealand. The purpose was several fold: first, to establish the most likely sequence of events on Friday, 9 February 2007. Then to analyse the search procedures to see if things could be improved upon – there were several factors that could have been managed differently. Also, of course, to establish cause of death.

It was a time of extreme tension and stress. Paul Hewitson and myself were called to the inquest as witnesses, and so we read our statements and answered questions from the coroner and the RCCNZ lawyer. Marsie, Poppa, Mike and Juliet also came over. I was deeply concerned that it would be too upsetting for them, especially Marsie, but they dealt with it well, all things considered. By the end of court proceedings the coroner reserved his decision to allow me the opportunity to provide my final summary of the inquest.

The inquest was harrowing in itself, but it was the aftermath that was so difficult to cope with. The whole experience of the inquest was surreal. It was like going back in time and having to relive it all but in a very clinical and analytical way, which is not the way I'll always remember that nightmare. The strict and formal courtroom atmosphere was such a weird juxtaposition to the reality of that time in Te Anau and Milford Sound.

Again, that elusive concept 'closure' evaded me. Many people had said that I should feel better after it was over, that the inquest was my last hurdle. Not at all. My biggest and seemingly insurmountable hurdle is trying to get on with life without my Ant. I'll be jumping that one for the rest of my life. The process didn't bring my husband back. I still have to live the rest of my life without him. Finlay still has to grow up without his father. The process simply brought the nightmare to the fore again.

I guess it did bring something. Not closure, as people expect, but something – the coroner would issue a death certificate after he announced his findings. That in some way would finalise things. And that, in itself, is a challenge to deal with. It's sort of like saying, OK, Andrew is officially dead, so now you have to just get on with your life. But in some ways I don't want to get on with life because I don't want to leave Ant behind.

Saturday, 15 December

The sense of loss and deepest, deepest loneliness is overwhelming. I couldn't sleep. I'm exhausted. I feel like this is living hell. I can find no peace. I just want to shrivel up and die, because I can't stand the pain. I miss my Ant more than ever. I feel such an overwhelming sense of loss, half of me is dead. I don't know if I'll make it through this.

It's 10 am and Finlay is sitting in front of the TV, eating a chocolate biscuit for breakfast. I need to talk to someone. Bernie didn't answer his phone. Robbie is away. Lurene is away. There's no-one else I feel that I can call when I'm feeling like this. I feel that no-one wants to deal with this. It's a warm sunny day outside but I'm cold. I'm shaking, my legs feel weak. I'm scared. I'm in a state of perpetual nervousness. I'm lost, totally lost. The emptiness, the hollowness is unbearable.

Monday, 17 December

I had an unsatisfactory meeting with Bernie. I came away feeling no better at all. 'This is the real grief now,' he told me, 'and there's nothing else for it but to work through it one step at a time – day by day.' Up until now there have been things, events to focus on – Finlay's birthday, Ant's birthday, *Australian Geographic* awards, culminating with the inquest, but now there is seemingly nothing left. And that's exactly how I feel – I have nothing left. I collapsed into bed, an emotional wreck.

Christmas Day

Our first without my beautiful Ant, Finlay's daddy. It was another of those days of mixed emotions. I didn't sleep last night – images of Ant kept flooding my mind. Last year's Christmas Day at Grandma and Donnie's held very powerful memories. I recall Ant's delight when I came back into bed to tell him that Finlay was awake and saw the pile of presents Santa had left at the foot of his bed, but he didn't want to open them till Daddy was up. Ant thought that was such a special thing for his little boy to say.

I remember Ant and Googie and Grandma and Donnie and me all playing cricket in the driveway with one of his two new cricket sets. Ant batted and Googie bowled. Such memories made sleep impossible last night.

This morning, as Finlay opened his presents from Santa, I was overwhelmed with delight and pure, unconditional love. He unwrapped a gift and excitedly and in all sincerity declared – 'Oh, wow! Just what I've always wanted!!' – there was a moment's pause, a puzzled frown, then, 'What is it?' After breakfast, the unwrapping frenzy began in earnest. His pile of presents accumulated so fast, and was so vast (we were all overcompensating, I think) that he simply ripped each parcel open, tossed the contents aside, and grabbed the next one! Could have saved a lot of money by wrapping empty boxes – he didn't even look at the actual gifts!!

CHAPTER 68

January 2008

The dawn of a new year, a chance for a new start, as around the world people made resolutions to kick bad habits, eat less, exercise more, improve their lives. But for me, I held little hope of leaving my heartache behind. It should be seen as an opportunity for renewal, to strive for a greater purpose. Ant's words echoed in my head, 'Whether you think you can or you think you can't, you're right.' And of course he's right. It's just so . . . so . . . I can't find the words.

I resolved to keep busy. I spent a lot of time in the garden, landscaping, weeding, pruning. It's a good creative and physical release for me, just mindless stuff that I can get lost in and shut down my overly active brain. I needed that more than ever as the first anniversary approached. If only I could weed out the nightmares and prune away the negativity. It was as if I had been transported back in time to this time in 2007. I felt all the same fear and my nerves were on end, yet that overriding sense of excitement was missing, because I knew the end result. Sometimes, though, I seemed to forget it was 2008 and I felt waves of anticipation, as if this time there would be a better outcome.

Finlay asked, as he helped me move boulders around the yard, 'Would you like a drink, Noonie?' (his new name for me, which I was horrified to learn actually means grandma), to which I replied that would be lovely, darling. He ran off to get me a drink and when he returned, I told him that I loved him more than anything in the world. He replied, 'I don't love you more than anything in the world, I love both you and Dadda the same amount, more than anything in the whole universe!'

Then, on Saturday the 12th, we needed to go to the shop to buy the paper (the *Sydney Morning Herald* was running a feature about Andrew's incredible yet heartbreaking journey), so Finlay decided he'd like to ride his bike. He hadn't ridden it for a while, so when I pulled the bike down from the hook in the garage the tyres were flat.

At first I couldn't find the pump, what with Ant's huge mess in the garage. When eventually I did, I couldn't get the stupid thing to work. Finlay wanted to help but I told him it was very difficult and if I couldn't do it, he wouldn't be able to. After several attempts with me getting increasingly agitated and cursing under my breath, I asked Finlay to get the phone. I phoned Neil. No answer. Oh, that's right, they were away. I didn't really want to have to call for help anyway, not for such a silly little inconvenience as my inability to pump up a little bike's tyres. I continued my attempt on those stupid tyres to no avail. Countless times I've pumped bike tyres. Never have I had difficulty before.

As I slumped in frustration, Finlay bent down beside me and looked up into my anguished face and said quite matter-offactly, 'We shouldn't have let Daddy go, should we, Noonie? We should have told him not to paddle to New Zealand.'

I grabbed my little angel, held him tight and cried so I thought the tears would never end. But at last, when my eyes were empty, I stood up with great determination and got that damned pump working, and pumped up the tyres, and put his little helmet on his little head, and opened the gate for him, and he sped down the driveway, with me running to catch up, and he pedalled, and I ran all the way to the shops.

CHAPTER 69

Anger is apparently one of the necessary phases of grief. The friends I mentioned – the couple I didn't hear from for six months – eventually revealed to me that the reason they didn't know what to do or say was because of their anger. They were angry with Andrew for leaving us. Both Juliet and Mike, at different times, had expressed their anger at him too. In our counselling sessions, Bernie tried to elicit an anger response from me. 'It's alright, and perfectly natural to be angry with Andrew,' he said. But one thing I will never be is angry at Ant for having the courage to pursue his dreams. How could I be angry with that? My anger is directed at the circumstances, not at Ant.

I vent my anger on the tyre that won't pump up, the night that never ends. Night time has become a torture. I still cannot sleep. My head is so full of unwanted imaginings. What happened in those final hours . . . minutes? It's the not knowing. Did he hear the rescue choppers? To hear and not see them would have been agony. What happened? Did he suffer? They say drowning is peaceful. How 'they' know that, I have no idea. Full of wisdom, 'they'. I was told that the sea of the west coast is home to many huge marine creatures. I can't bear to think of such an end. So sleep won't come, yet every morning I get out of bed, expecting to step out of the nightmare, but I never do. And then one night, while we were in the bath, Finlay grabbed his little blue boat and wanted to play 'daddy's sinking boat game'. I wondered if 'they' had any clues what to do now?

On 8 February 2008 the Coroner, Trevor Savage, emailed his findings, with a cover note stating, 'I now attach a copy of my final decision, acutely conscious of its date.' The 33-page document detailed evidence from the inquest, although I guess the most pertinent were paragraphs 7 and 8:

Finding as to death:

[7] the evidence in its totality leads to the irresistible conclusion that a person has died; that the person was Andrew Peter McAuley; that he died on or about 9 February 2007 in the sea off the New Zealand coast in the general area of a position defined as latitude 44 degrees 32.6 minutes south, longitude 166 degrees 50.3 minutes east, which is the best estimate of the position the kayak was at when Andrew made the radio call.

[8] The medical cause of death is not quite so clear. I find that Andrew was in the water when he made the radio call. I accept the evidence of Mr Seward that based on internationally accepted survival graphs Andrew's survival time would at best have been 12–15 hours before he succumbed to hypothermia. Andrew's voice in

the recording of the radio call is slurred, and I think it likely that in the choppy sea conditions that prevailed, with a 25 knot wind, Andrew would have drowned before succumbing to hypothermia. The possibility of some event such as a shark attack has not been excluded but is speculative. I find on the balance of probabilities that Andrew died from drowning as the effects of hypothermia increasingly made themselves felt.

On 9 February 2008, the ever-eloquent Derrick Mayoleth posted on his kayakquixotica.com:

A year goes by so quickly. On February 9th of last year a garbled distress call was the beginning of some dark days in the kayaking community. What was to be a celebration of an amazing accomplishment turned quickly into deep sadness. Andrew McAuley we learned had lost his life just miles off Milford Sound on New Zealand's south Island.

Since then his motives and actions have been filtered through the sieve of every opinion and world view. All the while his wife and friend, Vicki McAuley had no choice but to keep moving ahead. She of course had young Finlay to look after. Every one of us who has been through loss in our lives knows how the cycle goes. For a while and usually when you are too numb to really take it in, all the world seems to rally to your side. The world moves in a strange bubble that sits just outside of your reality. Then as time passes all but those most close to you slip away back into their own lives. There's no way around it. In the end, you have no choice but to take it all upon yourself and find a way forward. A year, as I said, goes by so quickly. I hope today we not only take a moment to remember Andrew and his great accomplishments, but we also can send a message out to Vicki and Finlay that they are still in our hearts and minds. Life is after all an adventure and we want to continue to encourage and support Andrew's family as they keep pushing ahead on their journey as well.

Robyn came down from Coffs to be with us on the first anniversary and we made another pilgrimage to the clifftop off the Pipeline track in the Wolgan. As we did for his birthday last year, we left photos, a painting and a card for Ant, and Finlay decided Daddy might like a dinosaur, so he mailed a little toy parasaurolophus down the slot in the rock with the envelope. Andre and his lovely wife Catherine made a little origami boat for Andrew, which they gave me to accompany Finlay's painting – such a beautiful gesture.

If there's one thing that the nightmare of the past 12 months has taught me, it's that there really are some wonderful, kind, thoughtful and considerate people in this world. I think sometimes that it's too easy to get caught up in our own problems, but there really are some truly compassionate people out there who are willing to go to huge efforts to help ease the burden of others. My amazing friend Lara managed, between chasing after her own three children, one being only six months old, to bake not only a delicious gluten-free orange cake for me, but an entire dinner that was enough for the next three nights. On countless occasions she took care of Finlay when she could see I needed some respite. She was a godsend.

As we hurdled that milestone, the first anniversary of the loss of my heart and soul, Finlay picked up his dad's guitar. A couple of strings were missing, and it was badly out of tune. No concern for a four-year-old though. He held that big guitar to his little body and strummed. And he sang. And this is what he sang.

I love Mummy. I love you so much
I love Noushka. And Mummy gives me lots of cuddles
  when I come back
And she loves me so much too
And I love her too-ooo-ooo-ooo
And she lets me brush her hair
And I have hundreds of pets – a humungous back yard
I've got pet frogs. I've got pet fish
And I've got a swimming pool, baby.
And I love my daddy so much.
He is the best kayaker and he is the best paddler
and he nearly paddled to the shore in New Zealand
but a big wave knocked him out of his kayak and he
  nearly sank
But he still got to hold onto his boat
But he still did sink and the dolphins looked after him
  and turned him into a star.
His best friend is the bunny rabbit in the moon
And the moon is all round and sometimes half all night.

Thursday, 20 March 2008

I've been taking a bit of time out these last couple of weeks to chill out and look after myself and not try to achieve anything or set any goals that I'll have little hope of accomplishing. I've temporarily put my book project on hold. I was getting so frustrated with myself because I simply couldn't do it, but my very wise friend Claire told me that I'm simply not ready to tackle that mammoth undertaking yet – it's not the right time. She's right. So I'm just trying to relax a bit and I'll get back to it when I feel up to it. Who knows when that may be, but it's not now. I'm starting to get back into my swimming though, which is a very good thing for me. Swam 4 km yesterday, then 5 km today. I'm finally starting to feel like I can actually swim again!

I'm starting trauma therapy with my counsellor next week. Bernie says that it will ultimately help me to sleep better and rid my mind of the nightmares that haunt me and allow me to move on a bit, and thus become ready to work on the book. That's what he reckons, anyway! I hope he's right. I worry constantly about the rest of the family – Marsie and Poppa, Mike, Juliet. We each have our own way of dealing with this gargantuan hole in our hearts. We each suffer differently. I can only pray that they can work their own way through.

And I worry about Paul. Is he harbouring any unnecessary guilt? I often wonder if he feels that Andrew might be alive today if he didn't build the boat. He surely must know that Ant would have sourced a kayak elsewhere if Paul had said no. Ant was determined. He still would have made the trip. Maybe at a later date, sure. But could that have made a difference? That's a question no-one can possibly answer. For my part – and I know I speak for Andrew too – I'm immensely grateful for Paul's involvement. He became an invaluable part of the team and a trusted friend.

Friday, 5 April 2008

I was in the middle of a yoga class when I collapsed from vertigo. So that was the end of my yoga practice and the entire weekend. I inconvenienced a lot of people. My wonderful yoga teacher, Ben, who has supported me through the agony of the past 12 months, took me next door to see Rick, my acupuncturist and another pillar of support. Rick phoned Stu Trueman, who had to leave work to come and pick me up and drive me home. Then I had to arrange for Lara to collect Finlay from preschool and she very kindly took him for the entire night. He was, thankfully, very excited to be having a sleepover. The next morning Teen and Mark drove up to Springwood (15 minutes further up the mountains) to collect my car and Neil called around to see if I needed anything. Yes. My husband. All the while I lay in bed until the world stopped spinning two days later.

Tuesday, 8 April 2008

The kayak arrived home today – well, it actually arrived last Friday, but the crate had to be unpacked. Paul drove down to Sydney today to pick it up. I feel relieved to have it home. Paul told me the barnacles are virtually disintegrated, which I found a tad disappointing. They played a part in that historic voyage, after all. Otherwise, she's in good shape. I'm looking forward to seeing her, although I know it will be quite an emotional moment. Paul said that it feels pretty strange having her back in the workshop.

Tuesday, 15 April 2008

In the early hours of this morning, my beautiful Noushka suffered a stroke. I stayed up with her most of the night, cradling her head in my lap to soothe her, then called the vet first thing in the morning. He gently advised that, with her other ailments and her great age (at 14 and a half she's by far outlived the life expectancy of her breed) she would not recover.

I sent Finlay off to a school holiday soccer clinic with Donnie. I didn't want him to be here when the vet arrived. As he was about to get into the car, he ran back and gave me a big kiss and hug, and asked me to give them to Noushka to pass on to Daddy when she found him up in heaven.

Blake very considerately gave me some time to spend with my little girl before he gave her the injection. She died very peacefully in my arms, and my heart was wrenched from my chest for the second time in just over a year.

I guess I should feel lucky that at least I had the chance to farewell her, and the fact that she lived so long is testament to a most loving and wonderful life. She never really was a dog. She always thought she was a four-legged human, and lived life in our household as such. Finlay will miss her. He's only known life with her, and it's tough for him to now lose his 'dog sister' after losing his dad last year.

I was touched to receive a beautiful email from 'Meister, Meister' Phil Dundas, a work colleague and close friend of Andy 'Meister' (it appeared that everyone in the IT department at Coca Cola Amatil bore the title 'Meister').

Never before has a dog been treated with such compassion – I recall that Andrew often made the comment that his dog was eating better than him. Whilst the quality of the food may have been his comment, I can say for certain however that Andrew definitely had the upper hand in terms of the quantity of consumption. Meister never seemed to stop eating! We often joked about the requirement for him to have a chaff bag at work to hang around his neck to permit him to freely graze 24x7.

Days blurred into weeks, the weeks into months. Finlay's fifth birthday came and went. I bought him a puppy. The household felt so terribly empty, first without Ant, then without Noushka. Our night-time reading at the time was the C.S. Lewis classic *The Chronicles of Narnia*, and thus Finlay selected the name Aslan for our new little Malamute.

The promised trauma counselling was delayed after Noushka's death. Not a good time to start what would be a gruelling couple of months, Bernie had said. Since I could imagine nothing to be more gruelling than what I had already come through, we began the process at the beginning of June.

Jen, bless her soul, sat in on every session, offering support and to help fill in gaps, since she was there at the beginning of the nightmare. She has been an absolute rock of support, especially on the night in mid-July, when we got to the worst of it. The theory is to recall in great detail the events of that horrific time in New Zealand, gradually building in intensity until I can hold the intensity of the trauma in a controlled environment and know that no harm will come of the thought. With Bernie's help I then reduce the level of pain, thus building an immunity, if you like, eventually enabling my mind to pass through the nightmares and ultimately find a release. In theory. It was during our fourth session that we arrived at the most dreadful moment of my life – when the police came into my room at the Milford Lodge to break the news that my husband's kayak had been found, upturned, and there was no sign of Andrew. To relive this was almost as excruciating as the actual event. My body shook, I broke into a cold sweat even though it was relatively mild for July and I felt physically ill for days afterwards.

When the session finished, I was so distressed that I could barely walk out of that room, let alone drive. Jen drove me to my brother's house and stayed for a long while to help me calm down. Jen was, by this stage, heavily pregnant, and I was concerned that this stress might transmit to the baby. I was, at that moment, really questioning my decision to allow Bernie to begin the trauma counselling with me. He was adamant about the process, though – it was a very necessary step in my recovery. Without going through this process, he felt it would be difficult for me to work through my grief and push beyond it to a point where I could begin living an almost normal life again. He believed that without enduring this course I might be stuck in a state of numbness and disengagement for the rest of my life, and it's too important for Finlay's sake, and my family and friends, that I become a fully functioning being again.

In reply to an email to my friend Gail in Melbourne, asking how I was, I wrote, on 18 July 2008:

> *Just trying to pick up the shreds of my life and glue it all together to make a new one. Pretty hard though – there are lots of crucial pieces missing!! Managed to get through the school hols with my sanity still intact (or what remains of it, anyway!). We went to Bathurst for a few days – I've forgotten how cold it gets there. Much colder than here. Mind you it's been freeeezing here too. I've been really feeling the cold since my beautiful Ant died. Took Finlay to see Kung Fu Panda, and he spent the rest of our Bathurst visit karate chopping poor old Donnie!*

The documentary about Ant is nearing completion. I saw a rough cut a few weeks ago and it was just so very hard for me to watch. Made me physically ill. Bernie, my counsellor, came with me to watch it, which was a good thing. Anyway this week I saw the fine cut – they modified a few things that I had concerns with. There's still a couple of little bits that I'm worried about, but the director Dave Michod and Jen, who is the producer and co-director, convinced me that those bits need to be there. Anyway, apparently all the broadcasters think it's an amazing story. Unfortunately for me it will always be too hard to watch because it's my beautiful Ant. I've been questioning whether I should have continued with this project after it didn't end the way it was supposed to, but the documentary was a very important project for Ant, as was the book, which I'm working on – very slowly – so I feel very strongly the need to finish his work.

My decision to have Ant's documentary completed was based, as I told Gail, on my belief that Ant started the project, and I truly believe he would have wanted me to see it finished, regardless of the tragic ending. It's tough, though. It's such a personal story. It's my very private world and I feel vulnerable in exposing it to the masses. Yet so many people from all around the world took such a keen interest in, and gained such inspiration from, his incredible voyage that the story of it really needs to be told. From another perspective, it is a way for me to allow my friends and family some understanding of Andrew's motivation in undertaking such an inherently dangerous expedition. Some of my closest friends still harbour anger towards him for leaving us, and I don't want them to feel angry – I just want them to understand him.

When I spoke with Juliet about the trauma therapy, she questioned, 'Why go through it all again? Why . . . why . . . ? What possible benefits can there be of dredging up all this stuff?' My answer was, I need to do whatever I can to help me through this grief. I'm not going to bottle it up, ignore it, let it fester. I'm not going allow that insipid parasite to cause me a complete breakdown several years down the track because I didn't come to terms with it now. I'm doing my best to tackle it head-on so that I can be more present and responsive for Finlay, so I can give him the life he so very much deserves, and that Ant would expect of me. I have to deal with Ant-related issues every single day – the mail; the documentary; the settlement of the estate; the kayak and all that gear; the garage; opening his side of the wardrobe to find half of his shoes covered in mould; his breakfast cereal still in the cupboard; the empty space in my bed; even just looking into my little boy's eyes every single day and seeing his father in those eyes. How can I cope with all this if I don't confront it? I would simply shrivel up and die, and while I felt I truly wanted to last year, I won't allow it to happen! And I would be failing Andrew if I didn't try my hardest now.

So on Monday 11 August, just four days after what would have been Ant's 41st birthday, I was able, for the first time in 18 long months, to get out of bed, open the blinds and say, 'What a beautiful morning!' I'd felt so lost for so long, and now I felt that I was finally gaining enough strength to help Finlay make the most out of this precious life. I'd turned a corner in the tunnel.

CHAPTER 70

Emails began flooding in after the screening of our documentary, *Solo*, on the National Geographic Channel in the United States. This one from James in the USA:

> *This goes out to the friends and family of Andrew McAuley.*
> *I cannot begin to understand what you all have gone through and are still going through, but I felt it necessary to extend my condolences for your loss and my thanks for filming the documentary which aired tonight. It must have been incredibly difficult to make. I am sure that you will receive many of these messages over the days for if you have a beating heart you cannot help being drawn in emotionally to Andrew's story. Through the strength that you displayed in the documentary and the strength Andrew showed up to the very end, you have affected every person who watched it and will watch it. Know that their lives and my life have been changed for the better. I'm sure that*

your loss is immeasurable, but know that the lives you have touched are far too many to count. Thank you.

From Jeffrey in Calgary, Canada:

I have never experienced such a powerful combination of emotions, feeling both tremendous empathy and inspiration. To be so awakened by a film was truly a new experience for me. So, thanks for that. I am aware that this gift to me and to others comes with a terrible price.

Yes, I may have turned a corner, but this tunnel continues to throw obstacles in my path. On 1 October, I took Finlay to Bathurst to Grandma and Donnie's, then drove the two hours home to pack my backpack and meet my friend Jedda at the airport the next morning. We were heading south to Tasmania to walk the Overland Track.

Nothing was in my favour for this trip. Firstly, I'd been nursing a torn cartilage in my left hip for some weeks, and I was concerned about how that would cope with a heavy pack. On the plane on the way down to Tasmania, Jedda and her sister-in-law Jenny were raving about the excitement of going to 'Tassie'. It was at that moment that I knew this trip was a mistake. Ant left from the east coast of Tasmania on his voyage across the Tasman, so going back to Tassie was not the right place for me to be right now – too much anguish associated with the place. And, even though I desperately needed some 'time out' for myself, it was hard being away from Finlay. I had a very irrational fear of something bad happening and me not coming back to him. What if the plane crashed? What if some disaster befell me on the hike? What if we had a car crash getting to the start of the walk? What if? Sounds pathetic, I know, but I simply did not think it was a good time for me to be away from Finlay. I missed him from the moment I left him.

As it happened, my hip didn't handle the loaded pack well at all. I slipped off a log on the first day and injured it even more. We had walked here on our honeymoon, and the memories of the amazing time we had back then were too haunting. I simply didn't want to be there without him. I limped into the hut at Pine Valley, stayed the night, then left the girls to continue north in the snow while I limped backed to Lake St Clair.

I managed to find a lift back to Hobart, although my spare clothes and wallet were in Launceston with the man who had shuttled us to Lake St Clair. I was dropped off in the middle of town at about 6 pm, only to find all accommodation in the whole of Hobart was booked out due to some Irish folk-dancing competition – who could believe it?! I was in tears as I limped around town with my heavy pack trying to find a place to stay for the night. I had a credit card and a total of $5 in cash, which I wasted on a payphone on hold to the airport trying to change my flight home. I paid a small fortune to get the first flight home next morning. What a waste of time, money and emotion this trip ended up being.

My next multi-day hiking trip will wait until Finlay is old enough to carry a pack. I won't go again without him. That's a few years away yet.

In the meantime, we continued to jump hurdles. Not long after the Tassie disaster, Rick my acupuncturist, who has through all this become a good friend and confidant, moved to the far north coast. The following week, as I practised yoga with my wonderful teacher Ben, he told me that he, too, would be moving north soon. With the loss of two of my most valued supports, my fragile world came crashing down again.

Mum phoned on 22 October to tell me that their dear friend Ian had died. I had known Ian and Judy Brownlow for as long as I can remember. And although it was expected, death is never easy to accept. When I visited Ian in hospital before my disastrous Tassie trip, I wanted to ask him to find Ant for me, and tell him how much we love him and miss him, but I couldn't ask – maybe Ian really didn't think he was dying. He joked about the nurses, the food, the uncomfortable bed – typical Ian – and spoke as if he were getting out of there one day.

I hope Judy can find some peace – at least she would have had the time to say all the important and precious things to Ian before he died. I wish I could have told Ant one more time how truly, deeply and passionately I loved him and will love him eternally. I wish I could have told him that he is my angel and how very, very lucky I am for meeting him, falling in love with him, and sharing the most precious and wonderful and exciting, and sometimes fearful, times of my entire life with him.

I lost all control when Finlay refused to get dressed after the bath, and I screamed and screamed and screamed until my lungs were on fire and my throat was raw. Poor little Googie was terrified and he just needed a hug and we both cried our hearts out. Later that night, just as I walked into the bathroom, the shower suddenly let out a strong burst of water for no explicable reason. I thought it was Ant crying for me, but I wasn't sure whether he was upset *for* me or *at* me. I felt so ashamed – maybe he was letting me know that he was disappointed in me. I had to ring Robyn at midnight, because I didn't know what else to do, I was so terribly frightened.

A couple of days later, I swore loudly because Finlay was being obnoxious. He asked, 'What does fuck mean?' I was mortified. I tried to explain that he must never, ever use that word, and must never tell anyone I said that. But as we drove to gymnastics, a car went through a give way sign in front of me, so I yelled abuse out the window at him. When we walked into the Y for gymnastics, my poor little boy started crying and said he wanted to go home because he was too upset. That was when I realised that I desperately needed to sort myself out. I couldn't live with this anger, or be like this for my little angel. I made an appointment to see the doctor. I'd been fighting going down the medication path since my Ant died – working so hard with counselling, acupuncture, yoga, swimming, but it was not working. I'm not too proud to admit defeat, not when I know what's at stake.

You can't put a time limit on grief. 'They', in their incalculable wisdom, say it gets better with the passage of time. But time is a great variable and it's something that no-one, not even 'they', can expect to limit. The loss of a loved one is limitless, the pain endless. It really boils down to that fact that there simply is no escaping, only working through, adapting, changing to meet the new circumstances. That, I think, can be done. It's easier to look at it that way at least. Because there is no 'getting over' it.

CHAPTER 71

The year 2009 disappeared in a blur of trying, and very often failing, to get to school before the bell each day. It was a major milestone year for Finlay – kindergarten. He thrived with the establishment of routine, the thrill of learning, the new friends. He looked so gorgeous as he marched with all the confidence of his father off to his first day in class, in his brand new school uniform, the shorts well below his knees, the crisply ironed blue shirt neatly tucked in, the shoes polished to a mirror shine, and his hair perfectly combed. Not a single tear. Not from him, at least. No turning back.

We took the day off during the second week of school to visit our spot atop the cliffs in the Wolgan Valley. It's a great comfort to me, being there. We were sweating after the hike up the gully and a scare from a huge diamond python blocking our path. As we sat there, immersed in the tranquillity of our special place, Finlay uttered, 'I wish the wind would blow.' And it did! We looked at each other, our eyes alight with excitement.

'I wish the wind would blow again!' he practically shouted. Again, it did! Amazing. Those beautiful eyes, so much like his dad's, grew wider and brighter. And together we shrugged our shoulders conspiratorially and we smiled very smug smiles.

Solo screened in the UK on BBCTV in late February and on several European channels, although under the quite pompous title of *Solitary Endeavour on the Southern Ocean*. Apparently there's an icecream in the UK called Solo. They didn't want to disappoint those preparing themselves for a confectionery documentary. I was overwhelmed by emails, numbering into the hundreds.

Stephan in Belgium wrote:

I've seen Solo *yesterday evening and it struck me to my core and I just feel compelled to write some words to you. I'm sorry if this seems weird or if it brings up grief, this is not my intention. I'm writing you to offer my condolences and thank you for realising or allowing this documentary to be made. I had a similar feeling watching* Touching the Void *but this blew me away. It was gut-wrenching, at times it was agony watching it, but yet so inspiring and heartfelt. Simply beautiful. Afterwards I lit a candle for a few moments, to wish all you guys well. I cannot exactly say why, but it helps me see that people can overcome anything, it breaks all boundaries, it helps me to see that I can arrange my life the way I want to.*

I've been a lifeguard myself for years and live by the sea in Belgium and I also need to touch my boundaries to feel alive and clearly see what is important in life and what brings me true joy. I want to tell you, and I'm sure thousands of people feel the same way, that your loss is not in vain. I've grown up without a father, he died when

I was one, and inevitably you keep searching for role models. People like Andrew are true examples as a human, as a man.

I wish you lots of courage and all the best in your endeavours and I feel privileged to have had the chance to share these moments with your husband and you.

And this, from Shona McKeen:

We talk of courage, and strength, and power, and absolute talent and skill of people who do things like play football, or rugby, or sprint for a living. Yes, I will say that I recall I did think 'what's the big deal' to cross the Tasman by kayak when I heard about the commencement of this challenge those years back, and honestly, I did also think that someone wanting to do this was a 'silly' man and could not imagine why someone would want to do something that can be done by boat.

But now, Andrew has probably achieved what he never expected he would – to live on as a hero, a true adventurer, a role model to the world today. Indeed, where would we be today without the likes of Captain James Cook, Burke and Wills, or other ground-breakers in fields of medicine and discovery and the like. As his website suggests, 'Man cannot discover new oceans unless he has the courage to lose sight of the shore'.

I just have no words – as I sat here crying at the end of the documentary – just full of admiration and sincere heartbreak that Andrew made his most incredible impact through his final challenge in life, which included his life. I hope that Finlay will grow up knowing his father did set new boundaries for the world . . . and that placing your feet on land is a technicality, as the journey was making it from one land to another, and that was achieved in every sense of the word.

May peace be with you.

As many people chose to, Dominic O'Brien in the UK addressed his email to Andrew:

I watched your documentary of the Tasman Sea crossing on the BBC last night and just felt compelled to write. I feel very privileged to have been able to glimpse into the motivation, passion, dreams and fears that led you out into and kept you company on the Tasman Sea.

As an armchair adventurer I envy your courage and drive. As a father I can only mourn the fact that you didn't have the opportunity to re-adjust the balance between adventure and fatherhood as the Tasman had perhaps encouraged you to. As a husband to an equally loving wife as yours I can only say that they know us better than we do ourselves and true love is based on accepting our flaws as much as our strengths.

In my mind you have certainly proved that the impossible is actually possible and based on that it is fair to say that you achieved your goal.

'Life is either a daring adventure or nothing. Security is mostly a superstition. It does not exist in nature.'
– Helen Keller

Sleep was still intermittent for me. The trauma counselling of the last year did have an effect, but it couldn't completely erase the nightmares and that deep hollow emptiness. And as sleep evaded me one night in early April, I stayed up very late answering the continuing flow of emails from across the globe. My Gmail froze. I turned the computer and the router off, then on again. The internet connection was fine, but my email wouldn't load. Ant's still trying to tell me to go to bed! He's still looking after me.

On Easter Sunday, we were at my brother's beach house at Culburra. The local surf life saving club was on the beach doing some training drills and they had a couple of buoys out the back, beyond the breakers. I hadn't swum in the ocean since Ant died, but I decided it was time to step outside my somewhat diminished comfort zone and swim a few laps around the buoys, since they were patrolling in the rubber duckie. I'd been swimming for about 40 minutes, and enjoying it. The water was crystal clear and I could see lots of little stingrays and fish.

I was about to go in to the beach, but thought I'd do one more lap. As I turned my head for a breath, there, no more than a metre away, was a big fin! There had been an inordinately large number of shark attacks along the east coast lately! My heart went through my mouth and I sprinted towards the beach, but ran into someone swimming out *towards* the shark. I looked up and to my delight I was surrounded by dolphins! There must have been at least 20 of them and they were calmly cruising around us – by then a few board riders had paddled over. I ducked under water to hear them talking. It was beyond amazing! What a privilege. When Ant was lost, I told Finlay that the dolphins looked after him, so they hold great significance for us.

CHAPTER 72

It's 2010 now. A new decade, and Finlay and I have just returned from what has become a biannual pilgrimage to 'our special place' in the Wolgan Valley, marking the third anniversary of the death of the most important man in our lives. It's an all-day venture for us, over two hours by car, then another two to walk along the track and up that steep gully to our clifftop vantage point where the wind blew for us yet again. It was after dark when we arrived home, so I checked the mailbox the following morning. It was 10 February. Three years ago today, James Ure walked into that room at Milford Lodge.

Amongst the bills was a hand-addressed envelope. Not a bill, obviously, so that pleased me. The colour drained from my face though, as I scanned down the poorly typed page. My entire body shook with stunned disbelief. 'To whom it may concern', some cowardly excuse for a man had written. Who else, I wonder, was he expecting it to concern when he addressed the envelope to Vicki McAuley?

To bring a child into this world and then to nurture and help that child grow into an adult is the greatest success that a man can achieve.

I took my 5 year old to his first day at school the other day and he looked at me for guidance as I set him on his way. I look forward to seeing him play sport in the coming years to helping him as he progresses through life and its challenges, I will be there and maybe just maybe when he is an adult he will do the same with his children and I will proudly say I have succeeded.

I watched a documentary on tv the other night about Andrew McAuley, if it was to be a portrait of a hero then it sadly failed, I know a few other workmates at the office I work in Melbourne all talked about it the next day…… what a failure of a man.

To bring a young child into this world and then to take such a risk which he admitted to doing so and then to lose his life while a young boy grows up to never know his father is the biggest failure of a man we could ever see.

Maybe if you are a bachelor then climb mountains, cross rivers, risk your life but to take such a stupid risk and to leave your wife and a young child to live years without your help, support and fatherly love is the biggest failings of a man ..in fact maybe a cowardly act to be so stupid to put your own goals and wants before your young boy.

Andrew McAuley proved to us in the documentary that he was a failure of a man and sadly his young boy suffers because of this.

At least a dozen of those that saw the show all agreed … what a fool but a fool that has caused others to lose out because of his selfishness.

While his wife will continue to tell the young child

that dad made it to the NZ coast ..other fathers will be helping their youngsters play cricket, helping them to get over girlfriends breaking up with them, help them to do their studies and get them towards a degree or likewise and maybe one day be a granddad to their children.

The documentary really proved what a fool and a failure Andrew McAuley was and sadly the young son suffers the most because of that.

GB

St Kilda East

I couldn't muster the strength to take Finlay to school that day, such was my state. We stayed home and together we played cricket in the backyard with our dog Aslan, we swam in our pool, climbed to the top of Finlay's favourite tree, did somersaults on the trampoline, we read together and played a game of chess. We did what we regularly do together, which, Mister GB of St Kilda East, is a great deal more than many parents ever do with their children.

My anger is directed at the GBs of the world, who have nothing better to do than to condemn others. To those people I say nothing, for nothing is worth saying to them that they could ever hope to understand. But I think of the words penned by the polar explorer Robert Scott, as he lay dying, frozen and starving with no hope of rescue: 'To my widow . . . what lots I could tell you of this journey. How much better has it been than lounging in too great comfort at home.' It makes me think of Ant in his final moments. And, for some inexplicable reason, it makes me smile.

Yes, extreme adventuring is no doubt contentious. It provokes vehement debate. Somehow I think that Andrew might be intrigued by the discussion his adventure has drawn. The

National Geographic website had a blog pertaining to *Solo*, when it aired in late 2008. Among the many gracious comments was a disrespectful response so shocking that it won't be repeated here. Freedom of speech, they call it. I guess that's what makes for such a diverse and interesting society.

The ever astute Dr Stiles, in another extract from his 'To Take a Risk' essay, sheds a different and confronting light on habits of risk and responsibility.

> People become soldiers, firefighters, miners, police, footballers, motorcyclists – all carry a real risk of injury, if not death. And yet we do not usually label them with reckless disregard for their lives. In fact society usually holds them up as admirable, if not virtuous, citizens. Do we justify their risk taking because it serves some 'useful' social function? Or is the conscious choice in taking on such a career not much different in essence to that of the adventurer? It can well be argued that adventurers also play a useful social role, though perhaps less tangible. In a similar vein, I note a certain inconsistency when there is a public outcry when a large financial and personnel investment is required to mount a rescue response to an adventurer. People seem to regard such expenses as 'a bit rich' when it involves conscious risk activities – and yet few acknowledge the billions of dollars we invest to assist others who have engaged in other risk activities that are somewhat more socially familiar. Smoking and other drug use, over-eating, under-exercising, risky motorised vehicle use are part of a gamut of social risks that we as a society have accepted the need to provide a safety net of services for. To be consistent with the line often proposed for adventurers, the public would need to advocate doing

either nothing to assist a drunk 20-year-old who has just bent his car around a tree on a Saturday night, or perhaps to foot him with a $15,000 bill for the cost of his rescue, retrieval, medical and rehabilitation services. While the odd remote rescue costs a motza, these pale into insignificance in comparison to the amount we are prepared to underwrite the rest of our more socially familiar risk taking activities.

To keep life in perspective, I weigh the positives against the negatives, another of life's valuable lessons the past three years has taught me.

A gentleman named Bruce Taylor from Bristol in the United Kingdom wrote:

I have always regarded myself as a lover of life and adventure and can completely understand his reasons for making such a trip. Those that ask why are of a different mindset. I'm now 42, but even when I was a boy I knew that the spirit of adventure is not something you grow out of. It is with you for life. Those that criticise your husband's decision making clearly never possessed that spirit.

I've met only a couple of people in my life with such spirit and I gravitated to them instantly. That common understanding and spirit is immediately apparent. If I had been lucky enough to have met Andrew, he would have been one of those people. I've never wept at a film or movie, but did so last night. Not directly for him, but for the fact that the world lost one such rare individual.

Your husband remains a provider of inspiration marking the limits of human ability. I hope your son turns into such a man and I'm quite certain his mother will not discourage him one bit.

A note from James in the UK ultimately overpowers the negatives. *This* is what Andrew was driving for – to inspire, to encourage, to ignite a passion for life:

Dear Andrew and all the contributors in telling your kayaking adventure, thank you for your help; I was contemplating suicide (really) and by chance watched you on BBC2 today. The last couple of years when people ask me what I want for Christmas I would say a canoe but I didn't get one, I'm gonna get one and paddle as much as I can, metaphorically, in my own life.

From Charlotte in the UK:

I have not been able to stop feeling incredibly humbled by his great determination. Thank you for making that documentary, I can see how important it must be for you, but also how important it is for others to share in Andrew's incredible journey. For if it were not for explorers and adventurers like him, we would still be living a very sheltered existence, and probably still thinking that the world is flat!

And from Mitch Beavis:

Having just watched Andrew's Tasman documentary, I must say that whilst only having a brief glimpse into the person that he was and how he lived his life he should always be remembered as a true embodiment of the human spirit. His story has not only moved me deeply but has also opened my eyes on the meaning of humanity and how one should live their life and the perspective at which we should view things.

Whilst I sit here and struggle to put down words which I hope are some comfort and bring some sort of happiness or a smile at the very least. Putting it simply I know I will not be the only one moved by his story or be empowered by his sense of adventure or thirst for challenge and discovery. I know no mere words on a screen can bring back what both of you have lost but please rest assured that the knowledge of what a great man he was has been passed on to a complete stranger and that you both are very lucky to have his legacy live on in your lives.

Finlay's dad left him an almighty legacy, an abundance of courage, inner strength, zest for life and, above all else, enduring love. And our little boy has a plethora of male mentors – his uncle Mike to teach him to surf, uncle Peter to play golf and tennis with, Poppa to play cricket with, Richard and Mark and Neil and Charlie to take him climbing, Paul to bring him model aeroplanes, and Donnie, in his seventies, with two knee replacements, who always gets down on the floor and wrestles with him whenever he visits. And of course he has his four-legged, 45-kilogram 'little brother' to leap onto his bed every morning to wake him.

Four days after the horrible letter, a car pulled into my drive, stereo blasting so loudly the house shook, and Aslan ran to the door. It was a florist deliveryman, with a beautiful bunch of roses and an anonymous note: 'To a brave woman with a courageous man in her heart.'

When I told Pam and Neil that night at dinner, Neil laughed his endearing wry laugh, 'Ironic, isn't it? I bet Andy never gave you flowers in your life.'

'Of course he did! He pinched them from a neighbour's garden!'

Indeed that courageous man who remains eternally in my heart endured incredible hardship for 30 days at sea in his tiny kayak and demonstrated almost inhuman resolve to weather the extreme conditions. It was a profound physical and psychological journey he travelled. I take solace in the thought of the indescribable feeling of euphoria that he experienced upon sighting the mountainous coast of New Zealand. I'm sure words could never express his emotions at that moment when the low-lying clouds appeared on the horizon, with the first glimpse of mountains rising above them. I take that thought in both hands and hold onto it, and in some small way it sustains me.

As for that ultimate question – was it worth it? For Ant, for Finlay and me, and for our collective family and friends – definitively NO.

For the many who followed Andrew's Tasman Solo expedition – those who have no immediate connection with the man or his family, who gained from Andrew's journey the inspiration and the courage to venture beyond their comfort zone – maybe, for the pain is short-lived but the inspiration endures. That, if I can look objectively, is a good thing.

If the outcome had been different, without doubt it would have been worth it, for as the man himself said, 'I could die a happy man, deeply satisfied that I had done something truly bold and significant for the world of sea kayaking.' Just as it was 'important to me to do this', so it was for those of us who love him so very, very much to let him go. It's a concept that's difficult for many to understand, and even harder to articulate, but that, in its bare simplicity, is the way it was, and is.

* * *

New friends have entered my life. Some have faded away, but the enduring ones remain. I've found new support, and formed ever greater bonds with those who have been there from the beginning. My own family, for instance, have become my closest and most valuable support. Not that they ever weren't. It's just a harsh reality that it can take a heart-wrenching tragedy to overcome the complacency of close relationships. I think back to my childhood – a time of total reliance on my family.

Strangely enough, with my overwhelming loss and hurt and pain, I feel like that child again. I need that support, that guidance from family, once again. I need to feel that boundless parental love. I need their emotional and pragmatic support. I need to have my siblings as my best friends. And they are. Robyn and Peter will always remain my truest friends.

And, being a mother, I can feel the pain of Marsie's soul-destroying loss. 'One of the greatest loves is that which a mother has for her child.' I don't know the source of that quote – could be a Hallmark greeting – but the truth lies deep. And it makes me want to hold on to Finlay and never let go. But I will, one day, just as Marsie did. And she knows that Andrew has always loved her and will continue to love her, to love us all, from a different dimension.

CHAPTER 73

As I delved through Ant's files – a torturous process – I was amazed to find that he had already written the ending of this book:

> Finally I landed. Vicki was there, along with a small crowd of others. I stumbled from the boat, fell over, and crawled to shore. 'Daddy!!!' yelled Finlay. I burst into tears. Staggering about, I held Vicki close.
> Later, I said to her, 'That was so risky, and so scary. I'll never, ever do anything as hard as that *ever* again. I really mean it.'
> She laughed. 'Yeah, right!'

Yes, he wrote it as it should have been. As it so very nearly was. Oh, how I wept.

Still, we have little choice but to go on. Life with Ant was never what you'd call predictable. Spontaneity featured prominently in my life from that very day many years ago when I first laid eyes on the man who was to become my heart, my soul, my life.

I am eternally grateful that he was able to leave me the most precious gift of all – the new little man in my life, who I have no doubt will follow in Daddy's footsteps, and lead me into another life of incredible adventures. That little man seems to have inherited, among many other endearing characteristics, his father's warmth and compassion. When, in a moment of doubt, a tear comes to my eye, Finlay wraps his precious little arms around me and whispers with great tenderness, 'It's alright, Noona. We'll be OK.'

Walking out of my yoga class the other day, one lady said to me, 'Your yoga is an inspiration to me. You are so strong. How do you do all those things?'

'Well, my husband had a saying, "Whether you think you can or you think you can't, you're right".'

'Can you fly?'

Ant gave me strength. He taught me belief. So yeah, metaphorically, I reckon I can fly.

And now, as Finlay and I walk hand in hand down that long, bleak tunnel of grief, we can see, still some distance away, but I'm sure it is there, a glimmer of light. The fog is lifting.

We're closer than we were before.

ACKNOWLEDGEMENTS

Andrew's acknowledgements

In achieving anything great, we inevitably stand upon the shoulders of others. Not to acknowledge those others would be to ignore those who have lent inspiration, advice, or a helping hand at some point during the long journey that is behind any accomplishment of significance. In my own long journey, there are many people to thank. Although these names may not be known to you, they are very important to me, and without their shoulders to stand upon, most of the events in this book would never have taken place. Some are climbers, some are paddlers, and some are people who lent encouragement along the way.

My sincerest thanks to: my wife Vicki and son Finlay, Carsten Birckhahn, Anke Clauss, Vera Wong, Rod Willard, Armando Corvini, Andrew Burns, Shane Woonton, Lian Woonton, Mark Windsor, Teena Windsor, Arthur Henry, Lurene Pollard, Neil Crabb, Pam Crabb, Charlie Cross, Jodie Cross, Greg James, Robyn Cleland, Simon Carter, Mark Wilson, Ned Norton, Paul Weber, Chris Mason, Rob Cowan, Mum, Dad, Mike and

Juliet McAuley, Warren Sandral, Lincoln Hall, Greg Mortimer, Elaine Prior, Al Bakker, Robert Swan, Kylie Gill, Christine Gee, Richard Jones, Richard Host, Phillip Dundas, Greg Caire, Duncan Chessel, Lisa Morgan, Lucas Trihey, Deborah Dickson-Smith, Joanne Diver, Sacha Dench, Ken Eastwood, Kieran Lawton, Julie Styles, Tom Gilliatt, Wendy Stevenson, Mark Baker, Stefan Eberhard, Graant Bennet, David Noble, David Forbes, John Fantini, Helen Thompson, Marie Sombart, Ken Luck, Richard Stiles, Sharnie Wu, Rob Mercer, David Winkworth, Laurie Geoghegan, Paul Loker, Stuart Trueman, Sharon Trueman, Darrel Day, Cath Hew, Angus Finney, Andrew Eddy, Vince Browning, Damien Gildea, Ben Deacon, Pat Spiers, Lachlan Beed, Pete Lynn, Peter Treby, Mark Heggie, Mick MacRobb, Ian Dunn, Peter Provis, Chris Bray, Julie Stanton, Roger Aspinall, Jemima Robinson, Mark Atkinson, Justine Curgenven, Jeff Jennings, Matt Watton, Dom Mee, Alby McCracken, Alan Whiteman . . .

Sadly, there are some who are no longer with us. I have lost many colleagues to the mountains over the years, though none to the sea. Those closest to me were Wade Stevens, Rod Willard, and the loss is still felt years after they have left us.

And my unequivocal thanks to . . .

Finn Murphy for picking me up out of the dirt and for giving me strength, courage and belief. Tod Hollebon for taking off the policeman's hat and putting on that of a friend. James Ure – the bearer of bad tidings – I don't hold it against you, and Melanie, for your compassion. Jen Peedom for reading Finlay to sleep, for keeping the media at bay, for making such a powerful documentary, for being my pillar, and for becoming such a close and true friend. Greg and Jane Turner, and of course Charlie and Jack, for your generosity and friendship.

All search and rescue personnel involved in the search attempts and subsequent retrieval of the kayak – John Seward, Chris Raley, Richard Hayes, Mark Deaker, Lloyd Matheson and the many others I didn't get to meet.

All the wonderful people in Te Anau for your collective efforts in trying to ease our pain – in particular Silvia and Brett Prentice and Bruce and Prue Fraser.

Martijn Kleinjes for giving up your Good Friday.

The Tasmanian police – Ross Paine, Paul Steane, Matt Wotton for your concerns.

Jo Scard and Andrew Meares for your encouragement and, of course, the photos. Ben Shepard for getting me through all the yoga practices. Rick Peterson for the acupuncture, the herbs, and most especially the words of wisdom. Mark and Teen Windsor and Neil, Pam, Nic and Bec Crabb for the Sunday dinners and all that entails. Artie Henry for chaperoning and Lurene Pollard for such incredible unparalleled compassion and empathy. Angophora (Richard Stiles) for taking the onslaught and not throwing it back, and Sharnie Wu. Charlie and Jody Cross for your honesty. Stu and Sharon Trueman for your ongoing support and friendship. Paul Hewitson for the kayak, the support, the lunches, the aeroplanes and the friendship. Jonathan Bogais for weathering the storms. Ben and Urs Deacon for finding Bernie. Bernie Brown for pushing me through when I thought I could go no further. Pat Spiers for taking care of Noushka and the dead bird. Kieran Lawton for making me laugh despite everything. Rob Easther for coming to our aid at such short notice. Wade Fairley and Fred Olivier for your generous Tassie hospitality. John and Jedda Totenhoffer for being such wonderful friends. Andre and Catherine

Janecki for all the beautiful things, except the mushrooms. Shane and Lian Woonton for continuing to be just around the corner. Shane and Gail Schwarze for your enduring friendship. Laurie Ford for hanging out with me all day and Elli Tappan for the pics and the consoling emails. Jeff Jennings for helping Ant with the filming, and for the footage. Chris Bray for your support and your mum's cake. Terry Davis for your unparalleled generosity and for your initiative in creating the 'Andrew McAuley Inspiration Award' for CCA employees. Dick Smith for your incredibly generous support and your passion for adventure. Meister Phil Dundas and Bron Dundas for the many midnight phone calls. Simon Baulderstone for the guidance and the Machiavelli lunches. Karel Vissel for putting life into perspective. Donna and Mark Ayres for the little book. Lara and Ben Penrose for the sleepovers and the cakes and brownies. Kate and Phil Win for the 'playovers'... again! Penny and Kevin Nadaragan for the worthwhile distractions. Claire Davis for giving me the best advice – to not listen to advice. Lulu Bull; Ben Silverstone; Helen Clear; Linda Rowntree for helping restore my yoga. Yacetta Cariolato for the peace of mind. All the wonderful St. Finbar's mums for making me feel 'normal'. Father Stuart Hall for the beautiful service and your support. Peter Kappelman; Mark Sundin, and everyone from NSWSKC for everything. Ben Eastwood for the crocodile tales. Oliver Dudley (the person, not the cat!) for the seeds of change. Shelly Madrid; Antonia Payn; Chrystel Llaona Baudere – my e-friends!

All of Andrew's sponsors (listed alphabetically) Australian Geographic, Aquapac, Blue Earth, Back Country Cuisine, Dick Smith, Fastwave Communications, Fenton Pharmaceuticals, Garmin, Gore-Tex, Global Marine Networks, GPSM (Global Product Supply Management), H2O Audio, Highgear, icom,

Lendal, Mirage Sea Kayaks, Merrell, Mountain Hardware, Paddy Pallin, Sailing With Attitude, SkyEye, Sea to Summit, Silverstorm, Solution, Walker Wilson Associates.

Tom Gilliatt for taking on this challenge. Joel Naoum and Mark Evans for scribbling all over my manuscript.

All my family – Mum and Dad (aka Grandma and Donnie); Peter and Jilly and Tom and Jess; Robbie and Markie and Em and Sam; the other Peter and Jilly (ie Marsie and Poppa); Juju (Juliet) and Sean, Olivia, Caitlin and baby Emily; Mike and Nic, Tom and Indigo; Noushka, Aslan – for so much I'd have to write another book to tell you about it.

And MOST especially to Finlay (my little angel) for your incredible patience – quite remarkable for someone your age – for all those hang-on-a-minute's. And to my Ant, of course, for helping me find the words, and for being you.